Y0-BRJ-239

ARCHIVE–LIBRARY
RELATIONS

CONTRIBUTORS

Robert L. Brubaker, Chief Librarian, Chicago Historical Society; formerly Assistant Professor, Graduate Library School, University of California at Los Angeles.

Frank G. Burke, Executive Director, National Historical Publications and Records Commission; formerly Assistant to the Archivist of the United States.

Robert L. Clark, Jr., Director of the Oklahoma Department of Libraries; formerly Director of the Mid-Mississippi Regional Library System and previous to that Director of State Archives and Records, Oklahoma Department of Libraries.

Miriam I. Crawford, Curator, Conwellana-Templana Collection, Temple University; formerly Catalog Librarian and Reference Librarian, Temple University.

Marietta Malzer, Research Archivist, Oklahoma Department of Libraries.

Frazer G. Poole, Preservation Officer and Coordinator of Building Planning for the James Madison Memorial Building, Library of Congress; formerly Director of the Library, University of Illinois, Chicago Circle.

ARCHIVE–LIBRARY RELATIONS

Edited by Robert L. Clark, Jr.

R. R. BOWKER COMPANY
A Xerox Publishing Company
New York & London, 1976

Published by R. R. Bowker Company (A Xerox Publishing Company)
1180 Avenue of the Americas, New York, N.Y. 10036
Copyright © 1976 by Xerox Corporation
Printed and bound in the United States of America

Library of Congress Cataloging in Publication Data

Archive-library relations.
  Bibliography: p.
  Includes index.
  1. Libraries—United States. 2. Archives—United
States. I. Clark, Robert L.
Z731.A76   021'.00973   76-18806
ISBN 0-8352-0770-6

CONTENTS

ONE. THE SETTING
Robert L. Clark, Jr.

TWO. SIMILARITIES AND DIFFERENCES
Frank G. Burke

THREE. COMMON ISSUES
Miriam I. Crawford

FOUR. SHARED CONCERNS
Frank G. Burke, Robert L. Clark, Jr., and Frazer G. Poole

FIVE. PROFESSIONAL COMMUNICATION
Robert L. Brubaker

ANNOTATED BIBLIOGRAPHY
Marietta Malzer

PREFACE

A distinct characteristic of man is the need to communicate and record knowledge. The tools of communication have ranged from clay to satellites. Civilized societies have taken great pains to place recorded knowledge in safe places and create archives and libraries for this purpose.

The importance of recorded knowledge for survival and progress is constantly being elevated as more and more information is presented. Without information and its necessary control, a society is not only stagnant, but regressive. With social memory, preserved and controlled by archives and libraries, a society is able to evolve to whatever future it is destined to experience in an ever-changing environment.

Archives were the forerunners of libraries. The ancient archives contained the best of society's accumulated knowledge; and as nations grew in wealth and security, archives and libraries became symbols of a country's aspiration to create a better society. Today, archives and libraries are necessities. These cultural institutions pass information to succeeding generations in a variety of forms of distributable media. In this way, archives and libraries preserve the memory of civilization and pass this memory on to living individuals. The materials in these institutions contain the written and graphic record of social memory and human heritage and provide society with information on which to base actions, develop policies, ascertain rights, educate, and entertain.

Currently, the archive and library carry out two distinct functions, but, in many cases, they are located in one institution. To be sure, there are elements of both functions in archives and in libraries. Both deal in information and, specifically, writing as a communication tool. Both control information by selecting from a mass of data portions which may be useful to society. It is for these reasons that common problems, issues, and concerns exist.

Shared concerns include education, materials, methodology, reference, collection building, public relations, networking, standardization, technology, legislation, access to materials, literary property and copyright, social responsibility, and professional status. With these concerns come common problems, better solved by communication and cooperation than by duplicated efforts. Despite this overlap of interests, archives and libraries are different because their specializations are diversified and varied. While they have distinct modern histories, each deals mainly with different formats of information, controls its information separately, and has a heterogeneous clientele. Depending on the type of library or archive, each is used for many purposes, subject to the extent and type of information desired by the user.

Increased communication and cooperation between the two professions will accomplish the same purpose—serving the user more efficiently. Because of the similar purposes of archives and libraries, the user may be quite unaware of the basic differences in methodology. The user is concerned with access to materials and also with some of the same issues confronting the librarian and archivist. Specifically, the user expects the problems of literary property and copyright, access to collections, and useless collecting competition to be solved before they create barriers to research. Also expected is adequate bibliographic control of materials by techniques such as catalogs, finding aids, bibliographies, lists, calendars, inventories, and guides. In addition, the user expects the professionals managing the materials to prepare themselves for the new technology which presents different formats of access to information and special problems in research.

Despite the need for interchange and communication, the formal relationship between the professions has proceeded slowly. Differences in membership, size, and history of the American Library Association (ALA) and the Society of American Archivists (SAA) reflect the variety in the professions, but also require that communication and cooperation exist where interests overlap.

The background of professional relationships sheds light on past and present attempts at cooperation. The International Congress of Archivists and Librarians, held in Brussels in 1910, was the earliest international meeting of importance to both professions. The congress was held under the auspices of the Association of Belgian Archivists and Librarians, and concerned itself with many of the same issues confronting the archival and library professions today. The issues were terminology, international standardization, photographic reproduction of materials, statistics, classification and cataloging rules, union lists and catalogs, interlibrary cooperation, international exchanges and loans, government publications in archives, archival acquisitions of academic theses and dissertations, archival education and training, archival methodology, bibliographies of finding aids, parochial archives, access, architecture, exhibits, and library systems. The reports and decisions of the various sessions of the congress laid the foundation for presently accepted standards and practices of archives and libraries. It was this congress, for example, which adopted both the Dewey Decimal Classification, as an international bibliographic classification, and an exchange program of inventories of public archives.

In 1912 Waldo Leland, president of the American Historical Association and a leader in the establishment of the American archival profession, spoke of the United States outdistancing other countries in library science, but falling behind in archives. He also predicted that the time would come when the United States would awaken to the realization of the value of archives and that our descendants would look with dismay on the results of our negligence.

It was not until 1936 that formal communication, other than the occasional appearance of a journal article, focused on the relationship between archive and library institutions. In that year, the ALA established a Committee on Archives and Libraries, an outgrowth of the Committee on Public Documents. The committee held regular meetings from 1937 to 1941 when it was terminated. Later, American archivists were the first to see a need for formally examining these relationships. In 1970 the SAA formed an Ad Hoc Committee on Archives-Library Relationships to study possible areas of cooperation between libraries and archives, such as education, preservation of paper, films, establishment of standards, legislation of shared interests, and other topics of mutual concern. In the same year, the possibility of forming a joint committee of the ALA and the SAA was explored by the SAA. In the fall of 1970 ALA's Executive Board approved the establishment of an ALA—SAA Joint Committee on Library-Archives Relationships.

The formal relationships are thus of recent origin; additional stature and responsibilities will develop in time. For example, the establishment of these relations will ultimately aid in the standardization and formalization of archival courses in library schools. This development will bring the professions even closer together in purpose, theory, and fact. For this to happen, librarians must realize the kinship of archivists and share their experience in standardization and legislation. Archivists must realize that their numbers are limited, and cooperate, communicate, and work with the library profession for the advancement of their own ideas. Both professions can learn from each other and, by doing so, benefit the user. After all, it is the use of the materials which is most important.

This is the first comprehensive book dealing with the joint concerns and relationships of the two professions. The reader will become aware of basic principles and issues concerning both.

This work is based on the premise that archives and libraries exist as cultural institutions for a common purpose: to collect, maintain, and make available the written and graphic record of man's intellect and experience. Recent technological, political, and economic developments reveal an increasing interest in closer communication between the two professions. The past tended to emphasize the differences, but now an established yet changing archival profession and a library profession with many generalists have created an atmosphere of cooperation and concentration on points of commonality.

This work contributes to the archivist's knowledge of libraries' involvement in education, legislation, funding, standardization techniques, technology, and commitment to service. It contributes to the librarian's understanding of the potential of original source materials, their value, uniqueness, and the methods by which they are collected, maintained, and serviced. It gives the serious user of the institutions an insight into current trends in the professional milieu of efforts in common areas, while increasing the user's understanding of discrepancies in methods which exist from institution to institution.

The text is divided into broad sections containing topics of interest to both professions. Authors selected had direct experience in areas of their assigned topics. An annotated bibliography of articles on archive-library related topics is included. The conceptualization is oriented toward today's society, emphasizing the place and importance of professional objectives in society's culture. We dwell on the current situation, not the retrospective, and suggest areas in which cooperation, direct and indirect, can be of mutual benefit.

Robert L. Clark, Jr.
Kosciusko, Mississippi

ONE

THE SETTING

THE ARCHIVAL SETTING

Archives, including manuscripts, are available for use in a variety of repositories. These include libraries of all types, historical societies, religious organizations, business and industry, federal agencies, state agencies, county agencies, and municipalities. The records contained in these institutions reflect both systematic and haphazard collecting and are administered under diversified circumstances. Reasons for the existence of repositories lie in historical and administrative requirements, and the methodology employed may differ depending on the traditional placement and organization of the records plus the nature of the material.

In each case, a relationship exists with libraries on the level of the repository. The National Archives and Records Service, for example, maintains close communication and working relationships with the Library of Congress. Whether or not state archives are combined with a state library into one agency, each must know the scope of the other's effort. Where a special library exists to serve business and industry, it is necessary for the parent corporation to maintain its own published information in order to form current policies and make effective decisions. Where a college or university has established an archival and/or regional manuscripts collection, it is necessary to maintain close coordination and communication with the library so the total informational resources of the institution can be made available to students and faculty.

NATIONAL ARCHIVES AND RECORDS SERVICE

The largest archival institution in the world is the National Archives and Records Service (NARS). In its building in Washington, D.C., NARS contains almost one million cubic feet of textual records; millions of pho-

3

tographs, maps, and charts; thousands of reels of motion pictures; and thousands of feet of microfilm. NARS also administers 14 records centers throughout the United States which contain millions of cubic feet of semi-current and noncurrent records, but even this large amount of records is small compared to that still in the custody of the various federal agencies. In addition to the records centers, NARS operates five presidential libraries.

When President Franklin D. Roosevelt signed into law the 1934 legislation creating NARS, he provided the nation with a cultural institution constantly contributing to government and scholarship. A distinguished historian, Robert Digges Wimberly Conner, served as the first Archivist of the United States, reporting directly to the president. In 1949 NARS fell victim to the Commission on Organization of the Executive Branch of the Government and was placed under the newly created General Services Administration (GSA), the housekeeping arm of government. Even though the archivists on the staff of NARS and the leadership of the GSA are highly competent, the placement of NARS under GSA has met with ill will from many scholars and archivists who maintain that NARS should be independent because of its primary cultural role.

H. G. Jones, in his book *The Records of a Nation*, objectively weighed the existing program of NARS against its potentials. Jones considered the placement of NARS under GSA a "fundamental handicap" since the GSA has additional responsibilities for the Public Buildings Service, Federal Supply Service, Transportation and Communications Service, Defense Materials Service, and the Property Management and Disposal Service. He considered this an illogical union.

The protest against the placement of NARS within GSA results from the cultural purpose of NARS and the housekeeping tasks of the GSA. One of the factors contributing to the placement, however, is an important housekeeping and cultural role NARS performs. The records management function of NARS is measured both in preservation of essential information and in dollars and cents, but the end result of NARS is measured in the "cultural enrichment of the American people."[1]

The assimilation of records management by NARS was a natural union. Records management requires appraisal and evaluation of semi-current and noncurrent records and is a job for a professional archivist, upon the advice of the records manager. Theoretically, the science of records management overlaps the science of archives, but is differentiated from some of the routine housekeeping tasks of recommending filing systems, equipment, computer applications, and methods of disposal of records. The United States is unique in including records management functions within the responsibilities of archives. This American phenomenon, the records manager-archivist, is the result of bold archivists who recognized the importance of records appraisal at the stage of records creation. Since NARS established records management as a proper archives function, several state archives have followed suit.[2]

In contrast to European countries which maintain close ties between their nations' archives and those of the lesser agencies and cities, NARS maintains no formal link with the states. There is no national archival legislation or funding administered by a national archival agency in the United States.

Despite the absence of NARS involvement in state and local archival activities, NARS continues to lead in archival theory and contribution to scholarship. We owe to NARS the concept of the "record group," a refinement of the French concept of "fonds." In the area of records description, we owe NARS credit for an ambitious program of inventories. In the area of dissemination of information contained in federal records of value, we owe NARS credit for the program of microfilm publication, which has brought federal records to the desks of many scholars.[3]

Other NARS activities include the planning and promotion of special programs. The public, when visiting NARS, finds satisfaction in viewing interesting and innovative exhibits and films. *Prologue*, the official journal of NARS, is an award-winning publication based entirely or in part on records in custody. Many research projects are stimulated by the articles appearing in this scholarly publication.[4] In addition, NARS houses the National Historical Publications and Records Commission which administers grants to libraries, historical societies, and nonprofit organizations. Also, NARS publishes the *Federal Register*, found on the shelves of many libraries, which contains an account of the multitude of bureaucratic rules and regulations promulgated by federal agencies.

If the NARS organizational status was tarnished by its placement within GSA, its cultural contribution has not suffered. Still maintaining the high dignity envisioned by Roosevelt, NARS continues to make unequaled contributions to the understanding of our government.

STATE ARCHIVES

By the time NARS was created, over a third of the states had taken action to establish some form of archival endeavor. In the process, the states did not bother to collaborate with neighboring states but proceeded independently. Today, state archives find themselves as divisions, branches, or departments of state libraries, historical societies, archives and history departments, or as independent agencies. Where strong historical societies did not develop, as in the South, state archives were placed under a commission with authority over archives and history. In the western states, archival functions found themselves as part of historical societies since the societies were established early and supported with public funds. In the older states, private historical societies preempted the development of public supported societies, so archival service usually became part of state libraries.[5] There are exceptions of course to these generalizations.

All but three states have established state archival agencies since 1901. Eight states have placed their archives under state libraries and ten have placed them under historical societies. The remaining states have placed them with historical commissions, departments of archives and history, or have created independent archival agencies. The holdings of all state archives, which total 931,000 cubic feet of records, are less than the holdings of NARS.[6]

As a result of the independent pursuit in establishing state archives, legislation, administration, and effectiveness vary from state to state. Many states have effective archival programs, but the majority are still quite small. In a few states, the official records are dangerously neglected and have little financial support. Inadequacies in the laws make enforcement of existing legislation difficult. It is generally easier to convince legislators and the public of the need to support historic sites and preservation projects than to support the care of official government records. The Society of American Archivists (SAA), through its Committee on State and Local Records, has encouraged better care of state records but has been generally ineffective in changing deteriorating conditions. The past scope of the problems of caring for state archives is described in Ernst Posner's book, *American State Archives* (1964).

Three major factors contributed to the founding of state archival programs. As soon as the American Historical Association was founded in 1884, it concerned itself with the preservation of historical source materials. At the 1899 meeting of the association, a Public Archives Commission was organized to investigate and report on the status of the nation's public record repositories. The commission's report increased interest on the part of the states to make concrete provisions for administration of their archives.[7]

Another factor of great importance to the advancement of state archives was the Works Progress Administration's Historical Records Survey, the first nationwide archival effort. It is unlikely that American society will ever again experience a records survey that touched every level of government in most of the states and involved institutions dealing directly with the people. It was during this enormous survey that Americans began to recognize the importance of archives, and, during these formative years, the archival profession gained recruits. Historical survey workers numbered 7,150 and engaged in the preparation of guides, inventories, lists, indexes, and similar methods of listing public records.

The objective of the survey was to create and publish the inventories of archives in the 48 states, 3,066 counties, plus the cities and townships. Soon after the survey, the founding of the SAA and the establishment of the National Archives secured more public interest and understanding in establishing and supporting state archival programs.

The third factor in the development of state archives was the interest of the National Association of State Libraries. As early as 1910 it established a Committee on Public Archives to exchange information on those libraries to be charged with the future care of archives. From that time on, the committee informed the association of new legislation and activities in the archives field,[8] and its role was historically instrumental in the inclusion of archival services in the 1956 publication of the association's *Role of the State Library*. The influence of state libraries' interest in archives is seen in the early development of the state archival programs of Alabama (1902), Illinois (1921), and Arizona (1937). The state library and the state archives were combined in each case.[9]

HISTORICAL SOCIETIES

The American archival scene on the state and local level is widely influenced by the proliferation of historical societies. O. Lawrence Burnette, author of *Beneath the Footnote: A Guide to the Use and Preservation of American Historical Sources*, goes further when he states: "The collective holdings of these organizations contribute significantly to the documentation available for the history of any modern state and are second in significance only to manuscript sources at the national level." [10] These societies are supported by both private and public funds and collect all manner of historical material. The collection policies of these societies vary and usually are confined to the history of their constituent area. Some large and prestigious societies are not confined geographically, such as the State Historical Society of Wisconsin which denotes on its informational brochure: "The scope of these resources encompasses the history of Wisconsin and the other states as well as many foreign countries."

Walter Muir Whitehill, an expert on American historical societies, has commented that historical societies are as varied as they are numerous, some without buildings or possessions.[11] Whitehill says of the privately supported societies: "Some are extremely valuable; others are worthless. Of the 2,000 listed in the American Association of State and Local History's *Directory of Historical Societies and Agencies* (1961), only a little over a third report ownership of libraries. Many of these libraries would prove to be a few shelves of miscellaneous books that might include somebody's set of Waverly novels. There are, however, a few dozen societies of paramount importance to the American historian."[12]

COLLEGE AND UNIVERSITY ARCHIVES

America was slow to develop archives for colleges and universities, and official neglect has taken its toll among the records of our academic institutions. Scattered efforts to preserve university records on an informal basis were generally ineffective. It was not until 1939, for example, that Harvard established its archives on a formal statutory basis. Since Harvard's establishment, university archives have received more and more attention. As in most university archives, it was historical, rather than administrative motives which led to the founding of Harvard's archives.

The importance of the university maintaining an archives and manuscripts program is seen by the number of institutions offering the Ph.D. in history. In 1941–1942, only 58 institutions offered the degree and in 1966–1967, the number had risen to 114. Also, a survey conducted by Walter Rundell, Jr., [13] revealed the importance of original sources to graduate students in history, the problems of their research, and institutional differences.

There are two activities commonly associated with university archives: the housing of the official records of the university and the systematic collecting of historical manuscripts. Many times these two activities are combined under one head and, in the majority of cases, are under the auspices of the university library.

The systematic planning for collecting manuscripts has resulted in some exemplary university programs. The regional historical collections of Cornell and the Universities of Texas, Michigan, and Oklahoma are examples of prior planning and geographical definitions in collecting. Many of the newer collecting institutions find competition with appropriate universities designed for certain records to be healthy, but activities purely duplicative and extravagant rivalries make the scope of collecting difficult to distinguish.

Many archive and manuscript collections at the university level supplement their holdings by purchasing microfilm copies of noted collections from other repositories. Also, many institutions are filming and photocopying parts of their own collections for the benefit of others and to enhance prestige and further cooperation.

Universities are leading the changing emphasis in collecting programs. Where libraries and repositories once concentrated on collections relating to politics, government, and military history, more attention is now devoted to records of businesses, labor organizations, authors, physical science, medicine, and the arts. Black studies programs and courses emphasizing ethnic groups have had their effect on manuscript collecting. The change in collecting emphasis is also seen on the agenda of meetings, articles in journals, reports on acquisitions, and the establishment of new collections for special subjects.[14] In addition, oral history programs are continuing to gain support from universities since communication on paper has been diminished by the communications revolution.

BUSINESS AND RELIGIOUS ARCHIVES

Another type of archive, the business archive, continues to flourish as corporations age and gain increased prestige. Corporate records are preserved for the same reasons documents are appraised as valuable in government or institutional collections. The business archive preserves corporate charters, contracts, minute books, and correspondence mainly for legal reasons and for researchers who are interested in understanding the role of business in society. A business archive may help management by providing data necessary for examining policy decisions and for making current decisions.

The first objective of the business archive is to serve the administrative needs of the corporation. The archivist is often part of a special library and information center team. Some of the best known business archives are Boeing, Walt Disney, Western Electric, Ford Motor Company, the Rockefeller Foundation, and the Bank of America.

Religious archives in America are the most neglected. The Director of the Concordia Historical Institute in St. Louis, August R. Suelflow, has stated: "I believe that I would be safe in saying that we have no archival agencies in the narrow, limited sense among our religious groups in America."[15] Suelflow goes on to say that the reason why so many of our church-related archival-historical agencies have not contributed much to the field of archival theory and practice may be that their status, function, form, and future have never been critically examined. The result is an absence of a systematic archival program for church records in America. Exceptions do exist. For example, the Mormons developed a sophisticated system of not only preserving, storing, and filming their own information, but of systematically filming many records in other types of archives. Now they have millions of frames of microfilm containing millions of names for scholarly genealogical research.

Few records give more insight into the life of a community than church records. They are valuable to the economic and social historian, and because of this have been collected by nonchurch-affiliated agencies.[16] The only comprehensive listings to date of ecclesiastical and institutional records of monasteries, schools, missions, foundations, and lay organizations are found in the inventories of the Historical Records Survey. Many individual churches had their records cleaned, arranged, and inventoried by survey staff.

PROFESSIONAL ORGANIZATIONS

Indications of the worldwide scope and importance of the archival profession are the professional archival organizations in various nations. Professional archival associations are common in Europe and America, but are by no means developed in every country. The Vereeniging van Archivarissen in the Netherlands, founded in 1881, recruits its members from archival ranks. In Spain, Belgium, and Poland, the professional associations consist of library organizations with which the archivists have united. The British Records Association, organized in 1932, recruits its members from ranks of archivists, librarians, and manuscript curators. The move in many countries toward the last half of the twentieth century is toward association with librarians for mutual development.

The SAA was organized in 1936 and has continued to grow in membership and activities. In 1971, figures showed that the SAA had doubled its membership in the past decade. The committee system evolved from planning workshop sessions to undertaking surveys and publication programs. Committee affairs have become productive and the society is more responsive than it was a decade earlier when a small group controlled activities.[17]

The SAA sponsored a study of state archival programs which resulted in Ernst Posner's book *American State Archives*. Still another void in the literature was filled with the sponsorship of Victor Ghondo's *Archives and Records Center Buildings*. The SAA journal, the *American Archivist* (1937–), appears quarterly and is the most comprehensive source of writings on the theory and practice of archival science.

The SAA was instrumental in founding the International Council on Archives, created under the auspices of UNESCO in 1948. The council meets every four years, but has a more intimate international round table which meets during the interval to exchange ideas among leading archivists of the various nations. The round table is a working group and is the only international group which meets to discuss matters of common concern to the archival profession.[18]

SUMMARY

The archival setting is complex, both nationally and internationally. The profession involves many specialities, organizations, institutions, and people. Users who frequent repositories may take for granted the complex activities which make the papers available, librarians may or may not understand the complexities, but archivists must be willing to collaborate and communicate their problems and achievements.

NOTES

1. H. G. Jones, *The Records of a Nation: Their Management, Preservation, and Use* (New York: Atheneum, 1969), p. 256.
2. Ernst Posner, *Archives and the Public Interest*, ed. by Ken Munden (Washington, D.C.: Public Affairs Press, 1967), p. 136.
3. Ibid., p. 135.
4. James B. Rhoades, "The Role of Archives in the 1970's," in *Louisiana State University Lectures in Library Science*, no. 17 (Baton Rouge: Louisiana State University, 1971), p. 4.
5. Robert H. Bahmer, "The Archival Function in the States," *American Archivist* 22 (April 1959): 203.
6. Robert L. Brubaker, "Archive and Manuscript Collections," in *Advances in Librarianship*, vol. 3, ed. by Melvin J. Voight (New York: Seminar Press, 1972), p. 248.
7. Ernst Posner, *American State Archives* (Chicago: University of Chicago Press, 1964), p. 19.
8. Ibid., p. 24.
9. Joseph Scammell, "Librarians and Archives," *Library Quarterly* 9 (1939): 433.
10. O. Lawrence Burnette, *Beneath the Footnote: A Guide to the Use and Preservation of American Historical Sources* (Madison: State Historical Society of Wisconsin, 1969), p. 168.
11. Walter Muir Whitehill, "The Libraries of the Privately Supported Historical Societies," *Library Trends* 13 (October 1964): 165–178.
12. Ibid., p. 167.
13. Walter Rundell, Jr., *In Pursuit of American History: Research and Training in the United States* (Norman: University of Oklahoma Press, 1970).
14. Brubaker, "Archive and Manuscript Collections," pp. 250–252.
15. August R. Suelflow, "Maximum and Minimum Standards for Religious Archives," *American Archivist* 32 (July 1969): 227.
16. Mabel E. Deutrich, "American Church Archives—An Overview," *American Archivist* 24 (October 1961): 387–402.
17. Philip Mason, "SAA at the Crossroads," *American Archivist* 35 (January 1972): 7.
18. Ernst Posner, "Round Table on Archives—Warsaw, 1961," *American Archivist* 25 (January 1962): 23.

THE LIBRARY SETTING

Library statistics for 1974–1975 reveal that there were some 28,000 public, academic, special, and school libraries in the United States. Public libraries alone accounted for 7,652 and had a total income well over one billion dollars. College and university libraries numbered 1,605 and served 8.6 million students. Academic libraries boasted a total of 455 million volumes and operated on an annual income of $909 million.[1]

To reduce the cultural, educational, and recreational value of the nation's libraries to statistics may be unimpressive. What is important is the increasing intricacy of the information profession as it attempts to respond to a society which is moving toward more complexity. This movement has forced changes upon institutions involved in the information profession, and they have tried to respond with research and experiments in attempts to manage information in varied and changing formats. Much of the research work now under way in libraries is influenced by the presence of technology, reflecting the movement of society into a highly technical era. As a result the librarian is becoming more and more a manager of information and finding the emphasis of the profession increasingly on the tools of information management. Perhaps the most important tool is the technology which can help solve communication problems by reducing the forces of distance and time.

In face of these vast changes, it is important that the profession has not yet lost sight of the purpose of its endeavors—service to the user. Emerging responsibilities still determine the direction of the profession's emphasis, and signs point to continuous involvement in a multitude of issues which confront libraries. Traditional library support of government, education, economy, and recreation are now supplemented by interest in the integration into society of groups now isolated because of their lack of access to and assimilation of information. This mission enhances the profession's cultural contribution since librarians, directly or indirectly, serve as essential elements in the intellectual growth of the people.

NATIONAL COMMISSION ON LIBRARY AND INFORMATION SCIENCE (NCLIS)

The importance of the present status and future directions of the library profession is seen in the work of the National Commission on Library and Information Science, an official government body created in 1970 to determine the status and future needs of the information profession. In 1975, the commission issued its final report. The basic underlying assumption of the report is that a national program for libraries and information science must be based upon a scheme of networking using the new technology. The commission believes the time has come to develop a national network of libraries and information centers as a total system rather than encourage the proliferation of information networks now in existence. Many of these proliferated networks are not compatible with each other.[2]

The commission goes on to say that libraries are in financial trouble, are crowded and understaffed, and are facing the withdrawal of categorical federal aid. They are unable to keep pace with current demands and have little time or flexibility to create new programs, to experiment, or to undertake studies of value to their patrons.

To correct the generally poor condition of library and information service in the United States, the commission sees a future national network involving the cojoining of general and specialized libraries throughout the country. The purpose of such a national network would be to permit users access to the total knowledge resources of the nation, while remaining in one physical location. This implies that the problem of information utilization is one of distance. The commission has stated that "Building a national network of libraries to promote knowledge and progress between and among people of the states will require the same foresight that Congress had when it invested in the Interstate Highway Act to promote travel and commerce."[3]

The commission is serious about the threat to the nation's libraries and information centers through lack of money and the inability to take advantage of the new technology on a large scale. "Unless we take steps now to develop a unified program of library and information service in the United States, the National Commission believes the current system of libraries and information centers will be unable to cope with the nation's growing information requirements."[4]

The work of the commission gives insight into the current problems and achievements of the library profession. As reflected by the issues confronting the commission, the library profession is embarking on a new stage in its development. The extent of involvement of other information professions, including the archival profession, in the new directions which are now taking shape is yet to be seen. It is logical to assume that any proven system, in this case a new national network, which can increase the availability of information will be used by other professions concerned with information dissemination.

COUNCIL ON LIBRARY RESOURCES (CLR)

Much of the research required to formulate new directions for library involvement is supported financially by the Council on Library Resources (CLR), sponsored by the Ford Foundation. Established in 1956, the CLR aids in the solution of problems of libraries and archives through grants, contracts, and other means. Examples of CLR projects achieving national support and recognition by finding better methods of information dissemination are the Ohio College Library Center and the New England Library Information Network. In addition, the National Serials Data program and the Cataloging in Publication program administered by the Library of Congress have been funded. In the field of archives and special collections, CLR grants have helped to identify regional archives and manuscript repositories in the Soviet Union and to create microfilm publications of rare materials. The council has also been heavily involved in the Library of Congress Preservation Research Office, which has undertaken a variety of research projects including archival qualities of ink used in ball-point pens, glue removal methods, paper bleaching, and microfilm storage. The CLR also funds the Cataloging Secretariat of the International Federation of Library Associations (IFLA) which is particularly concerned with international cataloging standards.

The IFLA has as its concept an integrated worldwide system for the exchange of bibliographic data. It contributes to various UNESCO library programs and works to cultivate relations with other international organizations, including the International Council on Archives, where cooperation is especially acute in areas of book preservation and public access to documents.

LIBRARY OF CONGRESS

The de facto national library of the United States is the Library of Congress. Created in 1800 for the sole purpose of serving Congress, the library has vast collections at its center of service. Among the many national functions it assumes are international exchange and acquisitions programs, the creation and maintenance of classification and subject headings systems which serve as national standards, and the distribution of cataloging information in a variety of formats. In addition, the library publishes and maintains the *National Union Catalog* and the *National Union Catalog of Manuscript Collections*; provides reference service by mail as well as in-house; participates in interlibrary loan; provides national and international photoduplication services; administers the national library service for the blind and physically handicapped; experiments and conducts research in all areas of library and information science; and promotes standards to increase accessibility to all kinds of library materials.[5]

Its collections are universal and the largest in the world, numbering almost 74 million items in 1974. The basis of these vast collections is a sophisticated system of bibliographic control which is used to distribute bibliographic information to subscribing libraries in the form of cards, proof slips (preprint copy), and Machine Readable Cataloging (MARC) tapes.

The most preeminent manuscript collecting institution, and the one which houses the largest single collection of manuscripts, is the Manuscript Division of the Library of Congress. Founded with a heavy emphasis on the American Revolution, the Manuscript Division soon developed a more contemporary scope. About 90 percent of recent acquisitions are from the period since 1900, a period during which records of enormous proportions have been created. The division's fame comes chiefly from its comprehensive collection of presidential papers, from George Washington to Calvin Coolidge. The entire collections of presidential papers of the library number nearly two million.

The problem of bibliographic control of manuscript collections on a national level has long concerned the Manuscript Division. The division has established standards for the description of manuscript collections, and these standards have been accepted by the American Library Association. As a result, two important developments in bibliographic control of manuscripts surfaced in the decade of the 1960s, the National Union Catalog of Manuscript Collections (NUCMC) and the MARC format for manuscripts. It is still too early to assess the impact of MARC on bibliographic control of manuscripts. The potential of MARC is so great because of its widely accepted standards and flexible format. It is logical to assume that as local institutions gain control over their papers and archives, and as they report these collections to the Manuscript Division, some funds will be appropriated for automated control of this data for inter-institutional communication of bibliographic information. (See Part Four, "Standardization and Technology," for a detailed discussion on the MARC format for manuscripts.)

Since the Library of Congress leads the nation in the collection of manuscripts, healthy competition for collections exists between the library and major repositories. The prestige factor of having one's family papers in the Library of Congress gives that institution a decided advantage. Complaints have often been heard over competition between the Library of Congress and major repositories, but a 1962 survey by Robert Brubaker reported that most competition affecting major repositories stems from universities and other local libraries.[6]

STATE LIBRARIES

Next in governmental hierarchy are the library services of state libraries. Strategic to the total American library system, the state library varies from state to state in legislative responsibilities, powers, and programs. In 1956 the National Association of State Libraries prepared and adopted a statement of its firm policy on the scope, goals, organization, and principles of the operation of state libraries. These policies are implemented to a greater or lesser extent in each state.

Named as basic functions of state libraries in the statement were: service to all agencies of state government; promoting library development; improving library standards; and securing legislation. The statement also recognized the state library as providing "general library service" and included archives, legislative reference, state history, government publications, law, and public library development as components of general library service. The statement also made it clear that the most effective state library is one which encompasses all library services of the state government "so integrated as to function with economy and efficiency."[7]

The state library is a major link in total library service to every citizen of each state. The establishment of standards for library development, the provision of specialized consultants for other libraries in the state, and the planning of library development of all types are common responsibilities of this agency. In addition, state libraries are expected to stimulate cooperative and coordinated library system efforts and administer federal grants. In the area of library service to state government, the state library agency provides service to the courts and legislature. A state library may publish a roster of state agencies, officials, and boards, as well as administrative rules and regulations. Included in service to state government is the archival function which in eight states is part of the parent state library agency.

The National Association of State Libraries included the following paragraph on archives in its 1956 statement:

> An integrated state library includes the archives and archival program of state government. Responsibility for establishing a records management program and disposing of state records might be shared with other appropriate state authorities, but the preservation, administration, and servicing of archives is a function of the state library. The library also advises local governments on the management of their records.[8]

The SAA lodged a protest with the National Association against inclusion of this paragraph. The society's reason for protest was the concern over the prospect of archival policies being determined by state library personnel with no training in the management and administration of archives. This has not proven to be a valid concern since state archives within a state library are headed by competent archivists. It is unlikely that such a protest would be heard today from the society.

Another legitimate function of a state library, also outlined in the 1956 statement, is the responsibility for collecting, preserving, and servicing materials relating to state history. This charge has led approximately 20 state libraries, whether or not they are the state archival agency, to undertake the development of manuscripts to supplement their collections of books on state and regional history.[9]

HISTORICAL LIBRARIES

Important in our discussion of the library setting are the libraries of the historical societies, particularly on the state level. These libraries are usually invaluable for research since the collecting activities have concentrated on publications and imprints of a state or local origin. The age of these materials alone makes the historical society libraries a research haven. Among the largest of the historical society libraries is the Massachusetts Historical Society Library, with holdings of over 500,000 volumes. Accompanying titles and books in these special libraries are scores of manuscripts and other nonbook items.[10]

Special collections documenting the history of a region, subject, person, or institution are found in every type of library. Throughout the nation (and in many parts of the world) public libraries have assumed as part of their responsibility the collection, preservation, and dissemination of local history. In smaller libraries, where archival training is not available, archival methodology is scarce. In the United States it is rare that a public library will concern itself with the care of official county or city records. But services of informed public librarians are needed where neglect and disinterest on the part of the county and city officials lead to the eventual loss and destruction of the records.

John L. Hobbs, in *Local History and the Library*, made a practical case for library custody of official records of the municipalities and for the employment of an archivist on the library staff. In Great Britain (Hobbs is British) an increasing number of archivists are employed by libraries. Still, Hobbs was concerned over the qualifications of persons responsible for archival work in libraries.[11] Hobbs asserted that "The old assumption that librarianship and archive science are twin professions is true . . . in theory rather than in practice. Certainly they serve substantially the same ends, but the practical means of achieving these are widely different; and the basic differences in methodology must be appreciated."[12]

RESEARCH LIBRARIES

It almost goes without saying that there is one type of library, not yet mentioned, that exists primarily for the use of scholars. It is the research library that has the most in common with archival institutions. Research libraries, the heart of constant research and publication, are parts of institutions notable for the variety and depth of their holdings. Their professional arm, the Association of Research Libraries, has over 80 institutional members (by invitation only), and their collections range in size from 500,000 to 8 million volumes.

The modern research library has two major problems in common with most archival institutions. First, while older books are surviving well, works published during the last hundred years were printed on paper with a high acid content and consequently, their disintegration will be a fact of life. Second, rising costs and decreasing financial support are threatening to cause mediocrity.

SUMMARY

It is apparent from this overview of libraries and their responsibilities for manuscripts that manuscript collecting is a legitimate function of libraries regardless of the type of institution. Library control over manuscripts is significant, as a study by Robert Brubaker revealed in an analysis of entries in Philip Hamer's *Guide to Archives and Manuscripts in the United States* (1961). With the publication of the *Guide*, the scope of library control and management of manuscripts became clearly evident. Twenty-three libraries reported holdings of over one million or more manuscripts. Six additional libraries that possess holdings over one million did not report. Since Hamer's *Guide*, several other libraries have reached the one million mark. Among the libraries of over one million manuscripts, 12 were major historical societies, 20 were major university libraries, and 6 were public, state, and independent research libraries. The New York Public and Yale University Libraries have approximately nine million manuscripts each and are without doubt the largest except for the Library of Congress which has over thirty million.[13]

Among the libraries which had at least 500,000 but less than one million manuscripts were five historical societies, two university libraries, and two other libraries. Many libraries had holdings ranging from a few manuscript items to 500,000. Among these were 21 major historical societies, 260 college and university libraries, 200 local historical societies, 220 public libraries, and almost 20 state libraries.[14] Based on 1961 data, these figures are given only to show the enormous influence library management has had over the administration of archives and manuscripts.

NOTES

1. "Library Statistics," in the *Bowker Annual of Library and Book Trade Information*, 20th ed. (New York: R. R. Bowker, 1975), pp. 216–229.
2. National Commission on Libraries and Information Science, *Toward a National Program for Library and Information Services: Goals for Action* (Washington, D.C.: NCLIS, 1975).
3. "A New National Program of Library and Information Service," *Library Journal* 99 (February 15, 1974): 451.
4. Ibid., p. 455.
5. Douglas M. Knight and E. Shepley Nourse, eds., "The Library of Congress as the National Library: Potentialities for Service," in *Libraries at Large: Tradition, Innovation, and the National Interest* (New York: R. R. Bowker, 1969), p. 444.

6. Robert L. Brubaker, "Manuscript Collections," *Library Trends* 13 (October 1964): 236.

7. National Association of State Libraries, "The Role of the State Library," *Illinois Libraries* 38 (October 1956): 201.

8. Ibid., p. 203.

9. Brubaker, "Manuscript Collections," p. 232.

10. Walter Muir Whitehill, "The Libraries of the Privately Supported Historical Societies," *Library Trends* 13 (October 1964): 165.

11. John L. Hobbs, *Local History and the Library* (London: Andre Deutsch, 1962), p. 91.

12. Ibid., p. 247.

13. Brubaker, "Manuscript Collections," p. 228.

14. Ibid., p. 232.

THE ARCHIVIST AND THE LIBRARIAN

Librarians and archivists are of the same family. Because of a common ancestor, the old clericus, a literal keeper of the books, kinship between librarian and archivist was very close until the invention of the press. After Gutenberg, the situation changed little until many books became available. Librarians, as they were called, maintained custody of both books and manuscripts[1] until the archival profession, developing on its own, emphasized the differences to maintain autonomy, and created a body of professional theory and practice.

Librarians have a longer history and have been involved in more specialities than the archivist we know today. The modern archivist is a product of recent vintage. In 1909 Waldo Leland said in his presidential address to the American Historical Association:

> The time was when anyone who liked books and was unfit for anything else could be a librarian, but that time has long passed. The evolution of the archivist will proceed somewhat as has the evolution of the librarian.[2]

Leland's comments have proven to hold truth. Applying commonly accepted tests of professional status, the librarian seems to hold an edge. The archivist, still excitingly involved in a maturing profession, lacks a formal educational vehicle for entry into the field. Both the archivist and the librarian claim a systematic theory which delineates and supports the skills that characterize their professions. Both possess a service orientation, another mark of professional status. A career concept, sustained by formal associations, is also a test of professionalization claimed by both groups. There is no consensus as to what extent librarians and archivists possess the remaining tests of professionalization. There is, to be sure, extensive education required of both in a systematic theory, but there is controversy over the intellectual content of the knowledge base for librarians, and controversy over what constitutes the knowledge base for the archivist.

The librarian has a formal accredited educational vehicle for entry into the profession, but the archivist must rely on specialized institutes, seminars, and meetings to supplement a solid base in the social sciences and humanities. Many archivists draw upon the vehicles of the librarian or the historian to fill the educational gap.

Archivists have interested themselves in the librarian since their beginnings, as evidenced by their annual meetings and literature. Like the librarian, archivists have attempted to find out just who they are, and the attempts of both groups have usually resulted in unscientific generalizations. If Leland's comments are indeed prophecy, then let us take a look at librarians to see where they have come from and attempt to gain insight into who they are.

Verner Clapp, a library leader, read a paper before the Society of American Archivists in 1950 and gave his view of the changes the library profession was experiencing. He said:

> Time was when a librarian was expected to be a bookman, with a wide acquaintance of books and authors, of languages and literature. His basic education was usually in the arts and his professional training a science. All this is changing. Librarians are now engineers, and no librarian worth his salt considers books as literature, but merely as the stuff (he calls them "materials" or "collections") which is to be subjected to engineering processes. His talk is not of authors, but of administration; he never mentions books, but, instead, bibliographic control or organization. His speech and his writings are turgid with the vocabulary of what is called "management" and with the clichés of many applied arts and sciences, with words such as communication, mass media, channels, data utilization, . . . and modules.[3]

True, librarians are now information scientists and the graduating library school student may choose, from a variety of specializations, the type of library work to enter. The profession is mobile, and the variety of experiences available in the field are broad enough to fit many differing personalities. There are specializations for building collections, controlling materials, applying systems and automation techniques, and answering reference questions from the simple directional to the highly complex ones involving literature searching. There are also those who specialize in administration, audiovisual materials, government publications, service to the disadvantaged, rare books, and special collections.

Stereotypes of librarians are without statistical evidence. Conjecture and suppositions concerning the personality and image of librarians still exist and haunt a dynamic profession. Intellectually, energetically, and methodically, the library profession is equipping itself to offset the old ghost stereotype by continually improving a professional theory in order to strengthen personnel practices, and by controlling entry into library schools.

A 1958 study conducted by the Association of College and Research Libraries ("A Study of Factors Influencing College Students to Become Librarians") revealed that it is the influence of other librarians which stands as the most important factor. Other factors named included publicity, use of libraries, work experience in libraries, and library education. Each of these factors has significant influence to the extent that it is combined with one or more other factors.

Paul Wasserman has stated that those who choose librarianship as a first choice are small in number, and the prospect of professionalization through education is reduced as a result. Recent studies indicate that nine out of every ten Americans in the major professions have elected their professions as the first choice. The ratio drops as one goes into the technical or clerical classes.[4] Many entrants into the library profession have been teachers, housewives, or have come from religious vocations. Whether the librarians disliked their first occupational choice or were failures in their tenures is not known.

Trends in library manpower have fluctuated drastically since 1966. In 1966 the number of professional librarians was almost 90,000, but an American Library Association study in 1964 indicated a shortage of over 100,000. A comparative study in 1968 by the University of Maryland School of Library and Information Services concluded that only 3,816 vacancies existed in libraries between 1962 and 1965.[5] Quite a discrepancy!

As federal aid lessens and financial crisis looms, library graduates face stiff competition for jobs and many are required to accept less favorable positions than they could have demanded five years earlier. One cause of this is the number of people not holding a professional degree who are called upon to assume library jobs. This practice adds to the job crisis, and vacancies become filled with nonprofessional employees.

Although more than 80 percent of librarians are women, more than 90 percent of library administrators are men. Inequality and lack of choice for women are evident. Many women librarians may feel secure in their knowledge that most of their colleagues are women, but a 1968 thesis by Ben Bradley at the University of Texas revealed that 86 percent of the heads of the 50 largest public libraries were men and all of the academic library heads of the 50 largest academic libraries were men.[6] Also, a 1971 survey by the American Library Association revealed that women librarians earn an average of $3,400 less than their male counterparts and the gap is widening. A 1973 survey reported in *Library Journal* (January 1974) brought the figure to $4,740. It is easy to see why a 1964 article in *Esquire* advised men to become librarians because "men fill most of the top administrative posts."[7] For any meaningful alleviation of discriminatory attitudes toward women, laws and attitudes must change.

Percentage figures indicate that women archivists are in a better situation than their sister librarians with regard to discrimination. Twenty-eight percent of the founding members of the SAA were women and today 33 percent of the members are women. Forty-seven percent of the men and 35 percent of the women state they occupy administrative or supervisory positions. It is interesting to note that for library jobs within archival institutions, women outnumber the men two to one.[8]

Because the archival profession is small in numbers, it is easier to survey the manpower makeup. This was done twice, once in 1956 and again in 1970. Ernst Posner, the dean of archivists, attempted a quantitative approach to the question "What is the American archivist?" His greatest difficulty was in distinguishing the archivists' principal activities because there were many who migrated between archives and records management and a noncatalogable unit consisting of history professors, librarians, and others not classifiable. Some of Posner's data was collected in 1956 and verified in a 1970 questionnaire mailed to members of the SAA, again attempting to identify the makeup of the American archivist.[9] A total of 423 responses were received from a total of 1,060 questionnaires. The responses placed the archival profession in a favorable light since most of the respondents identified themselves as administrative heads of agencies or programs, or professional administrative assistants.

The 1970 questionnaire revealed an interesting number of statistics. The average age of the 40 percent sample of the SAA membership was 44.9 years and the average length with their present employer was 12.7 years. The following principal areas of activity and their corresponding percentages reflected the heterogeneous makeup of the SAA: 34.3 percent identified with archives; 14.4 percent identified with manuscripts; and 12.1 percent were records managers. Five percent claimed archives and records management, and an understanding 0.2 percent (only one lone individual) claimed to be a manuscript curator and records manager. Three and three-tenths percent wore three hats; those of the archivist, the curator, and the records manager.

The survey also revealed that there was a low degree of mobility within the archival profession but that its respondents displayed an active interest in a wide variety of professional organizations (an average of slightly more than four professional memberships). The most frequently reported type of organization was state historical associations. Twenty-one and one-tenth percent were members of the American Historical Association, and 11.6 percent belonged to the American Library Association. Nineteen percent of the respondents indicated memberships in state library associations. There was very little change in the educational backgrounds of the members as compared with the Posner survey of 1956. An impressive 86 percent held academic degrees and 64 percent held advanced degrees.

A significant point involving the clarification of just who the archivist happens to be is the American phenomenon of records management as an important adjunct of archival work. American archivists possess authority over records from their creation to ultimate disposition and this far exceeds European archival prerogatives. Also unique to the American archive profession is that admission into the field is not as narrowly limited as in the older countries where entry is the result of years of study and preparation.[10] Still another unique quality, according to Posner (who began his career in Germany), is that American civilization seems to mitigate against the archivist's participation in scholarly activities. Posner attributes this in part to a lack of leisure time and to a barrier between official duties of the archivist and research work.

Posner, himself a contributor to American archival development, summed up his views of the American archivist's ingredients when he stated:

> We had to be and we must still be effective salesmen of our cause, in a world that suspected us of being mere antiquarians, lap dogs that society could easily dispense with. . . . We have successfully developed the methods and techniques of archival arrangement and description. Last, but not least, in entering the field of records management, we have displayed the elasticity of thinking and the dynamism that are characteristic of the American people.[11]

It is true that archival activities have yet to capture the imagination of the general public and there is very little concerning archivists in current literature such as plays and novels. Too many people assume that archivists are only familiar with past events and details of family history. Another misconception is the impression that archivists have no concern for the present, and perhaps it is their surroundings that lead to this notion. Many people recognize that archivists have interesting and exotic jobs, but they also are under the impression that archivists do not have many demands on their time.[12]

The changing nature of society and of the archival role in society has required archivists to cease being mere custodians (if they ever were) and to become actively involved in the creation and collection of records and manuscripts. It takes special education and training for the archivist to fulfill this role. Archivists need specialized information concerning the government, institution, or historical background of the collection they represent. They need experience in working with scholars and must be qualified in appraisal techniques in order to pass the life or death sentence over records. Archivists must have the ability to converse in the language of their colleagues in other departments and agencies. They must be able to explain what archives are, what the archivist does, and the services an archives can offer.[13]

The archivist must be able to converse with such diverse users as auditors investigating tax records of a public official, attorneys investigating petitions, surveyors examining original field notes, genealogists seeking pension claims, and entrepreneuring politicians determining voting patterns of districts.

Archival work is so broad that no one person can claim to have detailed knowledge of all its aspects. The archivist who works chiefly with government records has developed an expertise that curators of manuscript collections will not have. Conversely, the curator will develop expertise in the location and collection of diaries, personal papers, and literary manuscripts which the government archivist will not develop. There are specializations in records management, administration, oral history, collection building, and business, church, and institutional archives. Repair, preservation, description, arrangement, appraisal, and automation are other specializations.

Whatever specialization an archivist chooses, there is much satisfaction in the work, no small part of which is derived from the customers—the users. Helping others find the information they need, helping an official establish certain rights of an individual, or guiding a scholar in virgin research—all contribute to the joys of the archival vocation. Another source of satisfaction is the archives themselves. Archivists must know their collections well and from this knowledge comes satisfaction in digging into unknown events, persons, and places. Archivists also have an excellent opportunity to publish from their own archives.

There are differences in the work of archivists according to the type and size of the archives, the organizational placement of the archives within the institution, and the level of difficulty under which the archivist is expected to perform. There are several common functions which all archivists at one time or another, regardless of inherent differences in management situations, perform. There are the tasks of answering questions or inquiries through searches of records and consulting with researchers. An archivist also makes specific documents and information available. State archivists, in particular, find themselves interpreting and applying statutory authority and policies, attending conferences, and occasionally presenting speeches on subjects drawn from the archives. Archivists have always selected and acquired, through study and research, records and papers for preservation. All archivists have been faced with arranging and processing records and papers, preparing finding aids and publications, editing, proofreading, and handling correspondence.

Determining who is qualified to be an archivist is a problem which perplexes management of libraries and archivists themselves in need of professional expertise. The problem becomes critical in that the location of a qualified archivist and the recognition of an archivist from credentials require specialized knowledge concerning the current archival milieu. Herman Kahn, when he was president of the SAA in 1970, posed the question of how archivists identify themselves in terms of occupation when asked what one does for a living. He suggested that few archivists would say "I am an archivist" as one says "I am a dentist" or "I am an electrical engineer." He observed that few archivists are not also something else and that many archivists describe themselves as "historians, editors, librarians, educators, analysts, documentalists, information retrieval specialists, audiovisual specialists, and government officials."[14]

However nebulous the identification problem may be, the archival profession is a dynamic, growing field, boasting an influx of younger members and shaping its own future directions. The directions for the future will have to answer just what the archivist is, just as the library profession has had to grapple with the identity of librarians. Corresponding with the influx of younger members into both professions are indications that the future identity of archivists and librarians will be quite different from what we have experienced in the past.

The main winds of change are in social involvement. Both professions have traditionally seen their work as neutral. It is becoming increasingly difficult to separate professional identification and social issues. Already the late 1960s witnessed a resurgence of protest within the library profession, particularly over the Vietnam War. The doves asked for resolutions against the Vietnam War, and the hawks scrambled to defeat any statement from the American Library Association on nonlibrary-related issues. The Vietnam War was the hottest issue and divided librarians severely.[15]

Librarians are also continually involved in the fight for intellectual freedom, clearly a social issue which overlaps into professional concerns. Librarians, for example, opposed publicly, through the American Library Association, individuals like Gov. Lester Maddox of Georgia who once "advised Georgians to 'Burn those books'—especially books on subversive subjects like anthropology, political science, and human ecology."[16] Librarians revolted against the American Legion in Kingston, New York, when legionnaires asked for a ban on the magazine *Ramparts*. Librarians in Inglewood, California, fought back when the public library was attacked for having records by the Beatles and the Doors, which were thought to advocate drug use.

Archivists are not protected against the overlap of social issues and professional concerns. In 1970 Professor Howard Zinn presented a paper at the annual SAA meeting on "The American Archivist and Radical Reform" which elicited heated controversy concerning social involvement for the archivist. Zinn lamented United States involvement in Vietnam and gave a strong case for the archivist to become involved, through his profession, in social causes. Zinn stated:

> Professionalism is a powerful form of social control. By professionalism I mean the almost total immersion in one's craft, being so absorbed in the day to day exercise of those skills, as to have little time or energy or will to consider what part those skills play in the total social scheme.[17]

He pointed out that library and archival professions were connected with dissemination of knowledge in society and as such were important occupations in which to exert social control. He suggested that archivists not be so scrupulous about their neutrality, but promote through their profession "human values of peace, equality, and justice" by collecting the papers of the insignificant as well as the powerful and by instituting oral history projects of things happening at the time, such as civil rights movements and antiwar demonstrations, rather than giving attention only to past reminiscences of prominent figures. This argument has received the support of archivists who no longer want to ignore the poor, the obscure, the radicals, and the outcasts.[18]

As both professions continue to evolve, it is quite likely that the controversy of the late 1960s, the intellectual freedom questions of today and the future, and the demand by the users for significant data on the heretofore unknown will place the archivist and librarian more into the public eye and will enhance their image. The establishment will have to bend because users are expecting much more in unique methods of collecting and disseminating the information.

Because socially involved careers have no problem luring many into their ranks, archives and libraries should have no problem in recruiting those who desire jobs linked to human aspirations. It is a fact that archives and libraries offer more opportunity for a career which will contribute positively to the human condition than those jobs in the profit-making sectors.

NOTES

1. L. Quincy Mumford, "Archivists and Librarians: Time for a New Look," *American Archivist* 33 (July 1970): 269.
2. Cited in H. G. Jones, "Archival Training in American Universities, 1938–68," *American Archivist* 31 (April 1968): 135.
3. Verner Clapp, "Archivists and Bibliographic Control," *American Archivist* 14 (October 1951): 305.
4. Paul Wasserman, "Elements in a Manpower Blueprint—Library Personnel for the 1970's," *ALA Bulletin* 63 (May 1969): 581–589.
5. August C. Bolino, "Trends in Library Manpower," *Wilson Library Bulletin* 43 (November 1968): 277.
6. Helen Lowenthal, "A Healthy Anger," *Library Journal* 96 (September 1971): 2597.
7. Ibid., p. 2598.
8. Mabel Deutrich, "Women in Archives: Ms. versus Mr. Archivist," *American Archivist* 36 (April 1973): 174.
9. Frank B. Evans and Robert M. Warner, "American Archivists and Their Society: A Composite View," *American Archivist* 34 (April 1971): 159.
10. Ernst Posner, *Archives and the Public Interest*, ed. by Ken Munden (Washington, D.C.: Public Affairs Press, 1976), p. 165.
11. Ibid.
12. W. Kaye Lamb, "The Changing Role of the Archivist," *American Archivist* 29 (January 1966): 3.
13. Leroy Depuy, "Archivists and Records Managers—A Partnership," *American Archivist* 23 (January 1960): 52.
14. Herman Kahn, "Some Comments on the Archival Vocation," *American Archivist* 34 (January 1971): 4.

15. Eric Moon and Karl Nyren, eds., *Library Issues: The Sixties* (New York: R. R. Bowker, 1970), p. 392.
16. Ibid., p. 388.
17. Howard Zinn, "The American Archivist and Radical Reform" (Paper presented at the 34th annual meeting of the Society of American Archivists, Washington, D.C., September 1970), p. 3.
18. Ibid., p. 15.

TWO

SIMILARITIES AND DIFFERENCES

MATERIALS AND METHODOLOGY

MATERIALS

It would be easy to state that the differences between archives and libraries are that archives contain documents and libraries contain books. The statement, however, would be inaccurate and misleading. One might more reasonably state that libraries contain printed matter, and that the librarian must deal with printed matter in various forms. Although still inaccurate, it is closer to the truth. Archivists also must deal in a minor way with some printed matter, usually consisting of reports, printed enclosures, or publications that complement the documents either as interpretive histories, biographies, or edited publications of the documents themselves. It is also conceivable that a true archives could contain a significant collection of printed books, if it were the archives of a publishing house or a university press.

The distinctions between archives and libraries become even less pronounced when other than printed matter is considered. Both can be expected to contain maps and charts; both contain audiovisual materials. Thus, since it is evident that printed materials are not the sole province of libraries, it is clear that manuscript materials are not the sole province of archives.

Terminology is not settled in the archival profession, and there are shadings in meaning that are important to an understanding of materials, their custody, arrangement, and method of processing and description. It is important that some terms be properly used, not just for standardization purposes, but so that legal implications may be realized as one questions the authority to handle certain materials, the legal aspects of access or restriction, the formalities required for disposition, and the authority by which the materials are transferred to other caretakers. The basic differences between personal papers and archives are:

1. purpose of creation
2. ownership
3. legal provision for access
4. legal standing

The purposes for which personal papers are created vary. A doting mother preserves the letters of her son who is off to war; a socialite just automatically keeps most of her correspondence and invitations, as well as some record of her social expenditures. An unsuccessful author keeps long series of correspondence with a successful author because the correspondence is treasured. Teachers and writers keep files of their correspondence, diaries, lecture notes, and the notes and manuscripts of articles and books.

Records, on the other hand, are created and retained for corporate purposes. They were not intended for a general posterity, but for corporate reference. "While the value of public records to historians and other social scientists can hardly be overemphasized, their primary value is to the government which created them to be used in the transaction of public business."[1]

Manuscripts are the personal property of their creator or collector. They can be destroyed, sold, willed, or given away as the owner wishes. They become part of an estate at death and can have inheritance taxes levied on them to the extent of their appraised value.

Archives are the official records of a corporate body. The regulations of the corporation for handling corporate possessions must be applied to the records. An officer of the corporation cannot destroy or otherwise dispose of the corporate records without recourse to corporation regulations or the governing body. In the federal government and in some state and municipal governments there are firm strictures about disposition or destruction of government property. In lieu of a specific act, such as the Federal Records Act (44 USC 2101), the government property acts normally apply to records.

Since manuscripts are personal property, access to them can be controlled by the owner. Traditionally, the owner can also control access even after selling or deeding his papers to an institution. This is a questionable practice, but has had its benefits by assuring that a collection of important papers is saved where the donor would be reluctant to deed them if unrestricted access were to be permitted. It is also a practice that has long years of application behind it.

Archives, on the other hand, are controlled by a complication of legal provisions. If they are records of a private corporation, the corporation can restrict access to protect trade secrets, patent or literary rights, or anything else, and provide for no public use of the records unless in response to a law or government regulation, such as those of the Securities Exchange Commission. If the corporate body is the federal government, access is controlled by a variety of regulations and laws, including the National Security Act, the Freedom of Information Act, and Executive Order 11652 relating to classified documents.

It is clear that archives and manuscripts cannot really be treated the same way without modification. Although both a manuscript collection and an archival record group may consist of documents, maps, photographs, clippings, and printed ephemera, the specific approach that the manuscript curator or the archivist takes to the material is different. In addition, archival records that remain in the continuous possession of the creating body have a legal document aspect to them that does not apply to personal papers or records alienated from their originator.

Libraries and librarians are often made the caretakers of manuscripts and archives, usually in a special collection, which may also contain rare books and other special holdings. Too often there is confusion over the distinctions between the material under the librarian's care. The librarian feels that because rare books can fit into the general classification scheme used in the rest of the library—although they are housed separately because of their value—the same can apply to archives and manuscripts; or that maps, photographs, and other materials can be treated as library material no matter what their source. But it cannot be overemphasized that the distinctions between library materials and archival materials are not distinctions of kind. Rather, they are distinctions derived from the method and intent of creation.

The differences in creation, ownership, and access to library materials and archival materials also extend to differences in their description and the concept of interrelations regardless of form. Archives as well as libraries separate materials by form, and it is rarely that documents, film, photographs, and sound recordings are filed in the same shelf area. In a large institution each form may require its separate administrative unit. In this regard, libraries and archives follow the same practice, dictated by the practical necessity of different shelving, containers, handling, and user requirements. But the similarities of treatment do not extend to the description of the material.

Library classification rules are different for different forms of library material. In many cases even the main catalog does not reflect the existence of some material, which is cataloged only in the custodial unit. When the National Union Catalog of Manuscript Collections began its work in 1958, the original concept was to create a card for each manuscript collection cataloged and enter the card in the main catalog at the

Library of Congress. Cross referencing, subject headings, title veri-
fication and other technicalities posed such a problem, however, that the
procedure was soon abandoned, and the manuscript collection is now
cataloged only in the Manuscript Division.

If a manuscript collection comes to a major library accompanied by
materials in other forms, for the most part the nonmanuscript items are
sent to the appropriate custodial division. If they are cataloged, there may
or may not be a provenance note on the catalog card. More often, the only
way to reconstruct the provenance of the collection is to inspect the original accession record. If there were many accessions from the same
source, and if they were multimedia in nature, it might be impossible to
reassemble the collection, even intellectually.

In many cases it does not matter. If an estate bequeaths a mixed collection to a library, it might be irrelevant to have the books, maps, incuna-
bula, and photographs or prints in physical or intellectual relationships.
Each item or each form is discrete and can be cataloged and interfiled in
the general collections.

Archives present another problem, and archivists have reached another solution. In a later section on methodology, the specific descriptive
techniques used in archives will be discussed. In this section on materials
we will only say that while corporate records may be physically separated
because of their peculiar requirements, they are kept as a unit intellectually in the descriptive device used for their control. Therefore, if
the records of the public relations office are received in the corporate archives, the written records, statements, press releases, and other documents might be located in one stack, the photographs in another, the public relations films in another, and taped radio spots in a fourth. But the
description of the records prepared by the archivist treats all the records
as a unity, describes them in their proper organic relationships, and only
notes in passing that they are physically separated. This archival view of
respect of original intellectual order was summed up recently by one author:

> While an item among the records of an organization and another discrete
> item in a collection of private papers may look quite alike, their significance
> as historical evidence may be very different. Their relationship to other ma-
> terials is important. Official records have grown as bodies of material, often
> referred to as "files," representing the lines of organizations and preserved
> according to their functions and development.[2]

This is not to say that one will not find a separate detailed description
or list of holdings of a custodial unit of an archives, just as one finds separate catalogs in the various parts of a library. But these descriptions are an
elaboration on the general guide to, or a description of, the complete record unit, which should be the first entry point used by the researcher.

In summary, except for the quantity of books, there is little difference between the kinds of material found in a large library and in a large archives. The proportions by type differ, but the variety of types does not, to any significant degree. Differences are in the arrangement and description of the materials, with library practices generally treating each item as a discrete unit to be considered on its own merits, while the archives practice treats each unit in the context in which it was created.

METHODOLOGY

The ultimate aim of both librarians and archivists is the orderly placement of material within their holdings so that it can be easily retrieved when called for. In addition, librarians are obliged to keep itemized records of their holdings so that they do not unknowingly duplicate the acquisition of items. Since archivists deal mostly in unique material, they are not generally concerned about duplication.

In the preceding section we defined the difference between the materials handled by a librarian and an archivist as one based not on physical characteristics but rather on origin. Comparison of library-archival methodology makes it evident that the concept of origin affects the method of acquisition, processing, description, and reference service on the materials in the care of each.

Acquisitions

For the most part, libraries purchase books and most of their other materials. The source of their funding is unimportant to our discussion here. Whether that source is tax money, an endowment, institutional or corporate budgeting, or income from sales or other sources, most libraries must budget their expenditures to do the most good with their financial resources. This requirement leads naturally to an acquisition policy based on the needs of the library users or clientele. An astute librarian can select wisely within the framework of the acquisition policy; defer purchases when nearby libraries can be cooperated with to provide complementary or supportive collections; if possible, use serials exchange as a means of increasing certain coverage; and judiciously encourage interlibrary loan use for special requests. In short, with some cooperation from the users, an effective librarian has tight managerial control over growth of the collections, both physical and intellectual.

Some libraries depend heavily on gifts of books and other material, in addition to money bequests. The dependence on gifts, however, removes some collection control from the library administrator and introduces an element of whim. Unless the librarian can exercise tight control over unwanted gifts, the library will soon find its acquisition policy in a shambles.

The acquisition of personal papers is also an activity which, if poorly administered, could cause a manuscript curator, a historical society, or similar institution to go under. Curators of manuscripts run many hazards. They cannot plan acquisition growth except in general terms. The acquisition policy may be narrow or broad, but actual acquisitions are subject to conditions over which they have little or no control.

Most manuscript collections are built through gifts. Having once established an acquisition policy based on consanguinity of collections within the range of needs of the clientele or purposes of the institution, the manuscript curator must initiate the chase. The curator must be familiar with people who might have created or developed materials in the field; be aware of competition from other institutions seeking the same material; woo the prospective donor; and once having won, show everlasting gratitude by treating the collection of the great person with deference and respect. The manuscript curator knows that for every gift from a donor, there is an additional increment waiting in the wings from the donor's relatives, who usually are also relatives of the great person. The manuscript curator cannot be certain that more collections in a special field exist, or that they will not be given to another institution first. And, if a living subject does not wish to give up his private papers, there is often nothing for the curator to do but hope that the heirs look favorably on his bid for the collection.

Present laws relating to the gift of private papers add a measure of doubt as to whether live subjects will donate their own papers—even more doubt than existed in the 1960s and earlier. Few manuscript repositories have so far had a policy of purchasing collections of private papers, but the lack of incentive for a person to donate papers for tax advantage may drive more repositories to that recourse. It is only tradition that has operated in the past to impede purchases of personal papers. After all, libraries purchase other special collections—prints, rare maps, rare books—why not personal papers? If fair market value can be established for tax purposes, the same value could be used for sale or purchase purposes. Until now, however, most manuscript curators have had to rely on their persuasive powers in order to increase the growth of their collections.

A true archivist, that is, one operating as keeper of the permanently valuable records of a corporation, has none of the problems of the librarian or manuscript curator. Under normal circumstances the archivist is working under a retention policy that has been administratively determined. There is no need to purchase any materials, because the corporate records are already owned and are merely transferred to the archives when they are retired. This condition is evident in the change in terminology when shifting from library to archival discussions. Materials become "records," evaluation becomes "appraisal," acquisition becomes "retention," and so on. The emphasis also shifts subtly on the role of the archivist vis-à-vis records, as opposed to the librarian or manuscript curator vis-à-vis their materials. The latter select from a universe of books or papers those which they wish to add to their collections, and they care little about items that they do not select. Those unselected books or papers are available for sale or gift to other institutions with other collecting policies. The archivist, on the other hand, is the rightful inheritor of all records created by a corporate body. A decision on what to retain also implies the opposite responsibility—to decide what should be disposed of, and therefore permanently lost—and this adds a dimension to the job not shared by colleagues in library or manuscript work.

> Disposal—to my mind the most difficult problem relating to records management—is indeed far from being a simple matter. It involves nothing less than an attempt to judge the future need of scholars. . . . No change in the role of the archivist is more significant than the way in which circumstances are forcing him into a position in which he has a life and death control over much of the material. And the decisions involved can rarely be postponed. The volume of records is frequently so great that delays may be costly and even impracticable. The archivist must select—and select promptly—or lose all.[3]

With this responsibility to select, the archivist in the United States in the past 40 years has developed a few new professions from which to derive support. The supportive roles are in the area of records management. Government and business have developed positions of records administrators, records center operators, correspondence managers, forms administrators, and a full spectrum of other occupations concerned with the creation, use, storage, and disposition of records. At the end of the pipeline is the archivist, who works hand in hand with the records administrator to devise schedules of what shall be kept, and for how long.

The dimension of records control from the origin of the record to its ultimate fate—retention or disposition—is what sets archival practice apart from that of the librarian and manuscript curator. It could be argued that if the entire range of archival responsibility is not being exercised, then the person performing archival duties is not a fully functioning archivist. Just as complete library service has to include determining acquisition policy, acquisitions, cataloging, and reference service, so complete archival service has to include prearchival records activities. Without that function the archivist foregoes primary control over the appraisal, retention, and disposition process, since such decisions can be made by others, prior to sending corporate records to the archives.

Processing

The librarian catalogs and classifies a book. The process consists of applying a classification designation, which locates that book in a prearranged universal scheme of all human activities. The scheme is there as a guide to be consulted, and the librarian's intent is to fit the book into the scheme.

An archivist, on the other hand, has no scheme with which to work. When dealing with corporate records it is true that the scheme may be self-evident: the administrative or functional structure of the corporation. The archivist must recognize the structure, sometimes after arduous historical study of the development of that structure over a century or more, and make certain that the records arrangement or description conforms to it. There is no external imperative for putting the documents and other records in any preordained pattern. There is only an implicit imperative derived from the corporate structure itself. Each agency, office, division, or department whose records come to the archivist may have its own records arrangement or filing scheme. It is the archivist's responsibility to identify and understand these patterns and verify the order of the documents within them. The written description of the records, prepared in an inventory, register, or sometimes guide, should closely resemble the organization chart or organizational structure of the corporation at various points in time. Thus, the description may proceed from the records of the board of directors, through those of the offices of the president, treasurer, comptroller, chief sales manager, and so on through the branches and infrastructure. Such complex information cannot readily be subject classified and captured on a catalog card. If one thinks of the complexity of the describable units involved, one can see why archives have not adapted any form of library cataloging and classification techniques.

A major library may contain a million or more volumes, each a catalogable unit. It would be impossible to maintain such a large collection without at least descriptive cataloging. At one time there was an attempt to redefine the archival describable unit from the record group—which is essentially the records of a government bureau or other large unit of an agency—to the series, which is the equivalent of one file (i.e., Letters Received) of one office or function within the bureau. The attempt failed; probably because of the size of the project as compared to the resources available, but also partially because the influential archivists of the day (the early 1940s) felt that description at the series level was cataloging, and cataloging was a library technique not applicable to records, since it described them out of context. The depth of feeling for organic unity was expressed by one involved in the dispute: "Records have meaning only insofar as they are kept together and their organic relationship to each other retained. As long as that relationship is retained, that body of records has harmony, symmetry, and significance."[4]

This state of idyllicism remained undisturbed in major archives for almost 30 years, as series cataloging was abandoned. But perhaps the archivists who most vehemently opposed series cataloging were victims of their own prejudices and confused cataloging with classification. Even as late as 1942 there were strong advocates for classifying archives by library rules. At a meeting of the Society of American Archivists that year, Randolph W. Church of the Virginia State Library made the proposal that library classification be applied to archival series.[5] To classify archival series would, admittedly, be impossible, but to catalog them (for example, identify them by title, dates, and size, describe them in summary, and rearrange them intellectually for information retrieval purposes) is quite possible without destroying the concept of *respect des fonds* or inherent organic interrelationships.

The device that is now permitting such cataloging is the computer, which allows the archivist to have it both ways. Through data formatting and manipulation, the archivist can retrieve information either in full inventory or in series catalog format. Such an approach is now well along toward implementation at the National Archives and is being adopted or studied by other archival institutions.

The librarian dealing with a catalogable unit, be it a book, map, or sound recording, goes through steps of identification, description, analysis, and classification. In no way does the librarian change the basic structure of the material at hand by rewriting the title page, reorganizing chapters, changing the table of contents, modifying the title, or creating an index that does not exist. The work or item at hand is a manufactured product that needs to be described in such a way that it can be identified and retrieved when needed. Author names may be verified, variant titles may be noted, series affiliations may be documented, but these actions are all done externally and do not affect the structure or content of the book.

The manuscript processor is faced with completely different circumstances when confronted with a collection of personal papers. The processor's role is fourfold: to analyze, select, arrange, and describe the papers and materials at hand.

Since the papers are those of an individual, they may have only a superficial arrangement, and even that may have been disturbed in boxing and transporting them to the repository. The curator's initial analysis is for form—correspondence, scrapbooks, diaries, photographs, etc. The analysis then turns to variations within each form—business correspondence, personal correspondence, scrapbooks of clippings, photo albums, household receipts, legal documents, literary manuscripts, speeches, etc.

From this analysis the curator may determine that there should be a selection, with some items scheduled for disposal, usually by class but occasionally on an ad hoc basis. Ephemeral printed matter might be one class: printed advertising brochures, unannotated road maps, tourist pamphlets of little significance, and so forth. Bank statements, household bills, auto repair invoices, and related items might be evaluated very low and scheduled for disposal in the papers of a statesman such as Harold Ickes or John Foster Dulles but might make up the most important part of a collection of a socialite such as Evalyn Walsh McLean or Perle Mesta. Selection from a collection once it has been accessioned is a controversial subject among manuscript curators, with most taking the conservative view that once a collection has been received it is inviolate, and everything must be retained, resulting in a box or two of miscellany at the end of all the legitimate categories of describable items.

After analysis and the outlines of a selection policy or establishment of selection criteria, the manuscript processor proceeds to arrange the collection. This process is invariably required with personal papers, although the amount of arrangement necessary varies from case to case. Sometimes it means only placing well-organized correspondence in boxes, followed by diaries. At other times it means examining every letter, determining if it is personal or business in nature, separating the two, matching outgoing with incoming, and deciding whether an alphabetical or chronological order is preferred. It is probably necessary to put the papers in file folders and to label them. With a large collection this process can take many man-months, and the manuscript administrator has to determine the ratio of expended time to anticipated research.

When the collection has been arranged, the manuscript curator puts down in a descriptive device called a register a statement of what has been done. The register is not a rigid format, but a recent analysis of some 400 registers from over 50 institutions indicated that informally, and without any standards to apply, most manuscript repositories are preparing registers that present information in essentially the same format.

When an archivist accessions records he formally transfers responsibility for the records from the office of origin to the archives, and under normal circumstances the records are considered to be permanently valuable. If all the necessary preliminary work has been done by records administrators, forms managers, and the appraisal staff of the archives, there should be little for the archivist to do with the records except transfer them to archives containers, analyze the series, label the containers, and prepare a description based on the analysis and external evidence. In practice, the process is not so simple. Records management practices are not universal, and the records have often been poorly maintained by the office of origin. Archivists frequently receive old files that have been shifted from place to place, provenance is uncertain, and the archivists' dogma of respecting original order is rendered useless by the seeming lack of any order at all in the records. When the National Archives began operations in 1934 it started a sweep of government bureaus for archives. In a few years it had swept up 600,000 cubic feet of them. There was no history of good record keeping in most agencies, with a few shining exceptions. Forty years later, considering that records acquisition has continued at a fair pace, the National Archives is still in the process of digesting some parts of that first massive inundation of paper. This is not atypical, since many archives, state and local, have been established in only the past 40 years and are faced with accessioning and processing records accumulated over the past 100 years or more.

Unfortunately, most books and manuals on archival practice presume that the great day has already arrived when archivists have caught up on their backlog; have instituted appropriate preaccessioning practices; and receive only clean, well-labeled, orderly files, ready to be shelved and used. Such manuals, therefore, avoid the term "processing," shun "arrangement," and never discuss "selection" for disposal after accessioning. In the real world, however, most archivists will do their share of arrangement and selection in order to keep their records holdings under control. When they are engaged in such activities, archivists process along the same lines as manuscript curators.

But there are a number of significant differences. There are retention schedules that can act as guides to disposal of records already accessioned. Just because an agency's payroll records were scooped up in the records sweep and accessioned does not dictate that they must be kept, since the retention schedules for that agency probably provide for the disposition of all payroll records. Therefore, the archivist has explicit guidelines to follow. Secondly, public or corporate records contain a higher proportion of duplicate and carbon copies of documents than do personal papers. This fact contradicts the view that archives are, by their nature, unique materials. Almost every government document has a transmitted copy in one file, a retained copy in the file of the originating office, and a variety of other copies spread throughout the system. When a disastrous fire recently destroyed some 20 million veterans records, it was found that a good number of the files could be reconstructed from copies housed elsewhere by other agencies. It is true that this condition applies more to twentieth-century records than to older ones, but there is considerable evidence that multiple copies of correspondence were made in earlier days. In the diplomatic field it was very common to make and sign multiple copies of treaties and transmit them via a number of different ships because of the hazards of transportation.

The archivist, therefore, has considerable opportunity for selection or weeding of his records; perhaps not in the case of important treaties, but certainly in the case of carbons of routine correspondence and multiple copies of printed or otherwise reproduced reports.

Description

The purpose of description is the same for librarian, manuscript curator, and archivist: to provide sufficient information about the described information unit to permit a researcher to determine whether or not to look at the unit for research purposes. Secondarily, the librarian wishes to provide an administrative record of holdings so as to avoid unwanted duplicate acquisitions.

The librarian uses a number of descriptive devices: the catalog card, both descriptive and subject, filed in a main catalog; a shelf list; a public catalog; and often a special area catalog. The main catalog and shelf lists are almost exclusively administrative in nature, since they are rarely available to the research public. In the catalog the classification scheme has multiple purposes—to provide subject relationships and therefore bring like works together, and to encode the book with a unique identifier for location and retrieval purposes. The librarian will also describe materials in special bibliographies (usually centered on one class, or subject area), and contribute to the National Union Catalog or a state or regional cooperative catalog. Recent acquisitions lists, either locally distributed or published, round out the most common library descriptive materials.

When the manuscript curator has finished processing a collection and undertakes the descriptive task, he must make a number of decisions not required in library description. He does not have a self-contained book before him. There is no title to the collection, no date, no chapter headings, no index, no publisher, or place of origin. The curator, therefore, is compelled to provide this information. Based on internal evidence and buttressed by some external research, he decides what each piece of information will be and puts it together in a register.

The ideal manuscript register consists of seven parts, comparable to some sections of a book. They are: preface, introduction, biographical sketch, scope and content note, series description, container/folder listing, and occasionally an internal index. The purposes of these parts are to detail the collection provenance; restriction on its use; its size and span dates; how it fits into the institution's collecting policy; the interrelationships with other collections; a note on the important periods of the subject's life; a description of each of the forms of material found in the collection with indications of their quantity, dates and a brief analysis of their content; an essay on the person whose papers it represents; the extent to which the collection relates to that person's career; lacunae; location of supplementary material; a box-by-box list of folder titles and dates of each folder's contents where appropriate; and, finally, occasionally an index to the contents of the finding aid itself if it is a very large and complex collection. In some cases, especially with small collections, an item list will be incorporated in the box/folder list.

Item listing of manuscript collections was once a common practice that never quite attained universal application. The preparation of such lists is exacting and time-consuming. It requires a minimum of four pieces of information: the author of the item, date, number of pages, and, if a letter, the addressee. More complex indexing might include place where written, subject or subjects covered in the document, proper names mentioned, and enclosures or attachments. If an item index is prepared on cards, a card should be prepared for each information element of the item. Thus, if five elements are used, there are five cards to be prepared for each item, and five catalog listings are provided. Modern manuscript collections running to thousands or tens of thousands of documents preclude such a detailed treatment. But the physical difficulty of preparing such indexes is not the only deterrent. There is serious doubt about the benefits to be reaped from an item approach, since the great majority of documents in a modern collection are unexciting and even unimportant standing alone and only have meaning in context. A manuscript collection cannot be approached or understood through an item index. It must be read, and in the reading one can begin to piece together and understand the character of the person whose papers the collection represents and the succession of events in which the individual was involved.

It would be unrealistic, however, to believe that there are not times when an index is extremely useful. If one is searching for the scattered correspondence of a notable figure, it would be handy to know if any is to be found in a large complex collection. One would not expect to find letters of early film actress Mary Pickford in the papers of the architect of U.S. airpower, H. A. (Hap) Arnold, but an existing index to Arnold's papers indicates that there are some. And some collections are endowed with so much potential research value that an item index is a distinct benefit to scholars. Or the frozen arrangement of some collections is such that the only approach can be through an item index.

The last two attributes, research value and permanent arrangement, are what make the Papers of the Continental Congress such a prime example of a collection in need of item indexing. No matter what the original arrangement of the papers might have been, they were rearranged and bound in the middle of the nineteenth century. Since then they have been microfilmed, thus further freezing their order. Twelve partial indexes were prepared over the years, with the most recent being an attempt made in the 1940s. But until recently the 60,000 documents were enough to thwart almost any effort. A project to index the Papers of the Continental Congress with computer assistance is nearing completion at this writing. It is estimated, however, that the index will cost some $6 per document by the time the task is completed, with the bulk of the costs being the human analysis of the documents, not the computer processing time.

For this project the computer simply eliminates the necessity to prepare multiple cards and to keep multiple index files. One set of data is processed into the computer for each document, and the machine prepares the multiple lists according to program instructions. This is not a process recommended for collections of low research value, and costs must be equated with anticipated benefits to the researcher.

Registers and item lists are not the sole products of manuscript curators' descriptive work. If they are responsible for a large collection it might be appropriate to prepare a public catalog by collection title. Often the catalog will contain a single alphabet consisting of cards received from the National Union Catalog of Manuscript Collections (NUCMC), to which curators would have reported by preparing another descriptive device, the NUCMC data sheet. Some repositories prepare the data sheets, send the original to the NUCMC, but retain photocopies in looseleaf binders, available to the researcher. In such instances it is not unusual for curators to insert a copy of the collection register and perhaps an enlarged statement on access limitations after each data sheet. They have thus created a guide to the repository holdings, arranged alphabetically. A copy of this guide or any segment of it can be copied and distributed to inquiring researchers. It is then only a step to the preparation of a printed and bound guide, with perhaps an index of its own. But one must be cautious about carrying the process too far. It is preferable in many respects to have a flexible looseleaf guide than a printed and bound one that is out of date the day it is printed because of continuous collection growth.

The descriptive process does not end with registers, a public catalog, or a guide. The curator will, out of self-defense, almost always create a multifaceted accession file, by accession number, by date (sometimes unnecessary if accession numbers are applied chronologically), by collection title, and by donor. The donor list is especially useful when providing information to a donor for tax purposes, or when memorializing the gifts of a long-term donor.

In summary, the manuscript curator has certain administrative controls to apply to collections, as well as intellectual controls. But except when copying off a folder label or a literary manuscript title, curators do what librarians dealing with books never do: they provide the title, series titles, and sometimes the indexes themselves.

The archivist follows the descriptive process of the manuscript curator very closely. In the usage of the profession his descriptive device is generally called an inventory instead of a register, but its elements are very similar. The inventory usually contains a preface, which is a broad statement appearing in printed inventories about the institutional holdings and how the records being described fit into them. There follows an introduction, which is a hybrid—half general description of the records (scope and content note) and half institutional or agency history (biographical sketch). This is followed by a series and subseries listing, which provides a basic paragraph description of series. Normally, that is the extent of inventory coverage. There is rarely a container list of series, and almost never an item index of all items in the records described in the inventory.

In addition to the inventory, archivists prepare accession records and other administrative controls. They may find it appropriate to analyze certain series very closely, so they prepare a special list of records within one series. Or they might think it appropriate to analyze certain items of importance only, and they thus prepare a select list.

Each level of description[6] has its place in the hierarchical descriptive techniques of archivists. Where they differ from manuscript description is in the limitation for providing titles to archives. The name of the record group is the title of the organizational unit being described. The title of the series is usually a description of form (reports, accounts, correspondence, etc.), with some dates and an indication of size. Only in the narrative series description paragraph does the archivist get to expound on an analysis of the documents.

In summary, the librarian describes material by analysis, but classifies it into a prearranged universe according to a preestablished scheme or rules. The archivist uses external evidence, such as corporate or government structure to determine the proper arrangement and description of records. The manuscript curator uses logic, often individually arrived at, after analyzing the papers in question, to provide an arrangement and description.

Reference Service and Use

The one essential difference between libraries and archives is the concept of open versus closed stacks. It is this difference that immediately requires different reactions of staff to researcher. Open stacks have never been uncommon in libraries, and they have been most common in public branches and school libraries, while in universities, historical societies, and large urban reference centers stacks are almost always closed. Even this is changing, however, and as stacks open up and browsing is permitted, the need for reference service should drop. (I say "should" because I have seen no figures to indicate that this is actually the case.) The availability of open stacks can also result in simpler catalog configurations, since the reader is able to survey a class of works by actual inspection and does not have to rely on the catalog to provide clues to contents. Since one of the primary roles of a reference librarian is to interpret the catalog to the reader by giving hints for subject headings in the main catalog or appropriate class numbers in a shelf list, the opening of stacks and simplification of the catalog should reduce the duties of the reference librarian. We are speaking here only of general collections. In a special collection, and especially in rare books, the closed-stack rule is still almost universal, and the expertise of the reference librarian is called into play hourly.

I know of no archives or manuscript collection that has open stacks. The uniqueness of the material, the consequent monetary value of much of it, the fact that papers are loose within boxes, and the impossibility of arranging shelved items in any observably logical order all mitigate against allowing the researcher to roam freely through the stacks. In addition, it has already been noted that there is rarely more than a title catalog to manuscript collections, and no cataloging of archives. Relative shelf locations are unimportant, and records may be moved from one stack area to another for administrative convenience without users being aware of the shift. It does not often happen, but military records may be shelved next to agriculture, and records from the eighteenth and the twentieth centuries may share the same stack range. It is unimportant how records or documents are placed on shelves, so long as there is a master finding key for the archivist to use when retrieving them for the researcher.

It is also true, and has been noted, that descriptions of archives especially, and manuscripts to a lesser degree, are not precise. Quite often a series will be described in its gross dimensions, and no container list will be available to the researcher. In addition, the title of a series or the label on a box are not the clues for establishing subject relationships in archives. The subject content of a series and the institutional interrelationships of records are what will lead the researcher through the bureaucratic maze to the subject.

It is an adage, therefore, that the primary key to manuscripts and archives is the archivist. One can enter a public library anywhere in the country; take a few minutes to get oriented; determine if the card catalog is Dewey, Library of Congress, or some variation; look up one's material; fill out a call slip; hand it to the call desk attendant, or go to the stacks; and when the work is received begin to read and take notes. It is not necessary to say a word to a librarian or consult a reference specialist unless special problems arise in interpreting the catalog.

It is not possible to proceed in that manner in a documents collection. Typically, the researcher approaches the archives or manuscripts room, declares an intention to do research, is asked by a clerk or a professional staff member to fill out a registration form and present some identification. The researcher is then asked the nature of the research, and a dialogue between researcher and archivist begins. The archivist explains something of the corporate organization and history around which the records are organized, or the extent and complexity of the manuscript holdings. As the dialogue continues, the archivist may consult the files for information that will inform the researcher of previous research done on the topic, with an indication of what records were used by the previous researcher. The archivist, content with a grasp of the researcher's intent, presents the researcher with a selection of finding aids—registers, inventories, special lists, or indexes—and asks the researcher to refine the request for documents. By searching secondary works on the researcher's topic, the archivist and/or the researcher may come up with citations to record groups, series, or specific documents from the repository. When enough information has been gathered to provide both archivist and researcher with sufficient leads, the archivist will disappear into the stacks and emerge some time later with a few boxes or volumes of material. These will be charged out in various ways to the researcher who can then begin to browse, read, and take notes. In a complicated or obscure research project, it may take a few hours of conversation with the archivist before any records are forthcoming.

Most archivists are subject oriented, rather than procedure oriented. Their value comes not from their knowing the system of their institution, but from their grasp of the subject matter of a set of records or documents. They soon become specialists, both in the history of the agency or agencies of whose records they are custodian, and in the content of those records. Since the material with which they work is unique, their knowledge and expertise are nontransferable—a highly proficient specialist in the records of the colonial government of Georgia would be a neophyte if he transferred to the Colorado State Archives. Therefore, archivists tend to be stable and long tenured, unless they move into administrative positions. Researchers who enter an archival institution with the concept that they know exactly what is wanted and ask for only a specific set of records because they do not want to bother the staff, are not using the one basic facility that is imperative to archival research—the reference archivist. And since archivists are subject specialists, they will be interested in the location of other records relating to those in their custody. Manuscript curators are continually on the lookout for additional collections, and therefore are in continual competition with other institutions for the papers of the great and famous. During their careers they become aware of the collections that got away as well as the great catches that they were responsible for. They also remember where the collections got away to, and consequently they are a great source of information about related holdings in other institutions. Archivists therefore provide a useful reference not only to their own holdings, but act as almost a living union list of holdings related to their subject in other institutions.

We cannot leave the discussion of the role of the librarian and archivist on so narrow a base. It is true that both provide certain in-house reference services and that they are available for consultation and assistance to the individual who appears on their doorstep. But there is a larger role that is provided by each because, as custodians of vast information resources, they have important responsibilities to the community in which their institution is located.

In recent years the librarian has moved out of the stacks, and from behind the reference desk, and into the councils of the school, town, city, or corporation. Since a library is created to serve its public the librarian must be aware of that public's wants and needs and develop an acquisition policy to provide for those needs. The librarian, therefore, tends to become involved in educational trends, the growth of scientific areas of interest, popular sociology, or the changing character of the institution that the library serves. Today's librarian must be one step ahead of the community and when a demand arises be ready to meet it with available information. Immediacy is often the keynote. In addition to this role in society, the librarian "must have a firsthand knowledge of [books], their contents and their value; he must in himself and by himself be an intelligence agency, be the glowing point of contact between his library and the inquiring mind."[7] And, finally, it is almost unnecessary to cite the findings of a committee of professional groups: "Librarians perform a teaching and research role inasmuch as they instruct students formally and informally and advise and assist faculty in their scholarly pursuits."[8]

As librarians move into these roles more and more as a result of the desire to perform at a higher professional level, they naturally become more deeply involved in the councils of government and society, and in some measure move into the decision-making or policy-molding field in the social or corporate community.

Archivists are confronted with a different situation. They may have important roles in deciding what to retain or destroy, but can only work from the total body of materials for which they have responsibility, be they corporate records or the records of a single government entity, such as a state or municipality. They do not preserve these records because such records are required for immediate research purposes, but because they are the records of the corporation and may be needed only to satisfy some legal requirements. Also, archivists do not assume control over the documents until the records are retired, although in the role of records managers they may be concerned with their care until retirement. In most cases the social issues that archivists relate to are anywhere from ten to fifty years in the past and therefore find themselves more often dealing with the repetitions of history than with history as it happens. While a librarian might be looking for new materials on the energy crisis to meet contemporary research demand, the government or corporate archivist will be searching out materials on reactions and solutions to earlier energy crises which may have some modern application.

Curators of personal papers fall somewhere between librarians and archivists in response to contemporary social concerns. While naturally concerned with the past and the papers that document historical events, manuscript curators often look for collections that can be of use to the demands of the present. They follow research trends and the needs of their constituency, and modify their acquisition policy accordingly. Materials on black history went unsought in most institutions until the 1960s, when there was a sudden search for papers of prominent blacks or black organizations, and the Library of Congress added the records of the NAACP, the Urban League national headquarters, the Spingarn papers, and a number of other collections to its manuscript holdings. A university manuscript curator will work with graduate departments to determine relevance of research materials to course offerings. A respected professor directing a battery of graduate students in a certain field can strongly influence the development of manuscript holdings of a university library, and one can often trace collection subject strength to the existence of a strong department or the pressures of a particularly influential faculty member. To some extent this will also be true in printed material. While archivists can reevaluate their retention policy to answer anticipated research needs, they can exercise that prerogative only within the limits of the records over which they have archival control. Manuscript curators are not normally bound by such limits and can dramatically reverse the field or broaden out into new areas to meet new needs.

In a small institution the implementation of the acquisition policy and the decision on selection are in the hands of the same person as are processing and description. In large institutions there is a growing specialization that decrees special staff to provide these services. The use of full-time or part-time bibliographers is common in large libraries, with specialists in each field handling the task of keeping up with recent publications and evaluating them for acquisition. Manuscript collections have much the same service provided by specialists who may spend much of their time in reference work, but also engage in solicitations by keeping abreast of the availability of collections and contacting prospective donors to induce them to donate to their institution. In large archives there is a combination of assistance from records managers and archival appraisal staff to define and evaluate what should be permanently valuable and therefore accessioned into the archives.

In each field, therefore, there are the scouts, out looking for the materials appropriate to the collection, and each involved, in one way or another, with the sources for such material and at the same time with an eye on the eventual user of them.

NOTES

1. J. M. Scammel, "Librarians and Archives," *Library Quarterly* 9 (1939): 434.
2. Philip C. Brooks, *Research in Archives: The Use of Unpublished Primary Sources* (Chicago: University of Chicago Press, 1969), p. 8.
3. W. Kaye Lamb, "The Changing Role of the Archivist," *American Archivist* 29 (January 1966): 66.
4. Herman Kahn, "Librarians and Archivists," *American Archivist* 7 (October 1944): 247.
5. Randolph W. Church, "The Relationship between Archival Agencies and Libraries," *American Archivist* 6 (July 1943): 145–150.
6. Oliver W. Holmes, "Archival Arrangement: Five Different Operations at Five Different Levels," *American Archivist* 27 (January 1964): 21–41.
7. Jacques Barzun, "The New Librarian to the Rescue," *Library Journal* 93 (November 1, 1969): 3964, cited in Martha Boaz, "Some Current Concepts about Library Education," *College and Research Libraries* 33 (January 1972): 18.
8. "Statement on Faculty Status of College and University Librarians," drafted by a committee of the Association of College and Research Libraries, the Association of American Colleges, and the American Association of University Professors, *College and Research Libraries News* 2 (February 1974): 26.

EDUCATION

Considering the different requirements in solicitation, acquisition, processing, and reference service for library materials, manuscripts, and archives, it is not surprising that the education and training for these activities or professions is different. Although in many ways complementary, archival education and library education are in no way interchangeable. In this section we will look at the training of librarians and archivists to compare their similiarities and differences and to observe the current status and future trends in each field.

LIBRARY EDUCATION

It should not be surprising that during the early years of library education and training under Melvil Dewey, first at Columbia University in New York and later in Albany, the emphasis was on the primary tasks of the librarian—accessioning, cataloging, shelf listing, and what was then termed library "economy." Dictionary cataloging, and an appropriate apprenticeship in a library rounded out the curriculum. Sophistications crept into the curriculum with the addition of courses on book selection, reference service, and historical studies of books and libraries.

The practical approach to library education, to a great extent on-the-job training, was prevalent for the first quarter of the twentieth century. The ordinary library school was in a library, or if actually located in a university was often an appendage or an annex that might share some of the university administrative machinery with other departments, but not much else. There was little opportunity to develop a faculty devoted only to teaching, so courses were taught on a part-time basis by practicing librarians, with consequent lack of faculty control of standards and little opportunity to evaluate the student's overall instruction, especially that work done on the job or in workshops.

By 1936 some form was beginning to emerge in the library school curriculum, and a variety of tasks were compartmentalized into study areas. Much of this expansionist work was done by Ernest J. Reece, who was both a Melvil Dewey Professor at Columbia and a library education leader at the Carnegie Foundation. Reece formulated a library education curriculum out of four theme areas: "Fashioning a library collection," "Organizing and caring for a library collection," "Using a library collection," and "Directing a library enterprise." [1] These came to be the commonly known areas of acquisitions, processing, reference, and administration.

Also in the 1930s a dramatic shift began as "the pacesetting University of Chicago Graduate Library School included courses entitled 'Interpretation, Education, and Use of Library Materials'" which offered such

51

subjects as "The Library and Society," "Communication and Libraries," and "The History of the Public Diffusion of Knowledge and Ideas."[2] This approach was controversial, as were many others at Chicago, but at the same time stimulating and influential for the rest of library education. Recent curriculum proposals may seem new and innovative, but on inspection are just elaborations on the Chicago plan.

With the development of these early ideas through the postwar years, the evolution of library training continued but the purpose remained the same: to equip the librarian with the tools needed to handle the materials and provide the services required by library clientele. Despite the enlargement of responsibilities for some libraries beyond their four walls, or the requirement that some librarians become involved in social, scientific, or humanistic activities, "much of the work of librarians continues to be manipulative, requiring little professional knowledge, responsibility, and skill, and even at its presumably highest level—in selecting and organizing material, 'reference' work, and administration—performance is on a largely empirical basis, by rule-of-thumb, or by reference to codes, experience, and local regulation."[3]

Whether sophisticated or mechanical, however, the core of library education has to consider the distinguishing features of library activities, which in the broad sense are shared by archivists. One author has identified these as: "(1) the selection and bibliographic control over all types of recorded materials; (2) the retrieval of information from these materials; and (3) impartial guidance to these materials and their content, and stimulation of their use."[4] Significantly, the author notes: "Unfortunately, by custom and voluntary abdication, we must exclude archival materials from this list." It is doubtful that archival materials were excluded only for these reasons. It is more relevant to say that archives are excluded largely because they do not fit into the pattern of other library materials for the reasons cited in the earlier section of this chapter.

In considering the distinguishing features noted above, an approach to library education would then logically consider the prerequisites for students entering the curriculum, the curriculum itself, the use of materials and aids to teaching, and methodology. Because of the wide demand for library services and the wide range of services demanded, from the circulation desk of a public branch-library to the acquisition policy and administration of an Ivy League school research library, it is imperative that library training and education be available to almost anyone who wants it for whatever purposes they want it. For each level of training there should obviously be a concomitant level of prior education required. In praise of the liberal attitude of most library educators, one librarian has noted that there are not many professions that "would take students from all undergraduate disciplines, all ages, on a full- or part-time basis, for a second or even a third career, and often provide opportunities for work-study, internship or at least part-time work experience."[5]

On the other hand, John J. Boll complains that library schools for the most part have been shortsighted in their failure to provide students with controlled work situations and practical work experience associated with their studies. He feels that the schools avoid such training because it may "take away the aura of professionalism" that librarians seek, that it might impress on the students "too easy acceptance of the practical difficulties involved" in day-to-day library work, or ironically, "because practice is often an inadequate or poor model if we are trying to educate for good service and improvement."[6] In other words, don't do as I do, do as I say. In practice, however, one finds that many library school students do work in libraries. Perhaps these are not under controlled conditions, and the students' library education may suffer from that fact, but practical experience often accompanies the students' formal training.

While the library schools may be avoiding practical training, they are turning to a number of devices that the student may or may not encounter in the daily work situation in any one division of a functioning library. Modern education techniques, in almost any field, demand the use of advanced technology or equipment: the case study, the simulation technique, role playing, group dynamics, the systems approach, independent study, and a variety of other teaching tools. The better library schools are providing these, and therefore the student is getting what any student expects from the educational experience—a diversity of techniques and a broad range of exposure to the problems of the discipline.

In the 1970s the curriculum of many library schools is coming under fire by faculty, by library administrators, and by the principal theorists on library education. Neal Harlow voices the fear of many of these groups when he states that:

> Accepting that change is constantly taking place in the information base at society's disposal, in the informational needs of individuals and organizations, and in the potential for organizing and disseminating informational resources, it then seems unlikely that any parts of a curriculum which are a generation old can have current validity. Yet upon close scrutiny, the curricula of library schools look very much like those upon which the faculty themselves were raised.[7]

The theorists are giving consideration first to the prerequisites for entrance into graduate library studies. Whereas until now most graduate library schools accepted a subject specialization, a liberal arts background, and language training as the basic requirements, there are now some proponents for expansion of that base to include logic, interpersonal relations, and the principles of administration. It follows that the basis for such requirements is an expanded concept of the role of the librarian vis-à-vis job and public. This is borne out by the nature of what another author considers the stated objectives of the library curriculum, which include, in addition to the acquisition of professional knowledge and attitudes, and the development of intellectual abilities and skills: "conditions and problems of contemporary life to which [the problems of librarianship] relate; appropriate ethical behavior; and attitudes of scholarly concern."[8] This puts the librarian of today square in the middle of social, economic, scientific and humanistic problems and concerns, and implies that in order to be effective, every librarian, at any level, should be exposed to training in these areas. Certainly this removes library training from the limited definitions of Dewey and his earlier followers, and sophisticates it right out of the reach of the occasional or amateur practitioner.

These stated objectives are not being made by one person in a void. The core curriculum of a number of institutions is beginning to reflect Harlow's objectives, and the psychosocial aspects of library education are creeping into the graduate schools. In 1953 there was an invitational workshop on library school core curricula held at the University of Chicago Graduate Library School, and the educators and specialists who attended developed a core that had fewer than half the items dealing with library processes in the traditional sense. The seven areas of study that were proposed were:

1. the study of the library and of society and their relationship to each other
2. the meaning and characteristics of professionalism
3. the interpretation, appreciation, evaluation, selection and use of books, materials, and sources
4. the organization and characteristics of internal and external library services in relation to the users of the services
5. the basic principles and various patterns of library organization and management
6. an introduction to the characteristics and functions of the communication process throughout history and in the present
7. an introduction to the functions and methods of research, and the use of research findings.[9]

Only three items (3, 4, 5) are in the traditional mold of library science as known to Dewey, Reece, and others. The remaining four curriculum items deal with the questions of society, professionalism, communication processes, and the functions and methods of research. Although more than 20 years in the past, the concepts laid out in Chicago have not grown out of style. They were reiterated in a proposal for formulating library education for the 1970s in an article by Andrew H. Horn, published in *Special Libraries*, December 1971. Horn coincidentally also comes up with seven points, but does not lay the responsibility for all of them on the library schools. He believes that some subjects, such as foreign languages, mathematics or statistics, and computer programming, should rightly be in the area of prerequisite training for acceptance in graduate library schools. But the library school should be responsible for such areas as the philosophy and major problems of librarianship, the roles of librarians in society, the social value and educational relevance of libraries, dissemination of information, contemporary theory and practice in the use and development of human resources within organizations, theories, principles and methodology of research, performance evaluation, applicability of systems analysis and design, quantification, and mechanization or automation in the solution of problems of management, communication, and information retrieval.[10]

What is emerging is training for the new librarian—the social psychologist, information specialist, management analyst, administrator. There seems to be an impression that because a library requires computers, management, public programs, and building maintenance that all of these skills or techniques should be taught in library school and only one who qualifies as a librarian should be given the opportunity to perform these tasks in the library environment.

Commerce and industry have long abandoned the concept of the vertical person. At one time it was thought that the best airline administrator was someone who knew a lot about flying. The demise of many airlines soon decreed that philosophy to be false and erroneous. It is true that the heart of an airline is still its pilots, but when they go to flight school they learn to fly and need to know little about reservations, or fare structures, or personnel management. One must consider what the library school student is being trained for, and teach accordingly. If the student is to undertake a career in a school library or a relatively small public library system, while it may be true that the student will be required to have a rounded education in library operation and techniques, it is more likely that the skills required will relate to acquisitions, cataloging, and reference service than to information dissemination, computer technology, and paper preservation. Conversely, if the student is aiming for a major research library it is doubtful that the student will get to see more than the division or office selected or assigned, such as circulation, subject cataloging, interlibrary loan, or serials. Each one of these areas requires certain supportive skills, and supplementary training should be arranged. But to presume that a well-rounded library education will be relevant to all phases of a library operation is naive. Well-trained information specialists, management analysts, budget officers, personnel specialists, and administrators are as important to the functioning of a large library as they are to a corporation. But that training need not, in fact cannot, be received in a library school.

Fortunately, most library schools today have not departed from the concept that a good librarian must know books and book processing, with certain other courses in the elective area for broadening one's general knowledge, and perhaps as a way of justifying a full degree program. A recent survey of the curriculum of 50 library schools indicated that 84 percent of them had required courses in reference and bibliography, and cataloging and classification; 64 percent in selection and acquisition; 52 percent in introduction to librarianship—the library in society. In the same 50 schools courses such as research methods, history of books and libraries, information science, communication and libraries, administration and management, and systems analysis were overwhelmingly relegated either to the status of elective courses or were included in other courses.[11]

Whatever the course emphasis, library schools today are prepared to provide a continual flow of educated, if not trained, professionals to the burgeoning library system in the United States. But there are fears that library school accreditation and enrollment are rising faster than demand, and that the traditional curriculum is not changing enough to meet the problems of present-day libraries. In a controversial and critical analysis of today's library education, one author claims that "a quick glance at the catalogs of the new schools only confirms a general suspicion that the charmed circle is gained quickest by following the road trampled out by one's predecessors, having camouflaged one's naked conformity by a few fig-leaves of revamped terminology."[12] Certainly, some fears of overgrowth in library education are borne out by statistics. In 1970–1971 the awarding of 8,770 library science degrees in the United States posted an increase of 345 percent over the 1,967 degrees awarded in 1958–1959, while for the same period the total of all academic degrees increased only 132 percent. The addition of 10 accredited graduate library schools from 1968 to 1971 raised the total to 49, or an increase of 25.6 percent in those three years. The breakdown for all library education for 1970–1971 was 49 graduate accredited, 76 nonaccredited graduate, 195 undergraduate, 72 technical assistants, and 20 in the planning stage.[13]

The enrollment in library schools with a predominantly graduate program seems staggering. The figures for 1970 showed 4,067 undergraduates, 12,756 master's candidates, 222 intermediate students, 376 doctoral candidates, and 850 in special programs, for a total of 18,271 library students.[14] The ability of the American library system to absorb that percentage of the 18,000 who graduate will determine in the 1970s whether or not there will be a depression in the library market as there has been in some of the social sciences and humanities. In almost all categories—major, minor, and certificate-only library schools—and in full time and part time, women students outnumber men by ten to one. Again in 1970 the figures were: full-time men students, 429; women, 4,369; part-time men students, 287; women, 2,512.

In summary, one can state that library education has moved from basic on-the-job training in institutions with a heavy concentration in techniques of handling library materials, to a more sophisticated systems approach with a growing specialization and professionalization as the literature of the profession and interpretation of its role in society has been enlarged. Library degrees have grown to provide 0.8 percent of all graduate degrees awarded in the United States, and students have increased in significant numbers. There is a continuing debate in the profession about the core curriculum, with some movement toward providing librarians with an education that will equip them to manage all functions of a complex library system. On closer inspection, however, it appears that the schools are not implementing these broader programs as required courses just yet, and still deal with traditional material handling subjects.

ARCHIVAL TRAINING

If a considerable amount of information can be amassed about library education, including data on students, curricula, teachers, prerequisites, budgets, and enrollments, there is not much information available on archival training. I hesitate to use the term archival "education," because in the true sense there is none in the form of undergraduate or degree-awarding programs. A few institutions, such as Case Western Reserve University, offer a Master's in History and Archives, or a M.S.L.S. with a major in archives. Strictly speaking, however, there is no Master of Arts in Archival Science. There is a long tradition of archival courses in archival institutions, in libraries, or as a part of history department programs at a few universities. From the beginning, however, there has been a fear on the part of some archivists that such courses will be offered by librarians as an extension of library school education, and that somehow this would dilute the effectiveness of the courses or provide the wrong training. As early as 1937, less than a year after the founding of the Society of American Archivists, its Committee on the Training of Archivists, chaired by Samuel Flagg Bemis, stated in its first report that there would be a "distinct danger in turning over archives to librarians who are not at the same time erudite and critical historical scholars." The phrase is ambivalent and leaves one wondering if the committee would permit librarians to teach archival courses if the librarians *were* erudite and critical historical scholars, or if the report meant to condemn all librarians for not being such.[15] Dr. Bemis's fears were not immediately realized, because the first course designed with the sole intention of training archivists was given by Solon J. Buck at Columbia University in 1938–1939. Dr. Buck, who at various times held the estimable positions of archivist of the United States and chief of the Manuscript Division at the Library of Congress, pondered over what an archivist needed to know to function and consequently what

archival training should consist of. He concluded that a "workable outline" of topics of archival concern would comprise:

1. the nature and value of archives
2. the making of archives
3. the status and functions of archival agencies
4. internal organization
5. buildings and equipment
6. the recruitment and training of personnel
7. the appraisal and selection of personnel
8. the preservation and rehabilitation of archival material
9. the arrangement and description of archival material
10. the reproduction of archival material, including copying by hand or by
    typewriter, or reproduction by photographic processes
11. the editing and publishing of archival documents
12. the service of archives, including exhibitions
13. problems arising in connection with special types of archival deposits,
    such as local archives, business archives and church archives
14. problems arising in connection with special physical types of archival
    material, such as maps, motion and still pictures, and sound record-
    ings.[16]

When Dr. Ernst Posner left the Prussian Privy Archives and emi-
grated to the United States and Washington in 1939, he was appointed professor of Archives Administration in The American University Graduate
Library School, and the university joined with the National Archives in
offering a course entitled "The History of Administration and Archives."
Taught jointly by Buck and Posner, the course not only provided archival
training for anyone interested, but presented an excellent classroom training opportunity for the staff of the young National Archives, which was
only five years old and was not able to find enough trained archivists.

In addition to his "workable outline" of training, Buck felt that any
archivist, even before taking specific training, should be well-grounded in
history; should probably know the current workings of his government (or
the corporation for which he works); should have some knowledge of administrative history; must have an understanding of historical method;
and should have a smattering of knowledge of European archival methods
and fields, such as diplomatics, paleography, sphragistics, linguistics,
chronology, etc.[17]

What Buck and Posner and their contemporaries Herman Kahn and
Theodore Schellenberg were saying was that archival training is an over-
lay to a deeper education in historical methodology. Their tenet was that
an archivist is first a researcher and historical analyst, since the training
received in these areas is required for the archivist to perform the most
important and unique function—the appraisal of records for retention or
disposition—and also for the second most important function, the understanding of the records that are in his custody so that he can describe

them accurately and provide reference service on them. In almost 40 years of debate about archival training, no one has been able to get away from the fact that one can learn to be an archivist only after receiving training elsewhere in another discipline. Like Goethe's Faust, two souls dwell in the archivist's breast, and one is continually tearing away at the other. "Almost every archivist has a divided heart. Whether he is primarily an archivist or primarily something else seems to depend in good part upon where he is and with whom he is speaking."[18]

This dichotomy has been evident in the archival training courses offered over the years and accounts in good measure for the failure of any full-fledged archival education curriculum. The University of Denver experimented with a course in the management of archives as part of the curriculum of the graduate school of librarianship. After a few years it was moved to the history department. "The reason for the change was not that the librarians were incompetent or unwilling but rather that the philosophy inherent in the program demanded the widest possible academic selection of courses, both in the humanities and in the social sciences."[19] As Kahn put it,

> the training one receives as an undergraduate and graduate student in history or related subjects, which gives or should give one a knowledge of what scholarship is, what research is, how research is conducted—the relationship of the scholar to his sources, and the use and limitations of various kinds of sources—the whole story of man, and as a part of that story, how man has used the record in writing his own story—all of those vast areas of human knowledge that make use of the written record—it is when he is being trained in these fields that the potential archivist is receiving the truly professional part of his training.[20]

This is an accurate statement relating to the most professional activities of an archivist's career, and once that training has been received, the potential archivist need learn only some mechanical procedures about arrangement, description, and those few aspects of archival administration (i.e., security) that might differ from the administration of any other organization. Thus, there is really little that can be gotten from formal courses in archival science that cannot be picked up on the job in a medium-sized institution, and probably no need for extended courses so unnaturally expanded as to result in a degree, or even to be classed as a major field of study.

The natural order of things has led to exactly this situation. There are no archival degree courses, and there are only one or two major archives fields of study in American institutions. There are only a few full-time teachers who specialize in documentary source materials as their subject. Most archival teaching is done by practicing archivists who take time out from their already overwhelming duties to lecture for an hour or two on theory and practice in their specialized area—appraisal, arrangement, description, reference, etc. They do this for a number of reasons: because they like the classroom experience, because of their archival missionary zeal, or for the small extra income that such teaching provides. But without a professional teaching corps and a constant base for providing the learning experience, much of what the student learns is vicarious, and there are no standards by which to establish an acceptable level of instruction, no examination of what the student has learned, and no corpus of literature built from research and tested in the classroom. The curriculum for a course is usually shaped by the availability of specialists to handle a subject. The ad hoc nature of each training session leaves the archival institutes in a void, unassociated with the institution that offers the session because of the brevity of the usual course, only briefly affiliated with a formal institution of learning and the advantages that such association can bring, and separate and apart from other faculties and disciplines as would not be the case in a university environment.

A 1974 survey indicates that the prototype of archival training in the United States and Canada consists of training provided by archivists as teachers, in the facilities of a library school. At the introductory level instruction is for approximately one academic quarter (three months or less), with fewer than 40 hours of actual instruction for credit, and usually with an internship requiring experience with archival materials. (See chart.) Another survey indicates 12 institutions have multicourse offerings, 20 have a single-course offering, and 6 have institutes only.[21] The survey of courses reveals that, with few exceptions, the curriculum varies little from that provided in a joint American University/National Archives and Records Service Institute, which consists of:

Introduction to Archives: Archival Concepts, Terminology and Principles
Archivists, Librarians and Manuscript Curators: Comparisons and Contrasts
Archives Administration and Records/Paperwork Management
Records Appraisal and Disposition
Preservation: Protection, Storage Facilities, Repair and Rehabilitation
Arrangement of Archives
Description of Archives
Reference Service
Automation and the Control of Archives and Manuscripts
Microphotography and Archives
Administration of Cartographic and Related Records and Archives
Administration of Audiovisual Records and Archives

Archival Training in the United States and Canada

A survey of thirty-one institutions providing archival training in the United States and Canada. Twenty-seven institutions responded to the survey. Twenty-five provided data that could be statistically analyzed.

Questionnaire Item	Institutions Responding Positively
I. Is the archival training provided by:	
a. library school or equivalent	13
b. history department	7
c. a joint offering of two departments	2
d. other than library school or history department	2
II. Are the courses offered:*	
a. introductory	15
b. beginning	4
c. intermediate	2
d. advanced	4
III. Is the course length:†	
a. less than 1 month	3
b. 1 to 3 months	18
c. 3 to 6 months	3
d. longer than 6 months	0
IV. Is the course given for:	
a. credit	21
b. noncredit	3
V. How many actual hours does the course meet?	
a. less than 40	13
b. 40 to 80	4
c. 80 to 120	2
d. 120 to 160	1
e. more than 160	2
VI. Are the courses generally taught by:	
a. librarians	3
b. historians	2
c. archivists	14
d. combinations of the above	4
VII. Is there an internship associated with the course?	
a. internal internship	11
b. external internship	5
c. no internship	8

*Some institutions offer different levels of courses.
†These are for individual courses or institutes. Some institutions provide a sequence of courses that may run in total to a year.

Publication Programs
Exhibits and Public Relations
Specialized Institutional Archives
Oral History
Archives and Manuscripts—An Historical Overview
Program Planning and Development
Laboratory in Arrangement and Description

It is evident that any course or institute with a curriculum similar to this one is aimed at introducing beginners to archival principles and has little to do with training in sophisticated archival evaluation and judgment techniques. There are few instances today of seminars in archival rationale, or the philosophy of records retention, or research methodology in the use of original source materials. Some people are thinking of archives in terms of "institutional sociology," or the aims, purposes, and methods of an institution and its employees or staff, and how this affects the records that the institution creates, but no one is as yet teaching such a subject.

A committee established by the Society of American Archivists to study the future of the profession published its lengthy report in April 1972 on all aspects of the profession and the professional society. It is notable that in the area of archival education and training the eight recommendations of the committee recognize the nonprofessional nature of much of archival work and the inadvisability of attempting to establish archival training as a degree-oriented program. All of the committee's points are pertinent to our discussion here. They are:

1. That the society, through its Committee on Education and Training, formulate guidelines for courses, institutes, and training programs and that, in the development of such standards, due consideration be given to this committee's conclusions with regard to the following matters.
2. That the society urge that appropriate education and training, as well as direct experience in the administration of archives and manuscripts, be required of persons offering courses, institutes, or other training programs in archives and manuscripts.
3. That the society not attempt formally to endorse specific courses or training programs, but that it instruct its Education and Training Committee to develop a set of minimum standards to assist members and other interested persons in evaluating such courses. We further recommend that the Education and Training Committee seek the financial resources necessary to accomplish this objective.
4. That the society intensify its efforts in such areas as terminology and uniform archival statistics in order to facilitate the preparation of minimum standards, instructional materials, and curriculum design for professional education and training. We further recommend that the Committee on Professional Standards participate actively in these efforts.
5. That the council and the Publications Committee encourage special-area

and technical committees to participate in the preparation of publications dealing with basic archival functions.

6. That the society, through its Education and Training Committee, develop appropriate position descriptions that require and give appropriate recognition, in terms of status and remuneration, to the education and training essential to such positions.

7. That archivists do not develop separate degree programs in colleges and universities for archives administration, but instead, support the development of a sequence of introductory and advanced courses including closely supervised internships, specialized directed reading courses, seminars, and thesis or dissertation supervision for studies dealing directly with archives administration. Such a program would constitute a solid area of specialization within existing degree programs for an M.A. or a Ph.D. Even if combined with related courses in records management, information sciences, administration of general historical agencies or programs, the result, in our opinion, would still not constitute a sufficient intellectual discipline to merit a separate graduate degree.

8. That the society not attempt at this time to develop its own degree program or to endorse such programs should they develop. We are convinced that the most appropriate educational backgrounds for archivists are the fields of history, library science, and the social studies in general, and that archivists' background should include training and experience in the use of original research materials. As courses in the information sciences, specialized courses in the audiovisual field, and other relevant courses become available, we recommend that the society make every effort through its journal and newsletter to inform the membership of these training opportunities.[22]

The committee comes down hard on the side of the status quo as far as the education and training of archivists are concerned; what it proposes is better control over the qualifications of teachers of future archivists. In another part of the report the committee makes this point even stronger:

The administration of modern archives and manuscripts is neither an exclusively intellectual discipline, nor a craft, nor a trade, nor yet an art, but it shares elements of all of these. It is therefore essential that those who offer training to archivists not only have appropriate academic qualifications but that they themselves also have the training and experience necessary to give both substance and practical dimensions to their teaching.[23]

The long-range trend in popular archival education, from Solon J. Buck to the Committee for the 1970s, therefore, is away from theory and scholarly understanding of the archival material in custody, away from archivists as "erudite and critical historical scholars," and toward greater emphasis on methodology, administration, and procedure. This seems to be just the opposite trend from that in library education, which is aiming toward theories of acquisitions and the establishment of a library philosophy.

Perhaps it is axiomatic that the idiosyncratic nature of archives precludes general education in those fields that are most important to the archivist's decision-making role, since archives represent the holdings of a corporation or institution, and one can speculate about their value only in the context of their creation. Being unable to specialize in the important aspects of the archivist's task, courses and institutes have turned to the relatively unimportant and mechanical processes. The nature of archival work requires a great number of staff members doing arrangement, description, and preservation, while very few do high-level reference service and appraisal. Archival courses, by their very nature, therefore, are training grounds for the least professional activities of the archival profession. This condition can easily lead to a split, where the less professional tasks are relegated to a battery of course-trained archivists acting almost in the capacity of clerks, while the administration and direction of archival institutions and the establishment of archival policy is undertaken by administrators not trained in archival techniques and frequently selected from outside the archival community. A survey of some of the top administrative positions in the profession (except, of course, for the archivist of the United States) tends to confirm this.

Archivists have been aware of this dilemma for many years and have moved to strengthen and enlarge their ranks by the establishment of procedures, standards, a national literature, and educational requirements, and thus have created a certain mystique. In the federal government this mystique was institutionalized with the successful establishment of Civil Service Commission standards for archivists in the federal service (GS–1420). In part, these standards require that for grades 5 through 15 an applicant must have:

A. A full four-year course in an accredited college or university which has included or been supplemented by 18 semester hours in the history of the United States, or in American political science, or government, or a combination of these; and 12 semester hours in any one or any combination of the following: history, American civilization, economics, political science, public administration or government, or:
B. Courses in an accredited college or university as described in A above, plus additional appropriate education or experience which, when combined, have provided the candidate with the substantial equivalent of A above.

There are certain trade-offs permitted when experience can be substituted for education, but the substitutions do not apply once a person is hired as a nonprofessional at the National Archives. In other words, years of archival experience at the subprofessional level in the National Archives cannot be converted to credits toward becoming a professional archivist—only the minimum education requirements may be used to make the crossover.

The Civil Service Commission, therefore, does not explicitly recognize training in an archival course or curriculum as a requirement for becoming an archivist in the federal service. It is formal education—in American history, political science or related fields—that is the requirement for becoming an archivist, supplemented by on-the-job training after being hired. The commission thus recognizes that there are two levels of archival activity, and has limited access to the higher levels of the decision-making process to academically trained professionals whose main calling lies outside of the field of strictly archival practice. If these professional archivists do take training courses, it is usually after qualifying for and being hired as archivists, and quite often are for the purpose of familiarizing themselves with the work that archives technicians, who they must supervise, should be doing. This situation does not normally exist in smaller archives and manuscript collections because of the requirement that each staff member be versatile and operate over the full range of archival activity, but there are many medium-sized institutions, mostly among the state archives, where conditions similar to those in the federal system prevail. In many of the borderline cases, where requirements for professional archival activity are minimal, the archival mystique is a defense mechanism for insecure archivists, and it can be used to ward off attempts to downgrade the status of the staff through lower salaries, or, what is sometimes worse, lower prestige associated with less professional-sounding job titles. This threat is even worse where academic requirements for hiring are not as strict as they are in the federal government, and where the major credentials that an archivist holds are the archival courses completed at some institute. As long as those courses continue to deal with mechanics instead of issues, archivists will continue to be trained as clerks and will continue to live in fear of losing their status and consequently the respect and esteem of the professional scholars who use archives. Unless archivists can develop true professional qualifications different from those any graduate historian has, they will continue to be haunted by the suspicion that they are looked upon as historians who could not succeed as teachers, and so became archivists as an alternative. And, as long as the federal government and other agencies do not require the completion of an archival curriculum as a prerequisite for hiring as an archivist, the status of archival education will remain low.

Perhaps the most disturbing aspect of the archival training trend, as well as of the report of the Committee for the 1970s, is the total avoidance of any consideration of the use of archives in the educational process, or of relations of archivists with researchers, and the requirement to fill some of their needs. It is a purist's view that archives exist only for the institutions or agencies that create them and that all others take a back seat in the concerns of the archivist. The research rooms and correspondence files of any public archives or manuscript repository will refute that concept. And yet it is only in the past four or five years that one can discern any movement in the direction of archives as instruments of popular education except through public exhibits. It is not unreasonable to ask that archival institutes should include discussions on topics such as public archives as part of the cultural, socioeconomic environment; archives and education; photoreproduction (microfilming) of archives to meet the needs of popular education; and the implications of computerized records (data archives) for archival research. There is also a necessity for establishing some criteria for the retention of audiovisual archives which have great value for popular educational purposes but about which there has been little discussion in archival training programs.

Archives may not be social centers, as many community libraries are, but neither are they the sanctified preserve of advanced scholars, lawyers, and those interested only in moldy antiquities. One group that has discovered the value of original records is genealogists, who can be found occupying most of the seats in almost any archival research room on any given day. A recent (unpublished) survey of the readers of *Prologue: The Journal of the National Archives* revealed to the surprise of the staff that the majority of the 2,200 respondents were not the scholars, graduate students, and serious amateur historians at whom the journal was aimed, but were overwhelmingly composed of genealogists. Even with the evidence of their own clientele before them, most archivists are reluctant to admit who is making most use of their records and rarely include in archival courses any discussion of genealogical needs and how best to serve them. In the end, however, it is not the archivist's role to select the clientele. If there is an underutilization of documentary sources by historians, as there is, it is the fault of historical, not archival, training. The graduate history departments must bear the burden for this condition.

Archivists are presently concerned about the direction from which leadership in archival education should be coming. The Committee for the 1970s of the Society of American Archivists deftly avoided the question. It stated that there should be no degree programs, in or outside of the society, and that certain committees of the society should develop training standards, but it said nothing about where the leadership in training should come from. One institution that is invariably mentioned as a prospective training ground for archivists is the National Archives and Records Service. The archival education role of NARS, as the nation's largest and most comprehensive archives, has been to cooperate with The American University in offering a semiannual orientation for beginning archivists called "The Administration of Modern Archives."

The course is a two-week overview of all those areas of archival activity noted earlier in this chapter, from appraisal to public relations, and contains a full serving of readings, but no laboratory or workshop. Aside from the lectures in the National Archives building, the class has contact with the archival world only through a session in the Library of Congress

Manuscript Division and a tour of the Maryland Hall of Records at Annapolis.

There has been discussion from time to time about NARS severing its ties with The American University and offering the course on its own. From the national viewpoint there are implications that must be considered if this is done and NARS then decides to add to the curriculum the genealogical institute that it has been independently sponsoring, plus the records management seminars and a recently instituted one-week workshop in the use of archival materials for research purposes. Together these institutes would form an archival training center probably unmatched in North America. However, they would require long-term administrative and financial support, some full-time staff, and facilities not now available in the National Archives for a large, complex institute. These and other commitments might be difficult to sustain because of changing requirements of federal government standards and procedures relating to budgets, contractual services, promotion and publicity, printing, and other administrative details. There would certainly be some concern aroused at archival training centers now functioning that might feel undercut by the national effort. Questions would be raised about the federal government providing education instead of just providing for it. The relevance of an experience at the largest institution of its kind in the country when most education and training are needed to cope with the problems of small to medium-sized institutions would also be questioned.

Conversely, the National Archives has such a diversity of staff to call upon for instructional assistance (such a wide variety of professional activities directed by specialists that can be used as teaching examples) and by far the greatest financial resources of any archives within which to absorb some of the administrative costs of such an institute, that it would be difficult to deny its preeminent position as a possible instructional center. The existence of such a training center in Washington would not preclude smaller centers in other archives or educational institutions elsewhere because the teaching of archival theory is not necessarily affected by the size of the institution teaching it—theory is just as applicable to the Fairfax County Historical Society as it is to the Library of Congress Manuscript Division.

It is anticipated that this debate will be entered into in the next few years and by the end of the decade may be settled, at least for the foreseeable future. In the meantime, archival education and training lumber along, occasionally being innovative and inspired, but more often being a recitation by practitioners of "this is the way I do it in my shop." Its most grievous shortcoming, however, is that such training is not a requirement for being hired as an archivist.

NOTES

1. Sarah R. Reed, "The Curriculum of Library Schools Today: A Historical Overview," in Herbert Goldhor, *Education for Librarianship: The Design of the Curriculum in Library Schools* (Urbana: University of Illinois Graduate School of Library Science, 1971), p. 26.

2. Ibid.

3. Neal Harlow, "Designs on the Curriculum," in Goldhor, *Education for Librarianship*, p. 3.

4. John J. Boll, "A Basis for Library Education," *Library Quarterly* 42 (April 1972): 200.

5. George Bobinski, in comments responding to an article by Jeanne Osborne, "Innovation in Library Education," *Library Journal* 98 (November 15, 1973): 3348.

6. Boll, "A Basis for Library Education," p. 204.

7. Harlow, "Designs on the Curriculum," p. 14.

8. Ibid., p. 7.

9. Reed, "The Curriculum of Library Schools Today: A Historical Overview," p. 28.

10. Andrew H. Horn, "Time for Decision: Library Education for the Seventies," *Special Libraries* 62 (December 1971): 521–522.

11. Reed, "The Curriculum of Library Schools Today: A Historical Overview," p. 30.

12. Osborne, "Innovation in Library Education," p. 3342.

13. Frank L. Schick and Kathryn Weintraub, *North American Library Education Directory and Statistics, 1969–1971* (Chicago: American Library Association, 1972), pp. 2–3.

14. Margaret E. Monroe, "Graduate Library Education Programs," in Schick and Weintraub, *North American Library Education Directory and Statistics, 1969–1971*, p. 23.

15. Samuel Flagg Bemis, "The Training of Archivists in the United States," *American Archivist* 2 (July 1939): 157.

16. Solon J. Buck, "The Training of American Archivists," *American Archivist* 4 (April 1941): 86.

17. Ibid., p. 85.

18. Herman Kahn, "The Archival Vocation," *American Archivist* 34 (January 1971): 4.

19. Allen du Pont Breck, "New Dimension in the Education of American Archivists," *American Archivist* 29 (April 1966): 182–183.

20. Kahn, "The Archival Vocation," p. 7.

21. Society of American Archivists, *Education Directory: Careers and Courses in Archival Administration* (Ann Arbor: Society of American Archivists, 1973).

22. Philip P. Mason, "The Society of American Archivists in the Seventies: Report of the Committee for the 1970's," *American Archivist* 35 (April 1972): 207.

23. Ibid.

THREE

COMMON ISSUES

LEGISLATION

"It's the law" serves as a guide to the archivist far more often than to the librarian. Taking a cue from the statutory authority which created the agency comes easily to the archivist, whose professional responsibility is for the legal and administrative value of the records of that agency as much as for their broad research value.

Archives and libraries have developed along essentially different paths beyond their very early common beginnings. In the United States archives and libraries have shown contrasting patterns both historically and legally. Now interests are merging again as archival collections grow and diversify, and their research potential becomes more highly respected.

STATUTORY BASES IN THE STATES

The American public library, developing out of the nature of American democracy, has been characteristically a local agency, locally funded—whether by a governmental unit, by a voluntary association, or endowed by gift. The states have played a role, but, for the most part, this has been through the general statutes from which the local libraries draw their authority, through setting standards, or through the supporting services provided by the state library. Academic libraries, a few specialized institutions not privately funded, and, of course, state libraries have had a greater degree of state support.

Organized archives came late on the American scene, the greatest impetus coming finally at the federal level, although state archives had been organized previously. Responsibility for state archives became fixed over a span of many decades, resulting in different patterns of organization in the various states. The Society of American Archivists (SAA), organized in 1936, gave its early consideration to increasing the provisions made for public archives in the different states, hoping to have minimum standards adopted that would guarantee the preservation of essential records and to have legislation passed establishing archives in the states where none existed.

Particular aspects of the archives responsibility in the states were given increased impetus in 1960 when the Council of State Governments, responding to a suggestion of the Federal Civil Defense Administration, recommended to all states the passage of two pieces of legislation. The "Preservation of Essential Records Act" was designed to ensure the preservation, in times of disaster, of records essential to the continuity of government and to the rights and privileges of citizens. Unfortunately, it was enacted only in Oklahoma, Nebraska, and West Virginia. The second piece of legislation recommended—to provide a records management act—was more widely accepted and served as the model in a few states, particularly where the archival agency had not previously been responsible for the disposition of current or semicurrent records.

The number of established state archives has gradually increased until today almost all the states have made some official provision for their historical records, but the pattern of organization is still as varied as in the earlier period. The majority of states maintain their archives under the control of departments or commissions of archives and/or history, under the state library, or under the state historical society.

The uneasy existence of some state archives was dramatized with the news received at various archivists' conferences in late 1973 of a just completed survey of the Maine State Archives. As an economy measure, the survey had recommended the abolition of the archives as an organizational entity and the destruction of the six thousand cubic feet of records in its custody. Fortunately, large numbers of archivists, the SAA, and recently organized regional archival organizations sprang into action with strong words of protest to the governor, the two Maine senators, and the state's Archives Advisory Board. The survey's recommendation was rejected, but it was an indication of the perennial danger that exists for the preservation of useful records if an active public relations program does not serve to convince officials and laymen of their value.

While it is generally difficult to draw direct cause and effect relationships between pressure tactics and governmental actions, we might contrast these efforts and their positive result with earlier ineffective efforts of archivists to have specific legislation passed. The Uniform State Public Records Act sponsored by the SAA in the 1940s and the legislation recommended for essential records preservation in the 1960s had the organizational support of archivists although lacking an aggressive approach on their part. The more forthright position adopted in countering the suggested abolition of the Maine archives is today more acceptable than it might have been in an earlier period, but a strong position together with the added pressure of the regional archival organizations may have helped determine the result. One might also point to the more successful records disposition legislation of the 1960s, winning where other legislation failed, because it served an economy need in state administration at the same time that it achieved a goal of the archivist. Timing, sufficient expression of support, ready action in emergencies, and correctly judging the needs of the governmental agencies—all may be relevant factors in effecting results in the governmental sphere.

With state libraries playing a large role in the administration of state archives, we should examine the questions this raises for the relationship between the two professions. The report of a 1955 SAA committee on state archives called attention to certain problems in library-administered archives at that time. These agencies usually collected local as well as state records and also maintained collections of private papers and manuscripts, but the governmental archives were received on a voluntary basis, the implication being that governmental records received less-favored status. Even where the state law defined public records, it was generally not compulsory in its provision for records transfers.[1] The problem has eased, it appears, with the growth of state records and their assignment to a state archival unit within the state library, generally under the supervision of a trained archivist.

BASIC NATIONAL LAWS

On the national level as on the state, the historical pattern of archives and libraries has been dissimilar. Federal law created a much more clearly defined system of federal archives, although late in the country's national development. The organization of the National Archives in 1934 vested authority in the archivist of the United States to guarantee preservation of essential records, with the advice of the National Archives Council, of which the librarian of Congress was made a member under the law. Early recognition of overlapping interests, and cooperation between archives and library units, can be seen as the principle, rather than subordination of one to the other.

Efforts to place the National Archives under the administration of another agency were initially countered successfully by the expressed need to keep an agency responsible for the records of executive, legislative, and judicial branches free of all three divisions of the government. In the later 1940s the Commission on the Organization of the Executive Branch of the Government authorized a study which resulted in a reorganization shocking to most archivists and to historians concerned with national records. The National Archives was reduced to a unit of the General Services Administration (often called the housekeeping agency); the archivist, previously appointed by the president, was made an appointee of the general services administrator; and the National Archives Council was abolished and replaced with a weak Federal Records Council.[2] This drastic shift of responsibility for the nation's records has been attributed by some to the archival profession's failure to continue a strong relationship with historians and a simultaneous failure to establish increased cooperation with librarians on the firm basis of mutual responsibility to the research needs of scholars.

One of the most productive experiences for the preservation of documentary resources arose out of national adversity at the height of the economic depression in the mid-1930s. The HRS (Historical Records Survey) of the WPA (Works Progress Administration) was instituted to give paid federal employment to people without other means of subsistence, but it also provided a measure of self-respect in view of the work of permanent value that these people were creating. Luther H. Evans, later librarian of Congress, was instrumental in bringing the survey into being, building on proposals that had been under discussion among numerous scholars. Using unskilled, usually white-collar clerical assistants, and a minimum of professional supervisors, Evans put in operation the ". . . most extensive program of governmental support of historical research in America . . . an experiment in socialized scholarship."[3] Developing his own *Manual of the Survey of Historical Records*, his own forms and detailed procedures for the army of untrained workers, but drawing on frequent consultations with librarians, historians, archivists, and others, Evans directed for three years a history-making accomplishment.

A legacy that cannot be belittled remains: the organization of basic records that was created; the descriptions prepared for local offices; the training of new archivists begun in the survey; the development of methods adopted by other historical agencies; and the lesson of a mass utilization of unskilled workers. But it must be noted that few of the inventories, published as a rule in mimeographed form, have been given the extensive use by scholars that their planners foresaw. Librarians, it would seem, have been insufficiently aware of the rich resource created in these unprepossessing listings.

Greater knowledge nationally of the accomplishments of that survey could be of great help in speeding a second attempt, begun at the end of 1974, to collect and preserve the historic papers of the states, local governments, and private agencies. The expansion of function, funds, and size of the National Historical Publications and Records Commission (NHPRC), signed into law in December 1974, could achieve more complete control of the vast quantity of little-known state and local records scattered around the country. Activity on a national scale may stimulate local interest as well. NHPRC's authorized funds are to be doubled to $4 million annually for the years 1975–1979. However, if the added $2 million proves as difficult to obtain as in its first year, the commission is likely to spend a great part of its efforts juggling its publication and collecting responsibilities, to the detriment of both. Shared knowledge, combined support, and utilization of survey results by librarians and archivists are of paramount importance.

We can see in the existing national patterns a strong contrast between the system of federal archives, as now established in the National Archives and Records Service under the General Services Administration, and the generally uncoordinated federal libraries. The national records are maintained in a centralized system of archival units and records centers, all responsible to one authority even when dispersed geographically. An effort in the last decade to separate the records management aspect from the archival function was defeated and appears to have left NARS in a reasonably secure position as a unified agency.

The federal library system is a haphazard development, uncoordinated and without central plan, developed out of the internal needs of the various government agencies. The Library of Congress, although a highly respected institution, has often been challenged when referred to as a national library. It has not had the financial support needed to provide adequate services for scholars and at the same time to fulfill its responsibilities as the research arm of Congress. Nor has it provided the comprehensive leadership to the library world and the total range of services expected of a national library.

Without wanting to substitute the kind of centralization existing in the National Archives, but looking for a higher degree of national library leadership, many librarians have responded favorably to the 1975 proposals of the National Commission on Libraries and Information Science (NCLIS) in regard to the federal libraries. The NCLIS recommends designation of the Library of Congress as the National Library and incorporation of the major federal libraries into a national network, recognizing that effective implementation of such changes may require special legislation.[4] The NCLIS recommendations, however, should be examined against the backdrop of recent legislation affecting libraries and archives.

RECENT NATIONAL LEGISLATION

The tremendous surge of growth and inspiration that had benefited libraries and their patrons and—perhaps by a measure of marginal inclusion—archives and manuscript repositories for almost 20 years collapsed in the early 1970s. In the wake of the great increase in funds that had been made available to libraries, large segments of the population never before adequately served had learned to use the wealth of resources in libraries, and new kinds of services rarely if ever before envisioned had been provided for numerous library patrons. It will take strong advocacy in the late 1970s and perhaps into the next decade to preserve a good share of those gains for the enrichment of the future. As we show the gains made by the people who use libraries, attributable to the legislation and accompanying federal funds of almost two decades, can we also demonstrate the need for continuing that support? And can we, at the same time, illustrate the same need shared by archives and manuscript collections?

Federal statistics state that 20 years ago 30 million Americans, or 20 percent of the population, lacked library service, but that in 1973, 193 million had access to a library system, leaving an estimated 8 percent currently without service. Since the Library Services Act (LSA) was enacted in 1956, more than $560 million in federal funds have been made available to libraries, and another $1.5 billion provided in state and local funds, up to the end of 1973.[5]

More relevant to the concerns of archivists and manuscript curators are the gains accruing to academic libraries, often the institutional parent, or home, of an archival unit or manuscript repository. The Higher Education Act of 1965 (HEA), which provided $5,000 grants to accredited institutions of higher education for library acquisition of books and related materials, has benefited libraries to the extent of $135 million in its decade of operation.[6] Because libraries were often included in general college grants, the precise advantages to libraries are difficult to determine, but it is clear that over one thousand library facilities received grants from 1964 to the end of 1972. Graduate library facilities received almost $52 million from 1964 through June 1969. This period produced "the greatest flowering of academic library building experience the country has ever known or is likely to see," but came to an abrupt halt with the cutting off of funds at the end of 1972.[7]

It is worthwhile to note that the Library Services and Construction Act (LSCA), originally directed especially toward public libraries, now, late in its life, has been extended to include independent research libraries, among which archives and manuscript repositories might be counted. Signed October 19, 1973, PL 93-133 broadens LSCA's definition of "public library" so that an independent research library may be included if it: (1) makes its services available to the public free of charge; (2) has extensive collections not available through public libraries; (3) disseminates humanistic knowledge; and (4) is not an integral part of an institution of higher education. It would be gratifying to have a large number of archives and manuscript repositories take advantage of this late opportunity for federal assistance since they do not appear to have taken much advantage of the limited number of previous opportunities.

The HEA (Title II B), for example, provides grants to institutions of higher education and to library organizations and agencies for training grants (institutes, fellowships, and traineeships) and for research and demonstration projects relating to the improvement of libraries or the improvement of training in librarianship. There has been little attention paid by archivists to the utilization of federal grants, particularly for training, although education and training are among the recognized major needs of the profession. While public archives cannot be defined within the limits of this act, it is very likely that archives and manuscript repositories within a university or a historical society, especially those that are administratively or, perhaps, physically within a library, could be so defined. Archivists and library school faculties could perhaps cooperate on such useful training projects.

The future outlook for those dependent on federal library funds has been unstable. Two alternatives to the previous categorical aid programs have been suggested as substitutes for federal funding of library programs. One is the general revenue-sharing program, officially the State and Local Fiscal Assistance Act of 1972, designed to provide general financial assistance to state and local governments. Critics of this substitute for direct aid to libraries point out that its purpose is quite different and the financial aid is therefore used very differently on the local scene. Not only do libraries have to compete with the many pressing needs of the states for funds—pollution control and law enforcement, for instance— but, since a provision of revenue sharing requires no matching funds from the states or local communities, this money may be used as a substitute for funds previously available from the local source. Reports show that less than 1 percent of general revenue-sharing funds spent by the states and local units has been allocated for library purposes, "despite the fact that libraries are specifically earmarked in the general revenue-sharing legislation as one of eight 'priority' categories."[8]

The passage of LSA in 1956 was considered by many librarians to be the beginning of a partnership between libraries and government which was enhanced in the next decade by additional legislation. The attendant publicity helped the nation to focus increasingly on the importance of libraries to the nation's healthy growth. A succession of executive bodies was named to analyze the role of libraries in national perspective. The core of a national policy first began to take shape in the report of the National Advisory Commission on Libraries in July 1968. One of the chief recommendations of that commission was the creation of a permanent planning agency on national library policy. The National Commission on Libraries and Information Science (NCLIS) was then established by law in 1970.

Its charge affirms "that library and information services adequate to meet the needs of the people of the United States are essential to achieve national goals and to utilize most effectively the Nation's educational resources and that the Federal Government will cooperate with state and local governments and public and private agencies in assuring optimum provision of such services." The commission faces serious difficulties in carrying out that charge. Its budget is not large enough for completing its various surveys, studies, hearings, etc.; it has a very small staff; and it must rely on the services of HEW for all its administrative help.

Early drafts of its national program for library service received much criticism chiefly for its stress on network concepts and technology at the expense of user needs. The same emphasis appears in the final program, with added attention to user need through continuing federal support, and specific references to a strengthened LSCA as a current priority; to legislation assuring equal access to knowledge regardless of economic, cultural, or social conditions; and to federal funding of fellowships and training institutes for the personnel of libraries and information centers. But a commission statement is not federal policy. The work of other commissions has died with the issuance of a report. The recent history of library legislation leads one to think that strong professional and lay support will be needed to bring the commission's recommendations to life.

There is here an opportunity to involve large sections of the library world—defined in its fullest sense—in developing a national information services program that would include all types of institutions responsible for the collection of recorded knowledge and its dissemination, combining the different approaches to our common responsibilities. The final paragraph of the NCLIS program states that "recorded knowledge is a national resource and its nationwide access a national responsibility." Can archivists allow the unique records in their collections to be excluded from this consideration? In its stress on the value and needs of research libraries, the NCLIS program opens the way to the inclusion of such collections. They are not mentioned specifically; the concern is with publications, to the extent that types of materials are described in a limiting manner. But the emphasis on the breadth and variety of media that must be encompassed in a national information services program calls for the inclusion of original source materials. In working toward the goal of nationwide access, librarians, archivists, manuscript curators, media specialists, and many related communications workers can learn to coordinate activities and strengthen common interests.

It appears that the inclusion, or exclusion, of unpublished materials in the concept "library" has not previously been considered in federal legislation. Certainly, a manuscript or archival collection which is a part of a recognized library will not be excluded from any benefits available to that library. But there are no known instances of any archives not affiliated with a library applying for aid under federal library legislation. Within the concept of research library and the larger umbrella of information services, it is now worth defining the identity of research function in archives and libraries, with the professionals most involved taking the leadership. Archivists responsible for public records will probably rise up in sharp disagreement at throwing in their lot with librarians. For them, a separate arena may well be necessary. But the separate and distinctive development of American nonpublic archives requires serious attention to the common interests of librarians and most American archivists.

An added vehicle for drawing attention to the needs and common goals at this time is the prospect of a White House Conference on Library and Information Services before the end of 1978. Such a conference is downgraded by some as a ploy, but it is a useful and appropriate device, scheduled for a time likely to gain the necessary support—following the ALA centennial year and the national bicentennial. Remembering the effectiveness of earlier White House conferences on children, on youth, and on the aging population, and the subsequent attention and support for specific needs, one can think more positively of the desirability of this attempt.

Many individuals and organizations expressed strong approval at the 1973 Congressional hearing on the proposed conference. Noteworthy for our purposes was the presentation of Dr. James B. Rhoads, archivist of the United States, who pointed out that "the resources of archival agencies and manuscript repositories comprise the very bedrock of the library and information science community itself. . . . Any consideration of the issues of information science should include the problems of archival agencies and manuscript repositories. Like libraries and information centers, they, too, provide basic information and educational services."[9]

A brief review of various other pieces of legislation recently adopted which affect or could be utilized by both archivists and librarians may help to strengthen understanding of our identity of interest on the national scene. One area of concern relates to the availability of personnel and possible provision of federal funds for their employment. The Comprehensive Employment and Training Act, signed in December 1973, enables state and local agencies in areas of high unemployment to use federal funds for the creation of jobs. A few libraries have been able to obtain additional paid help with such funds. An adventurous archivist might retrieve the *Manual* of HRS and adapt the most practical of its methods for utilizing untrained personnel in a records survey.

A similar program is available under the 1973 amendments to the Older Americans Act of 1965, which, in Title IX, authorizes federal funding for the employment of persons aged 55 or older who have poor employment prospects, and who could be employed in community service projects, specifically including educational, library, and similar services. Another related program is now encompassed under the Domestic Volunteer Services Act of 1973. A number of different volunteer programs are administered under this act, including the Retired Senior Volunteer Program from which public libraries involved in oral history and other projects with senior citizens have drawn help.

Of relatively minor effect in practical terms, but more interesting as it relates specifically to studies in the historical realm, is the Ethnic Heritage Studies Program, authorized by the Education Amendments of 1972 to provide grants to public and private nonprofit educational agencies, institutions, and organizations. The grants are intended to assist in developing programs that will enable elementary, secondary, and college students to better understand the differing and unique contributions to our national heritage made by each ethnic group in the United States. Drawing lessons from the "outreach" activities that a few archival institutions have developed in the last few years, more institutions could profit from the support offered by this act.

Postal regulations are a mundane but ever present aspect of the activities of any institution today, affecting many operations in libraries and archival institutions. The former national policy of providing favorable postal rates to newspapers, magazines, books, and other educational materials on the principle that their dissemination was in the public interest was abandoned in 1970 with a U.S. postal reorganization. By delegating to the new independent Postal Rate Commission the right to set rates for most classes of mail, the Congress has, in effect, permitted a 126 percent increase for second class mail (newspapers and magazines) and a 70 percent increase for books and other educational materials, spread over a five-year period.

Various amendments to the Postal Reorganization Act, chiefly aimed at spreading the total increases over a longer period, have brought little help to libraries. A more important amendment would require the Postal Rate Commission to take into account, in setting rates, the educational, cultural, and scientific value of mailed materials, bringing the possibility of substantial relief. In working toward legislation of such immediate importance to both libraries and archives, the combined efforts of the two professions could be of the greatest value.

A POLICY OF LEGISLATIVE ADVOCACY

The American Library Association, 60 years the senior of organized American archivists, now has a well-oiled legislative machinery. There may be many lessons it can teach the archival profession in helping to influence the making of laws or in creating a national climate responsive to a particular profession.

December 1973 marked 25 years of ALA's Capitol Hill coverage. There were ALA legislative activities before 1948, but the assignment of a permanent staff made a decisive difference in the ability to keep librarians and friends of libraries informed, and in the ability of the association to respond quickly, both organizationally and individually, to moves of the Congress or of a particular administration.

It took ten years' active work before the first Library Services Act was passed in 1956. That fact emphasizes the point that no legislative activity of importance is likely to be accomplished without years of diligent pursuit of information and people and an endless chain of contacts to make the efforts effective. Since the 1960s, legislative activity has been a cornerstone of the ALA program; the Washington staff keeps librarians around the country better informed and in closer touch with their legislators than is true for many professional groups.

Their most effective tool has been the *ALA Washington Newsletter*. Its modest, inexpensive appearance (mimeographed but highly readable) gives little indication of its value, based on its prompt delivery of the latest information, its accuracy, amount of needed detail, relevance to the concerns of its members, and usually effective layout of information. Its publication is irregular, but often biweekly or even weekly during congressional sessions, and its information is specific in terms of bills, their titles, numbers, status, appropriate committees, and how, when, and whom to contact. Its tone is not dogmatic or militant, but positive and highly informative. The masthead courtesy line "Any or all parts of the *ALA Washington Newsletter* may be reprinted for distribution" is itself inviting.[10]

The ALA's effectiveness in its mission to sell the value of libraries to the nation's legislators can best be judged by the whole range of library services supported federally from the 1950s to the present and by the substantial improvement in the quality and extent of library service made possible throughout the country. More immediately, between January and December 1973, those active on the scene saw the results in a reversal of policy following President Nixon's announced policy of zero funding for libraries. The Washington office of ALA makes clear that in its efforts toward continued funding it had the active support and participation of numerous librarians in the field who contacted their local legislators and fed supportive information on local activities to Washington.

In considering the ways in which librarians and archivists have responded to legislation, one must note certain different characteristics of the two fields of work that are likely to result in different responses from a legislature. Many types of recent legislation are more applicable to libraries than to archives, since the concerns emphasized have had popular, recreational, or basic educational purposes, and were more characteristic of library objectives than of archives. Perhaps SAA can help the profession to define the ways in which archives serve the broader educational needs of the population, or to relate research services provided to these needs. Archivists are responding in more of their activities to broad educational needs—to minority questions and to women's history—and may wish to direct more attention to the youth and to the popular aspects of their records, in order to serve the needs of larger segments of the population.

Another difference concerns the historical relationship of the broad institutional framework to the central government. Because archival agencies took shape most fully within the federal government, the professional association has tended to depend on that authority for leadership. Many members have long felt the need for SAA to assert its independence of the federal influence, and to take a position when appropriate, whether it pleases those in the government hierarchy or not. Libraries, on the other hand, began as private institutions generally; the government supported units came later. Even the early public libraries were often not government financed. Their professional association could therefore develop more independently, without fear of government pressure.

While archivists may envy the achievements of the ALA Washington office, the smaller size of the SAA appears to preclude a comparable development by the latter organization. There may be various alternatives if archivists decide that they need to be a more direct force on the laws affecting them. One method lies in the role of the new full-time executive director of the society who has already been heard on Capitol Hill on legislation important to archivists. Another may be to establish an SAA Committee on Legislation, utilizing to the fullest the many members located in Washington and in the various state capitals, to alert the rest of the membership to proposed legislation, and to assist in carrying through any position adopted by the society that might be translated into law. Archivists in government employ will remind us that current state and federal laws hamper the legislative activities of those holding government positions, requiring that their roles receive careful consideration.

Still another alternative which needs exploration is expanded cooperation between ALA and SAA, whenever possible, in the whole field of governmental and legislative relations, building on each other's strengths, without duplicating efforts. A good deal of membership education is required on both sides to make such a venture successful, but an increasing number of members of both ALA and SAA recognize mutual interests and could aid in that educative process. Strong arguments can be offered for weaving all three of the foregoing alternative solutions into a legislative policy for the SAA, beginning with the first two, and gradually developing the third method for greater cooperation with ALA.

The specific methods of cooperation will need close analysis by the leaders of both organizations. But an archivist active in both ALA and SAA thinks of what might be accomplished, for example, by a Washington office that considered archives one of its direct responsibilities because it recognized the clear interrelationship of archives and libraries, and because SAA was contributing to its upkeep; or, how effective up-to-date legislative information to archivists would be, channeled to them either through the *ALA Washington Newsletter* or through selective additions from it to the *SAA Newsletter*; or, how much more forceful the voices of an SAA Executive Director and an ALA Executive Director might be if, when they spoke on issues of mutual concern, their voices were combined.

Inherent in any such close cooperation is a clear understanding of the relationship of archives to libraries. On this question there is yet no general agreement. Archivists will need to take the lead in educating those outside the field to the character of the research function performed by archives, supplementing the activities heretofore seen as a function of libraries. American archives are unique institutions, going beyond the public record responsibility characteristic of their original European models, in developing collections based on many kinds of institutional and personal records, and therefore welcomed by scholars for their research value. We now need greater recognition of this function of archives, as allied to the traditional library function, and meriting the same public support that libraries have gained.

NOTES

1. Edna L. Jacobsen, "State and Local Government Archives," *Library Trends* 5 (1957): 397–398.
2. H. G. Jones, *The Records of a Nation: Their Management, Preservation and Use* (New York: Atheneum, 1969), pp. 58–65.
3. David L. Smiley, "The W.P.A. Historical Records Survey," in *In Support of Clio: Essays in Memory of Herbert A. Kellar*, ed. by William B. Hesseltine and Donald R. McNeil (Madison: State Historical Society of Wisconsin, 1958), pp. 3–4.
4. U.S. National Commission on Libraries and Information Science, *Toward a National Program for Library and Information Services: Goals for Action* (Washington: U.S. Government Printing Office, 1975), 106 pages.
5. John R. Ottina, "USOE and the Library Role," *American Libraries* 5 (1974): 315–316, 318.
6. Ibid., p. 315.
7. The quotation is from Jerrold Orne's "The Renaissance of Academic Library

Building, 1967–1971," *Library Journal* 96 (1971): 3947–3967. The rest of the information comes from Edward B. Stanford, "Federal Aid for Academic Library Construction," *Library Journal* 99 (1974): 112–115.

8. Eileen D. Cooke and Sara Case, "ALA Washington Notes," *Wilson Library Bulletin* 48 (1974): 624.

9. U.S. Congress, House of Representatives, Committee on Education and Labor, Select Subcommittee on Education, *White House Conference on Library and Information Services in 1976*, Hearing on H.J. Res. 734 and H.J. Res. 766, 93rd Congress, 1st session, November 29, 1973, pp. 65–67.

10. The *Newsletter* is available at $8.00 per year from the ALA Washington Office, 110 Maryland Avenue, NE, Suite 101, Washington, D.C. 20002.

COPYRIGHT AND LITERARY PROPERTY RIGHTS

Knowledge of the principles of copyright and common law literary property rights has long been considered necessary to any archivist or manuscript curator. Librarians, on the other hand, have taken the concept for granted, without great attention to its complexity, until recent challenges to the use of photocopy.

Recent technological developments directly affecting the manner in which copyright is applied, the use of new media by archives and libraries, and the broadening scope of their actvities give both groups of professionals new cause to examine the issue in terms of their overlapping and merging concerns over both statutory copyright and common law literary property rights.

There is some validity in separating the major roles of archivist and librarian as they approach the question of copyright, the former representing principally the needs of the scholar for access to research materials, the latter focusing to a large extent on the layman's needs for access to information for daily living. But as they attempt to satisfy these needs along their separate paths, the activities constantly merge and they find themselves looking for common solutions, for greater standardization or uniformity in responding to copyright, and the recognition of literary property rights.

Copyright is the protection offered by the law to the creator of an intellectual or artistic work, assuring the individual the exclusive right to the fruits of that work for a limited period of time. Publication of the work—making it available to the public in some way, usually by sale or public distribution—with a notice of copyright included in a specific manner, is necessary to secure copyright for books and similar writings and for certain other kinds of publications.[1]

In considering these basic provisions of copyright, we are immediately plunged into the issues that have agitated publishers, authors, librarians, and archivists, and, since its attempts at copyright revision beginning in 1962, the Congress of the United States. What is "a limited period of time" for which the creator of a work is entitled to its exclusive control? The long-standing 1909 law provided a term of 28 years from first publication, with the opportunity of extension for another 28 years, this being the limit. Current proposals for revision, receiving strong support, provide for a copyright term extending to 50 years beyond the life of the author of a work. Librarians have generally opposed this revision, on the grounds that it would usually further hamper the availability of needed materials. Archivists and manuscript curators have been silent, as though concern for published materials was out of their realm. But this narrow view is also shortsighted.

85

In the proposals for copyright revision, there is, for the first time, legislative recognition of the literary property rights inherent in unpublished creative works. The term of copyright could thus be of equal concern to archivists, manuscript curators, and librarians. Fifty years beyond the life of the creator, if imposed also on unpublished works as the limit of literary property rights, as has sometimes been suggested, would at least greatly modify the indefinite period which has been previously accepted for such works. Literary property rights, heretofore protected by common law, and existing in perpetuity, have often required extended search for an author's heirs when the rights were not transferred to a manuscript collection with the manuscript itself.

An even more basic element of copyright has on occasion concerned those dealing with original materials. What constitutes publication of a previously unpublished work? The printing of a work is not alone a guarantee of the general publication the courts have required, since works printed for private distribution without notice of copyright have been accepted as still carrying their common law literary property rights. Greater clarity is therefore needed on the many kinds of limited distribution which may be open to a writer or artist today. In addition, for certain types of works, such as dramatic or musical compositions which may become known even without publication, copyright is possible simply by registering a claim in the Copyright Office. What is the effect, then, of a public library performance of a work not so registered upon the creator's exclusive rights? The courts have generally held that such works remain the property of the creator until published in the usual way. Such lesser known aspects of copyright are important in view of the wide current use of the tape recorder and the possibility of an unauthorized recording being misused.

What constitutes publication is a question of particular importance for the manuscript curator. Archivists and manuscript curators must be alert to the whole question of copyright and literary rights at a much earlier stage than will generally be true for librarians responsible only for book collections. The manuscript curator needs to be alert to questions of literary property rights from the time of the first offer or receipt of materials, in order to make provision for an appropriate agreement with the donor. And since, in small institutions particularly, the librarian may often be the person accepting donations of gifts which may include manuscripts, that professional must also be well informed on the meaning of the literary property rights in unpublished materials.

Occasionally, unorthodox arguments have challenged the concept of personal literary property rights when posed against the rights of the public and posterity to preserve the heritage of the past. Since literary property becomes a part of the public domain upon general publication, when unprotected by a notice of copyright, and if general publication, as sometimes defined by the courts, is achieved by the placing of the material before the public in any unrestricted way (that is, by granting access to the general public) then deposit in an institution whose resources are open to the public has sometimes been said to constitute general publication.[2]

If one accepts this view, all manuscripts or letters deposited by their creators in institutions open to the public—at least when no specific restrictions are placed on their use—are in the public domain, freely available for all kinds of use. Nevertheless, since the courts have not been consistent in the interpretation of what constitutes general publication, the researcher, writer, or publisher who uses this as a working rule runs a very definite risk of legal entanglement. Ethical considerations require the curator who accepts such a standard to inform potential donors of the effect of deposit of their own works on their future literary rights, difficult as that may be when it could mean the loss of valuable literary and historical materials.

Since only the author or creator of a work, or the heirs, can claim ownership of literary property rights, only they may transfer such rights, regardless of who has ownership of the physical object embodying the creation. Thus, most of the literary works given to manuscript repositories by collectors, or letters given by those who received them, carried with them no transfer of literary property rights, regardless of the contents of any certificate of gift, unless signed by the author of each work or the heirs. Even the papers given by the individual or organization which created them contain many letters written by others who may retain literary property rights therein. It is in these cases, when transfer or donation of literary rights may be unobtainable, that the proposed 50-year limit, plus life of the author, would be most useful.

The specific character of gift or deposit agreements varies widely. The form probably most preferred by repositories is that used by the Library of Congress which has the donor, when willing, assign the rights to the public. Many other repositories prefer to have the rights transferred to the historical society or parent institution to which they are subsidiary.

When this type of general transfer of rights to the literary property in manuscripts or personal papers is not possible, a repository will usually accept the gift with whatever restrictions may be imposed by the donor, attempting to make these as few and reasonable as possible. In the past, such restrictions often might mean screening by the donor of those wishing access to the documents, but this practice is now discouraged, the principle of equal access for all scholars receiving strong support. Restrictions may specifically require the donor's permission for reproduction of manuscripts or for quotation for publication.

Wide variations in practice among institutions on donor agreements, on access to source materials, and on photocopying have made clear the need for guidance. Responding to this need and hoping to stimulate greater uniformity of practices, the professional associations have now formulated statements of standards. The Committee on Manuscripts Collections of the Rare Books and Manuscripts Section of the Association of College and Research Libraries (ACRL) has developed standards on both access to research materials and on the reproduction of manuscripts which were approved as policy by the ACRL board of directors in January 1974.[3] The same committee has more recently prepared a standardized form to be used by curators in transferring legal title to papers acquired by manuscript collections.[4]

A statement on "Standards for Access . . ." in language very similar to the ACRL document had been endorsed by the SAA council in December 1973.[5] The emphasis of these documents is on uniformity of regulations for all researchers, the minimum of restrictions, and clearly stated information on literary property rights and copyright provided to the researcher, whose responsibility for securing permission is specified. The proliferation of standards simultaneously from several different quarters underlines the great need for merging of these activities by librarians and archivists. Further coordination between SAA and ALA (specifically, its ACRL division) should make possible a single document acceptable to both professional organizations on a matter of such common interest, thus simplifying its use and applying a single standard less subject to varying interpretations.

It is over the copyright holder's right to exclusive use of the fruits of his work for a specified period of time that the greatest dispute has arisen in recent years. The copyright holder has the exclusive rights to print and copy the work, to sell or distribute copies, to transform or revise the work, to record it, and to perform it publicly. There are minor limitations, but, in a literal interpretation, the rights are fairly inclusive of any profit or use that could be made of creative works, leaving only another individual's right to read, listen, or look. The 1909 act does not expressly permit any use of copyrighted material without the permission of the copyright owner. The courts have nonetheless allowed certain limited uses as fair use, without obtaining permission, when this was considered reasonable and not harmful to the copyright owner's rights.

The extension of that doctrine to the use of photocopy and the increasing dispersal far and wide of reproductions of the printed work, lacking any control by, or financial return to, the author or publisher of the original work, have led inevitably to the present strong challenge from the publishing industry. If one looks back at the beginning of the copyright concept, this reaction can be seen as part of an unbroken development inherent in the origin of copyright, and tied directly to the investment of the entrepreneur in the machinery responsible for the reproduction of original works, making possible their dissemination. "The growth of the law of copyright protection closely followed the development of mechanical means of reproduction. Literary copyright was protected only after the invention of printing; artistic copyright was only established with the expansion in the use of engravings and lithographs."[6] At the heart of the current dispute, in direct opposition to each other, are the acknowledged right, in a capitalist economy, of the investor to profit from his investment, and the manifold needs in that increasingly complex but, hopefully, democratic society for the electorate to have at its command all the information it can possibly get. That may be called a highly simplistic statement of the problem, but it does contain the kernel of the dispute.

Libraries, as the instruments of popular education, became the natural focus of the publishers' efforts to regain control of their products. The much-publicized case of the Williams & Wilkins Company, publishers of medical books and journals, directed against the National Library of Medicine and the library of the National Institutes of Health as a result of the libraries' photocopying of journal articles, finally forced the issue to decision in the courts. But, in allowing a Court of Claims decision to stand—in effect, upholding library photocopying practices as fair use—the 1975 Supreme Court decision simply underlined the need for swift action in Congress for passage of a new comprehensive Copyright Act.

Certain issues raised by the Court of Claims are important in weighing arguments on both sides. The court pointed out that the photocopying was not done for the profit of the libraries, and that there was little chance that any libraries or individuals would purchase subscriptions to the journals if photocopies were not supplied. Although the court recognized the large amount of photocopying done by the libraries, it took favorable note of the controls exercised in the process to prevent copying of entire journal issues, to limit responses to requests to single copies, and to avoid photocopying from journals that were widely available.[7]

The strong minority dissent of Chief Judge Wilson Cowen charged "wholesale, machine copying . . . on a scale so vast that it dwarfs the output of many small publishing companies." He favored a licensing system with royalty fees paid to the copyright owner, as recommended by the publishers. The Special Libraries Association (SLA), unlike ALA and the Medical Library Association, has been supporting the principle of a fee paid for photocopies to recompense the copyright owner. Most library representatives contend that such licensing fees would cost more to administer than would be collected and would impose serious financial burdens on libraries and scholars.

Proposed revision of the Copyright Act, likely to become law in the immediate future, affects libraries, archives, and manuscript collections in its approach to the issue of photocopying. Privileges of reproduction of copyrighted works by libraries and archives (the latter inclusion not a common practice in previous federal legislation) are being spelled out, generally along lines supported by ALA, except for one controversial clause that particularly disturbs librarians. This makes the library liable to prosecution when "systematic reproduction or distribution of single or multiple copies" occurs, and could greatly hamper present interlibrary loan practices. An active campaign has been waged by ALA to exclude such a liability. If passed, further interpretation will clearly be necessary.

A new concept introduced permits reproduction and distribution of a single copy of an unpublished work, "solely for purposes of preservation and security or for deposit for research use in another library or archives" when the unpublished work is currently in the collections of the library doing the reproduction.

The principle of fair use has been for the first time defined in proposed legislation, including consideration of the use to be made of the copy and its effect upon the potential market for the copyrighted work. Such a provision could become more decisive in the future—and of particular value to libraries and archives—if current proposals become law. Likewise of interest to archivists and librarians is the inclusion of phonorecords as a form of copy allowed whenever photocopy is permitted.

Knowledge of the copyright provisions for sound recordings—covered since 1972—is obviously useful to librarians and archivists, many of whose collections now contain phonograph and tape recordings, and who may find easy duplication via the tape recorder an inexpensive method. Oral history programs and collections, of increasing interest to archivists, pose particular kinds of problems, analogous to the questions of literary property rights.

Knowledgeable oral historians have held that the words of persons interviewed are their creation and that the speakers have a kind of literary property right therein. Most institutions consider it important to obtain a waiver or transfer of the speaker's rights, in order to protect the institution in its transcription of the taped interview, and to assure public access to the transcription and tape. But, faced with sensitive and cautious interviewees, and eager to get a program under way, an archivist may settle for the development of collections laced with restrictions. Many oral historians, however, accept the value of restrictions on access to tapes and transcriptions for a specified period of time, particularly when there are any taped references to public persons, and in order to secure many interviews otherwise not possible.

In this area as in others, at least until there are clearer legal guidelines, and as a means to establishing reasonable laws, standards formulated by the professional associations are needed. But a greater weight of authority is also needed to achieve observance of these standards, all too often ignored in actual practice by even the established, prestigious institutions.

NOTES

1. The three most useful works for an explanation of the copyright provisions are publications of the U.S. Copyright Office: *General Information on Copyright*, Circular 1, 11 pages; *Copyright Law of the United States of America*, Circular 91, U.S. Code, Title 17, revised to January 1, 1973, 27 pages; *Copyright Time Limits*, Circular 22x, 1973, 1 page.

2. Seymour V. Connor, "The Problem of Literary Property in Archival Depositories," *American Archivist* 21 (1958): 143–152.

3. "Statement on Access to Original Research Materials in Libraries, Archives, and Manuscript Repositories" and "Statement on the Reproduction of Manuscripts and Archives for Noncommercial Purposes," *College and Research Libraries News* 35 (May 1974): 114–115. Single reprint copies of each statement are available free, and multiple copies for 20¢ each, from the ACRL Office, 50 E. Huron Street, Chicago, Ill. 60611.

4. "Universal Gift Form and Instructions," *College and Research Libraries News* 36 (March 1975): 95–96.

5. "Standards for Access to Research Materials in Archival and Manuscript Repositories," *American Archivist* 37 (1974): 153–154.

6. F. E. Skone James and Alan Daubeny Russell Clarke, "Copyright," in *Encyclopaedia Britannica*, vol. 6 (Chicago: Encyclopaedia Britannica, 1958), p. 425.

7. U.S. Court of Claims, *The Williams & Wilkins Company* v. *the United States*, [Decision] no. 73-68 decided November 27, 1973 (Washington: U.S. Government Printing Office, 1973), 104 pages.

ACCESS AND CONFIDENTIALITY

It is the issue of control of public access to the documents and books in their custody that shows the greatest contrasts between the librarian and the manuscript curator or archivist. The self-image is of the ideal librarian making all materials freely available to all patrons and of the equally dedicated archivist doling out selected manuscripts only after cautious perusal of the researcher's credentials.

Many repositories have traditionally served only scholars with advanced degrees, or graduate students, and require identification and the completion of a detailed application form stating the use to be made of the specific material requested before making it available. After this procedure has been followed, the researcher may still be refused access to specific documents for a variety of reasons. These may include the archivist's judgment that the document is too fragile; that the request violates institutional policy or the donor's restrictions; that the document may be closed to use for a specific number of years, due to the literary property rights of the author of the document; that the content of the document may be damaging to the reputation of living persons; or that it contains confidential information. If the repository is a government agency, restrictions may exist on classified documents not open to the public, or on others restricted by law or regulation. Even when made accessible for consultation, additional restrictions may be placed on the use of particular documents for publication.

The archivist, entrusted with the permanent preservation of original documents (many in long series of loose sheets), looks for assurance as to the character of the individuals in whose hands the documents are placed. To ensure the safety of the records, the archivist asks for sufficient maturity and knowledge in the researcher to recognize the value of original sources, to handle them with care, and to retain their order as presented. The archivist assumes the researcher has honorable intentions and the integrity not to deliberately damage or abscond with the records. An archivist could certainly be challenged in attempting to prove that possession of an advanced academic degree is sure evidence of good intentions, of knowledge, or of any other reliable status. But the degree nevertheless provides an easy rule-of-thumb criterion for judging researchers in many repositories.

With the increased attention given to original sources for historical research, the broader use of university facilities which house many repositories, and the upsurge of interest in topics of research formerly neglected, screening of researchers has become less acceptable. As an example of the shift in attitude over a twenty-year period, we may compare the 1974 standards on access of ACRL and SAA (discussed in the preceding chapter) with a 1950 statement of the Ad Hoc Committee on Manuscripts of the American Historical Association (AHA) which recommended the screening of applicants to consult recent collections.[1] Restrictions based on type of researcher are now often viewed as too subjective and possibly discriminatory in their application to minority persons, to young people, or to others outside the immediate experience of the archivist. The SAA standards specify that researchers are entitled to equal terms of access. (The ACRL standards use the traditional phrase, "qualified researchers, as defined by the respective institutions.") We shall have to wait to see, however, whether these apparently relaxed standards have sufficient effect in encouraging a large number of institutions to open their doors to the nonacademic researcher, infrequent though the request may be.

Does a repository have the right to ask researchers the purpose for which requested materials are needed? Granted, straightforward answers may gain researchers access to riches that they had not known the repository had available. But, if researchers choose to preserve their privacy for good reasons, is there sufficient justification for the repository requiring knowledge of the use to be made of the information, as has customarily been done?

This is the point at which archivist and librarian part company most clearly, the librarian generally committed to defending the intellectual freedom of the reader and the right of privacy, both of which have been the subject of specific ALA support actions in somewhat different contexts. Historically, the archivist and manuscript curator have taken the position that because they are responsible for unpublished personal and official papers and, sometimes, confidential records, they must preserve the implicit trust given in the deposit of those records by assuring that only those who will use them in scholarly fashion—sometimes interpreted to mean in friendly fashion—may have access to them. Certainly we can recognize that information transmitted in contemporary personal letters may be injurious to other living persons, or damaging to their reputations, perhaps libelous, or simply untrue. But there is considerable question as to whether an archivist can really determine whether a researcher's intended use of materials may be injurious to the public interest. There is an obligation to make sure that the researcher is aware of the hazards of publication, but, aside from such precautions, it may be wiser to prohibit access for a requisite number of years, and then to make a collection available to all who wish to use it, rather than to attempt to distinguish between reputable and disreputable intentions in use.

The objective of open access to research materials is based on the assumption that the contents of these papers are of potentially significant general research value—that we are delving into the history or records, not of an individual (unless this is an historic figure), but of a movement or historical period or of some social development. In direct opposition to the principle of open access to such historically significant records is the responsibility recognized by the archivist to protect the privacy of personal records—particularly those of living persons—the more so when these are not persons of public reputation. The privacy of public persons is also to be respected, but there is a recognition that an individual sacrifices a degree of privacy upon accepting public office or a career in the public eye. In the interest of protecting the individual, institutions have worked out varying methods: totally prohibiting the use of certain records for a period of time; blocking out names and other specific identifying information on individual records; or sometimes making them available to qualified researchers in full, with the understanding that no identifying information is to be used in publishing the data.

The inclusion within many institutional archives of vast quantities of data drawn from personnel files, from student records, medical records, credit files, etc., has forced archivists to take a strong position respecting the privacy of such files, and to develop policies and procedures which can assure their privacy. The entrance of the computer into record keeping and the subsequent development of both current data banks and social science data archives have compounded the intensity of the problem. Not only does the security of files in a particular institution require safeguards, and questions to be resolved as to who may have access to those files, but there are additional threats to privacy in the tremendous ability of the computer to amass data, in its ability to codify information about individuals from many diverse sources, and in the accessibility of that information to a host of computer technicians as well as to all kinds of officials and institutional personnel.

One challenge that should be anticipated is the possibility of a legal subpoena ordering records to be produced in court. How will the institution protect the privacy of an individual threatened by such a subpoena? If the archivist has not prepared for that eventuality by developing a policy that has been approved by legal counsel and supported by the highest authority in the institution, the archivist may be unable to muster support in an emergency. And, in fact, even with adequate preparation, one cannot count on institutional backing against the threat of a lawsuit—particularly in an agency of the government or one supported by government funds. Knowing the laws which may offer support for the safeguarding of particular kinds of information is a great asset. An archivist working within a library organization may also find some limited support in the position taken by ALA a few years ago in regard to the confidentiality of library borrowers' records.[2]

The vast and very loosely formulated needs of national security place additional severe restrictions on the scholar's access to historical documents. With the involvement of many nonmilitary U.S. government agencies in World War II, the use of security classifications was extended far beyond the military agencies. Various executive orders have had relatively little effect in limiting the proliferation of security restrictions on many federal records. A Pentagon security expert told Congress in 1971 that the government had 20 million classified documents on file, "including reproduced copies" and items elsewhere available, such as published commercial information and newspaper clippings. He estimated that release of more than 99 percent of these documents "could not be prejudicial to the defense interests of the United States."[3] But both classification and declassification are time-consuming and costly.

Many scholars now see the vast quantity of classified records and the bureaucratic complexity of the system that maintains this classification as far greater deterrents to access to important historical records than any true considerations of national defense or foreign relations. Not only is the researcher denied access to key sources for an analysis of events, but, more important, the American public is denied reliable information on how major decisions that deeply affect their lives were made. Increasingly disturbing to historians as well as to journalists is not the lack of access for research alone, but the selective leaking of information from closed sources, as it serves some public official's purposes, or the access to documents allowed selected individuals for the writing of memoirs, when others cannot consult the documents for analysis or rebuttal.

Following the unauthorized release of the Pentagon Papers, President Nixon issued a new Executive Order 11652, signed on March 8, 1972, on Classification and Declassification, ostensibly to allow greater public access but still subject to administrative interpretation. While all documents over thirty years old are intended to be declassified, any agency head may use the national security argument to prolong a classification. Citizens may request a formal review of documents for declassification, but only of those more than ten years old, and, in order to do so, must specify the document with considerable particularity. But—"catch 22"—how can you specify a particular document if its very existence may be kept secret?

An increasing number of scholars are now pressing for automatic declassification of all classified documents after ten years. The SAA council in December 1973 approved a resolution of its Committee on Reference and Access calling for the automatic declassification of all classified records "except the most highly sensitive" after ten years. Similarly, the AHA in 1971 went on record in favor of a ten-year limit on classification, amending a proposal for a twenty-year rule. To answer objections on grounds of national security, it recommended a review committee, appointed by the president, consisting of representatives from the National

Archives, government agencies, and the general public, with final authority for allowing exceptions to the ten-year rule when requested by a federal agency.[4]

A democracy governs with the consent of those governed. To have value, that consent must be based on an informed awareness of relevant facts, most of which are in the custody of the government itself. Moreover, our government is now the greatest storehouse of information of the most varied kinds found anywhere in the world, much of it of a very practical nature, useful to the citizen for many daily needs. To meet both types of informational needs, the Freedom of Information Act was adopted in 1966, making it mandatory for all federal agencies to publish rules and appeal procedures which govern the release of information from their respective agencies. The act gives "any person" the right of access to agency records without having to state a reason for wanting the information, and the burden of proof for withholding the information rests with the agency.

But, as most adults have learned, the adoption of a well-intentioned law does not automatically produce the desired results. Major problems of compliance met by citizens requesting information have been somewhat remedied by amendments made in 1974, although many roadblocks still exist in the pursuit of information. It has been shown, however, that persistence has very often achieved the desired results, because the agency will find it disadvantageous to go to court over most requests, and because in a majority of cases taken to court the right of the private citizen to information has been upheld.

Government agencies are now required to publish indexes to all matters or information issued, adopted, or promulgated by them, and to report them in the *Federal Register*. As an aid to improving access to this information, the *Register* has recently requested both agencies and the public to aid in improving its indexes to federal regulations, so that the language used will be more responsive to the average person's needs and understanding. This is an area in which librarians, knowledgeable in both subject headings and the public's difficulties in coping with them, could be of practical assistance to the larger public. The newer breed of people's librarian and direct information specialist might easily help in suggesting good indexing terms.

Librarians have a particular responsibility to provide their patrons with a knowledge of the Freedom of Information Act and to assist in its utilization. They should also become more familiar with and have available all useful government information that will enable patrons to make proper use of the act. But archivists should not lose sight of the fact that the act refers not alone to published information, but covers primary sources as well, therefore making possible its use as a challenge to the withholding of records within any government agency, or after transfer to the National Archives.

In considering the researcher's plea for access to records of historic significance, we need to be reminded that the question is not debatable when there are no records to be made available. The ability of the repository to obtain appropriate records and the judgment of the archivist in retaining those that have research value are elements in the right of access. Nowhere has the question of availability as a condition of access been so well pinpointed as in recent interest in the fate of the papers of public officials. American legal opinion and general practice follow the principle that manuscripts, correspondence, publications, and other works created in the course of employment of one individual by another are the property of the employer, and therefore are not the source of any literary property rights credited to the actual author. This principle has been applied to most public employees and to minor public officials, who are expected to leave their office files and correspondence intact, as the property of the agency, when they leave the position. Leading officers of the federal and state governments, however, from the earliest period have been permitted to treat their official correspondence and records—the product of the business conducted as an official of the government—as personal papers, and to remove them from government custody when they leave office. There is no law that specifies that they may do so, but without laws stipulating that the records of the governor of each state, the president, vice-president, cabinet officers, and other leading officials are public records and public property, no authority has been sufficiently strong and knowledgeable to alter the practice.

With the establishment of the Franklin D. Roosevelt Library at Hyde Park in 1940 a new precedent was set. The idea of the presidential library originated with President Roosevelt, apparently in response to his own strong sense of historical commitment, and as a solution to the overwhelming quantity of materials amassed during the earlier years of his public life, and increased dramatically by the surge of documents that descended on him as soon as he had taken office in 1933.[5] While Roosevelt's intention was apparently to guarantee the permanent preservation of his papers as a basic resource for American history, he fell short of the full recognition of presidential papers as public records. The new concept of presidential archives (which they should be called, rather than presidential libraries), without the assurance that future presidents would be compelled to transfer their records to public custody, appears to have motivated the American Historical Association to go on record in 1945 in support of the principle that presidents should take with them, upon retirement, "only that correspondence which is strictly personal in character."[6]

The argument has frequently been advanced that leading public officials—especially the president—must be allowed complete control of their public papers, or they and their subordinates and those with whom they transact important public business will no longer put down on paper, or otherwise record, the information that will enable historians or the public to ever know what actually transpired. Archivists reason that if there is fear that such information may be made publicly available soon after the event, nothing of importance will be recorded. The argument cannot be ignored, since such fears do exist. But, noting the various hazards that have beset the papers of presidents and other officials, and the loss of essential records to the nation, some archivists question the old argument. It can be assumed, for instance, that even if there was acceptance of the rule that the papers of the president are public records, their custody would be in the hands of the National Archives, perhaps even administered through presidential libraries as at present, and that time restrictions or other limitations would be placed on their use. The basic difference would be in the legal obligation of the president to turn over all records accumulated in office.

There is no question but that the development of presidential libraries has made much more readily available a far greater amount of research material related to each administration than was accessible in the past. But it must be noted that threats to the availability of presidential records still exist, in the right that each president since Roosevelt—or his heirs— has claimed to screen and select from the papers to be deposited in a presidential library. Archivists should weigh this against the fears expressed for the existence of any records if the public official does not maintain control. They should also note that, in spite of the presumed decrease of correspondence for the transaction of official business, by substitution of the telephone and tape recorder, many records of conversations, agreements, and events are preserved that the historian might expect would not have been documented out of a sense of caution. The evidence appears rather strong that the arguments for continued private control of the papers of public officials accumulated in the course of official duties have been overstated, and that renewed consideration needs to be given to the assertion of public control over all such papers.

Conclusions of this nature, based on what had been observed in the handling of the nation's records up to that time, had been drawn by a relatively small number of archivists by 1973. The events that have since occurred in the Nixon and Ford administrations, including the disputes over control of the presidential tapes, the tax deduction for Richard Nixon's vice-presidential papers, and the August 1974 agreement for disposition of his presidential papers, have served to strengthen or to alter the opinions of a larger number of archivists in this direction.

It now appears that there are a substantial number of legislators who may also be convinced of the need for a federal law establishing the right of federal control over the public papers of the president and other federal officials. Two major steps in this direction were taken by Congress at the end of 1974, first in establishing control over the tape recordings and presidential papers of President Nixon, and, second, in setting up a study commission to examine in depth the question of the disposition of the records of leading federal officials.

Today's librarians have a well-developed body of principles relating to open access to materials, principles of intellectual freedom put forth in the 1920s and 1930s, as the social mores of the country relaxed. The lesson of book burning in other parts of the world and countermovements in this country resulted in the adoption of the first Library Bill of Rights by ALA, and forced leading librarians to gradually evolve the principles of intellectual freedom.

In an oversimplified fashion, early and recent library history has provided two contrasting approaches to book selection for libraries: one called the value theory—"give them what they should have," only those books which will educate in some way, or enrich life; the other, the demand theory—"give them what they want," i.e., whatever readers are likely to request, justifying such acquisition with the view that citizens' tax support entitles them to get what they want. The Library Bill of Rights supports neither position in full, but puts the responsibility on the librarian to select what best suits the needs of the total community, allowing free access to all people and to all points of view, and permitting none to obstruct the same free access for other persons. The weight of the policy is therefore toward inclusion of the broadest spectrum of materials, rather than on some arbitrary standard of what is good for the community.

NOTES

1. "Report of the Ad Hoc Committee on Manuscripts," in *Proceedings of the American Historical Association*, 1950 (Washington: U.S. Government Printing Office, 1951), pp. 68–69. Quoted in Philip C. Brooks, *Research in Archives* (Chicago: University of Chicago Press, 1969), p. 66.

2. "Confidentiality of Library Records," Item no. 101.2, January 1971, in American Library Association, *Position Statements and Policies and Procedures* (Chicago: American Library Association, 1973).

3. James Reston, "The Secrecy Tangle," *New York Times*, June 25, 1971, p. 35.

4. Carol M. Barker and Matthew H. Fox, *Classified Files: The Yellowing Pages, A Report on Scholars' Access to Government Documents* (New York: The Twentieth Century Fund, 1972), pp. 89–90.

5. H. G. Jones, *The Records of a Nation: Their Management, Preservation and Use* (New York: Atheneum, 1969), pp. 147–148. Dr. Jones provides a full and absorbing account of the origin of the presidential libraries, as well as a broad, knowledgeable defense of the principle of presidential papers as public records, in the chapter, "The Records of the Presidency, 1938–1968," pp. 144–171.

6. T. R. Schellenberg, *Modern Archives: Principles and Techniques* (Chicago: University of Chicago Press, 1956), p. 123.

SOCIAL RESPONSIBILITY

One would not expect any justification to be necessary for the social responsibility which any member of a profession claims, and that, in fact, showing a sense of responsibility to society is one of the distinguishing marks of a professional. Yet, in the late 1960s and in the 1970s some librarians have found themselves on the defensive as proponents of social responsibility, accused of weakening the ALA.

In essence, social responsibility is generally understood to encompass three major aspects: the sharpened recognition of ethical obligations to broad sections of the general population and to its individual representatives; the responsibility of the profession for guaranteeing fair and equitable treatment to all those who practice in the field; and the need, on occasion, for the collective position of the members of the profession to be expressed on questions of public importance, when its expertise creates knowledge of special value and may aid in the achievement of socially desirable goals. Implicit within the point of view of the majority of those who espouse the concept is also an acceptance of the view that, to survive, society must constantly adapt its practices, and that the needs of humankind demand that we support social change, not oppose it through stolid continuance of the status quo.

There are those who believe that many librarians and other professionals suddenly became socially responsible in the late 1960s, apparently after having worked in isolation from all of the social movements flowing around them up to that time. However, if one remembers the adult education movement that flourished some 30 years before, in which many librarians integrated their activities, it appears otherwise. The terminology and the specific forms developed were different, but the outlook and function of the readers' adviser or of the adult education director in a library at that time show great similarities to those of the "outreach" programs or of the people's librarian in existing institutions. Throughout the years there have been librarians and library programs that displayed a strong concern for the basic pressing needs of the library user, and attempted to reach out to the large number of nonusers. There could have been many more librarians and programs to prove the library the democratic institution it claimed to be. Today's activist librarian tends to be more aggressive and, very possibly, is able to achieve more by being willing, if necessary, to cut through red tape to meet the needs of the patron.

ALA AND THE LIBRARIAN

The rebirth of responsiveness to social concerns on a large scale in the profession presaged by only a couple of years a similar development among archivists. This responsiveness occurred in many other professional groups at about the same time, reflecting the social upheaval affecting the country. The archivists and their professional organization have thus far escaped the excessive polarization experienced by ALA in this period. In the library field, encompassing a much larger population, more fully organized and probably including a larger proportion of young people, the evidence of change was much more obvious. Several loose organizations of students and young librarians had been meeting to discuss issues of better library service to disadvantaged sections of the population, democracy in ALA, and more opportunity for young librarians.

From these meetings developed ALA's Social Responsibilities Round Table (SRRT) in 1969, which spread quickly throughout the country. Its arrival on the scene apparently answered a rising need of the new generation of librarians who felt neglected in the vastness of ALA. Their goals of intellectual satisfaction and social purpose were too often unfulfilled in the pettiness of a beginning-level job and in the closed-door bureaucracy of ALA.

Acceptance of the Round Table within ALA gave it national organization support, but more freedom in operation than the larger divisions of ALA. Membership within ALA has been an ongoing point at issue, however. Many SRRT members find the organizational structure too confining. From 1969 on, members have periodically suggested the need to establish a separate organization, but few have considered that a desirable route, believing the strength of the SRRT voice within ALA was more effective than it would be as a possible splinter organization. The membership of SRRT within ALA has not exceeded 2,000,[1] but its impact on association activities has been considerably more far-reaching than that fraction of membership would indicate. The activists who have led SRRT can claim a good deal of credit for the elements of internal democracy that have become operative within ALA, as well as for the enactment of policies extending association activities into areas protecting the rights of the individual librarian more effectively, and for encouraging library service on new fronts.

Achieving a new breadth and greater variety in the contents of library collections has been one of the gains made in recent years, through changes brought about by the demands of library patrons for new materials and by the eagerness of young professionals to broaden the scope of their collections. The more active policies adopted by ALA in support of unfettered book selection have aided the development of collections of contemporary culture, which have saved for the historian of the future a substantial output of the "alternative" presses.

More open access to library materials has also been the objective in various projects—in volunteer service to prison libraries, in service to migrant farm workers, and in efforts to serve the practical informational needs of the unread residents of the inner city. Activist librarians have been accused of being bleeding-hearts or frustrated caseworkers, attempting to do the social worker's job and neglecting the duties of the librarian. Yet, among the most active of the SRRT leaders one can find attention concentrated on specific library problems, with new insight brought to old questions from the user's point of view. Sanford Berman's study of subject headings,[2] for example, considered extreme in its attitudes by some librarians, nevertheless forces us to give new thought to terminology and to library usage that for years has belittled women, minority groups, and the less respected elements in society.

The parallels between library and archival professions become readily apparent. A similar broadening of the content of collections has been an increasing characteristic of archives and manuscript repositories in the last few years, particularly as curators and archivists have become concerned with contemporary records. Documenting the history of women seems to be the first objective of many curators, perhaps to compensate for long years of silence on this score. Working-class history and the histories of ethnic minorities appear to run a close second in publicized records. The nonhero, the little known farmer, immigrant, or worker is the new hero of the archivist's collecting efforts. There is little doubt that attention to the lesser known groups in the population is spurred on by the added impetus such materials give to the growth of collections coming late on the scene. Diaries, photo albums, and scrapbooks kept by previous generations of ordinary citizens are likely to be easier for the new repository to acquire than are significant collections from families of noted persons. But the former will also help to document the day-to-day habits of sections of the population insufficiently studied in the past.

The similarity of objectives of these new collections in libraries and archives gives us the opportunity to consider ways in which separate collections might cooperate to produce finding aids that will direct the reader to both published sources and unpublished materials in particular subject areas. That kind of cooperation has been uncommon, but offers great possibilities, for instance, for providing undergraduates with a stimulating introduction to primary source materials.

Simultaneously with the beginnings of SRRT, and spurred on by its rising young leaders, the ALA began an effort to democratize its internal organization and to make its policies more responsive to the needs of librarians and to social issues. The Activities Committee on New Directions for ALA (ACONDA), authorized by the executive board, upon resolution of the membership on June 25, 1969, was instructed to "recognize the changes in the interests of ALA members . . . reinterpret and restate the philosophy of ALA . . . [to reflect] the beliefs and priorities of the profession . . . [and] to create a structure that will involve a larger number of members in the programs and committee work of the organization."[3] As a result of the ensuing ACONDA recommendations, six current priorities were established for ALA: social responsibilities; manpower; intellectual freedom; legislation; planning, research, and development; and democratization and reorganization of ALA itself. Looking back, one can see progress in most of these areas, although more often as policy statements of ALA than as practical achievements within libraries; and, even within ALA, only a limited commitment of association dollars to specific activities that carry out such policies.

Concern for individual professional welfare has been shown in the establishment of the Office for Library Personnel Resources in 1973 and in policy statements adopted in support of fair hiring and administrative policies, the most far-reaching being the Equal Employment Opportunity Policy and the Security of Employment in Libraries statement, both adopted in 1974. A policy adopted in 1971 had set up a new committee, the Staff Committee on Mediation, Arbitration and Inquiry (SCMAI), to investigate disputes involving fair employment practices, tenure, due process, intellectual freedom, and other issues spelled out in ALA policies. Enforcement of that program has been a thorny and time-consuming issue within ALA, but it contains the means to move the association slowly into more decisive action in support of librarians suffering unfair employment practices. Most critics of ALA would probably concede that improvement in the employment practices among minorities in the Library of Congress is being achieved as the result of one long SCMAI investigation.

In adopting its six current priorities on the basis of ACONDA's recommendations, the ALA council did not alter its previous Goals for Action adopted in 1967. The latter emphasize the need to improve library service, but state this in traditional terms, and therefore provide a wedge for dividing the older service-oriented librarians from their younger counterparts. Although social responsibility, as a stated priority, became a test of many programs and proposals, on one aspect of social responsibilities, as defined by the membership vote—"the willingness of ALA to take a position on current critical issues"—one must admit less achievement of the goal. In this area of activity with political overtones, the sharpest division of opinion arises, cutting into the support for the issues of social responsibility.

Labeling an action political in nature, and thus possibly endangering the association's tax-exempt status, has become a potent argument. That threat has become much more real as the Internal Revenue Service has moved to investigate many organizations and foundations which claim tax-exempt status, to determine their compliance with the criteria established by the Internal Revenue Code.

The issue of tax-exempt status was a key question in debates in 1969 and 1970 over whether ALA was to be an organization for libraries or for librarians; or whether it could be both. Its constitution states that the object of ALA is "to improve library service and librarianship." How to interpret that has not been settled, although many recent actions are intended to improve the lot of librarians, expecting also thereby to improve library service. The complaint of those who attempted to revitalize ALA was that it had become too institutionalized, putting its emphasis on its services to the larger institutions rather than to the patron and to the individual librarian. The effect on ALA's financial structure of a change in direction was not fully understood at that time, and reference to the tax issue was viewed as an effort to divert the discussion from the main issues.

The executive director's report to the 1974 conference was the occasion for the first specific review given the ALA council of what it would mean to ALA to lose its present tax-exempt status, as granted under the clause of the Internal Revenue Code giving the greatest exemptions, Section 501 (c) 3. Enumerated as the possible results of the loss of such status were: elimination of present educational discounts on certain types of equipment and supplies; required payment of sales and use taxes and real estate taxes; loss to ALA employees of participation in the TIAA-CREF retirement plan; and, considered most important, the loss of support from most government agencies and foundations for ALA projects, once they are no longer under an organization with the Section 501 (c) 3 status. As Executive Director Robert Wedgeworth stated, "The consequences of not being tax-exempt are serious . . . [but] ALA should not allow the IRS or any other outside agency to define its interests."[4] It is now up to the members to define the goals of the association in terms of social purpose, major objectives, acceptable limits of government control of the organization's activities, and how much members are willing to pay for the right to determine their own activities.

There is a recognized difference between political education and political activity, the former attempting to stimulate the electorate to take action along whatever road it may choose in the electoral sphere, the latter generally aiming at influencing action in a particular direction. The IRS may not view each action as the organization does in developing a program for improved library service that must be achieved chiefly through legislation. Many organizations and institutions claiming tax-exempt status now have representatives in Washington and in the state capitols. Some accept the designation of registered lobbyist, while others appear to consider alternative designations essential. Eileen Cooke, director of the ALA Washington office, admits to being a lobbyist, and sees no difficulty with the term. Her rationale is that as long as the funds expended for this purpose are no more than 5 percent of the association budget, there should be no problem.[5]

SOCIAL RESPONSIBILITIES AND ARCHIVISTS

The foregoing analysis has immediate pertinence for archivists and for the SAA, which, at its 1974 annual conference in Toronto, engaged in one of its most political debates. This revolved around the public ownership of the president's papers and those of other public officials, and, while resulting from current political events in Washington, was related directly to the archivist's knowledge and sense of professional responsibility for public records.

Many questions with considerable political import have risen as issues among archivists, as must inevitably be true from the nature of the records in their custody. But the way professionals deal with those questions determines their influence on the outcome of the issues more than the specific nature of the records. Private records raise as many questions as public records. Shall tax deductions be allowed for personal papers created by an individual? Manuscript curators and archivists certainly have an important point of view to contribute on this question, and, through their organizations, have already expressed themselves on the issue. But is that not a position which threatens tax exemption? Wouldn't the individual institutions that belong to the SAA or to the ACRL Rare Book and Manuscripts Section benefit if tax deductions were restored for the contribution of self-created personal papers? Of course, the world of scholarship, the donor, and posterity would presumably also benefit. But there is cause for concern in realizing how easily the tax-exempt status may be endangered. There is a most disturbing threat to the independence of the professional organization implied in that fiscal weapon. That threat—real or implied—may well be the ultimate question which professional organizations will need to consider and challenge if they are to remain independent and professional.

Comparing the development of social concerns in archival and library professions, one is impressed with the differing responses of the two professions and their professional organizations to the challenges created by the new demands of the public, by greater freedom in communication, and by a heightened awareness of the rights of individuals and groups often given little recognition in the past. If we allow for a delayed reaction time among archivists, there appears to be a greater willingness among leaders in that field to adjust to change than has been evident among librarians in the leadership of ALA. There may be some question, however, as to the speed with which changes within the archival institutions will take place.

It was the provocative statement of conscience offered by one non-archivist to the SAA in 1970 which, more than any single event, moved that organization into current response to the changing society of which it forms a part. At least so it has seemed to the archivists who heard in the statement the call to a new commitment to the profession's obligation to society. Howard Zinn, speaking at the 1970 annual conference in Washington, D.C., on "The American Archivist and Radical Reform," broke new ground in stressing that "professionalism is a powerful form of social control."[6] He noted that by "simply doing his own job," divorcing his specialization from the needs of society, each professional allows the full-time politician to dominate the society, and thus perpetuates the status quo with its corruption and continuing inequities. Zinn's address and other related events which had helped to produce it brought forth two important results within the SAA.

The ferment among the American people in the 1960s showed its effect on the SAA in 1970, as evidenced by the ground-breaking programs presented at the Washington conference. More far-reaching in effect was the appointment by the SAA president of a special Committee for the 1970s, to analyze the structure of the society, its program and objectives, its relationship with other professional organizations, and its needs during the coming decade, including ways to make the society more democratic, responsive, and relevant to its members. The changes that have resulted from the work of the committee, whose final report was submitted in April 1972,[7] have been largely internal to the society, and, as with ALA's ACONDA, have resulted in a more democratic organization. The improvement in representation is gradually bringing about other changes in the activities of the society.

Howard Zinn's talk at the Washington conference had a vitalizing effect on a portion of the SAA members who heard him. These were the individuals already committed to achieving changes in society, and in whom his words struck a common chord. The impact of those words served as a kind of rallying call to bring together those of like mind at an informal gathering during the 1971 San Francisco conference. Stimulated also by the previous experience of a few members with SRRT, by the same type of young professionals' eagerness to make a greater contribution in their chosen field, and by the wish to influence the changes envisioned for SAA through the Committee for the 1970s, they organized into a caucus of Archivists for Change, known also as ACT. The group has continued to function, largely through an irregular newsletter, and through informal, well-attended sessions at each of the annual conferences. It has exercised considerable influence on efforts toward further democratization of the society by raising issues of broad concern during conference sessions and in discussion with leaders of the organization.

The Archivists for Change caucus was a leading force in influencing President Wilfred Smith in 1972 to appoint an Ad Hoc Committee on the Status of Women in the Profession, in achieving passage of a resolution in 1973 committing the society and its affiliated institutions to eliminating discrimination in employment in the archival profession, in developing support for the initial commitment to the position of executive director, and was probably influential in the election of certain councillors. Because of the relatively small size of the SAA and its easy informality, it has been possible for ACT supporters to be elected to leading positions where their influence may be seen more clearly. But such positions often carry with them limitations on the individual's ability or willingness to speak out as forcefully. It remains to be seen whether the presence in leading roles of individuals committed to reform makes any appreciable difference in the policies of SAA.

There have been other progressive influences on the archival profession and on the SAA. The Women's Caucus within SAA has operated as a very informal collective since 1973, serving to feed ideas to the society leadership for the improvement of the status of women in the profession and to focus increased attention on records pertaining to women. The flourishing regional archival organizations, providing opportunities for less experienced archivists to learn the craft and to contribute new ideas, have been the source of healthy injections into the national archival scene. A couple of independent newsletters have increased communication and provided informal forums for raising provocative questions.

Archivists have moved into the 1970s with an increased awareness of the social change to which they may contribute, and a willingness to adapt to changes imposed on them, but not many of them have taken the lead in developing the climate for change, or in effecting specific improvement. A last word about the issues still to be faced may be useful preparation for the period ahead. A proposal presented to the SAA executive committee in November 1973 and referred to the Committee on Education and Professional Development focuses attention on one group of problems still to be faced. It calls for study of the workplace situation, training, and employment prospects of archivists. This could result in the collection of needed data that can help solve the difficult question of the proper training for archivists, and of the role that the SAA must play in setting standards for that training. It should also call attention to the lag among archival institutions in recruiting minority candidates into the profession and the need for vast improvement in the working situation for many groups of archival employees.

Questions of greater public import still to be faced by archivists, if they are not adequately resolved through legislation, relate to the public ownership of the papers of public officials, and to questions of access to personal records and other restricted or classified materials. These are troublesome issues that express, as clearly as any that may be mentioned, the obligation of archivists to work for the social good of the larger public as actively as for the specific benefit of their own institutions. One issue not often discussed openly is the competition in collecting that has developed among manuscript repositories. Would we not be acting in a more professionally and socially responsible manner if repositories defined the broad areas of collecting in which they would each concentrate, and would refer potential donors to more appropriate locations in the normal run of their activities, rather than on very rare occasions? David C. Duniway's 1961 article still proves useful as a guide to planning more responsible collecting policies, and serves to remind us that social responsibility improves our professional performance in the long run.[8]

One other issue recognized by archivists but not yet adequately analyzed is the need for greater cooperative relationships with the other professional societies—not only with ALA, but also with the American Association for State and Local History (AASLH) and the historical organizations. It is an issue to which ALA has only begun to address itself. One positive sign is the agreement concluded in 1973 by ALA with the University of Illinois for deposit of the ALA archives at that institution. It is very possible that this practical relationship with an archival institution will do much to improve the understanding of librarians of the different but related character of archives, and will create a greater awareness of the common interests of the two professions. The close parallels that appear in the increased recognition of social responsibility within ALA and SAA offer specific opportunities for working together on issues still before both groups.

NOTES

1. Included in the total SRRT membership are those ALA members who wish to join, at a cost of $5.00 beyond the ALA membership fee, and nonmembers of ALA (who constitute the bulk of the membership of SRRT affiliate groups) who may become nonvoting members of the national SRRT upon payment of $3.00.

2. Sanford Berman, *Prejudices and Antipathies: A Tract on the LC Subject Heads Concerning People* (Metuchen, N.J.: Scarecrow Press, 1971), 249 pp.

3. American Library Association, Activities Committee on New Directions for ALA, "Final Report and Subcommittee Reports," mimeographed (Chicago: American Library Association, 1970), p. 25.

4. Robert Wedgeworth, "Excerpts from 1974 Report to ALA Membership," Information Report #2, Attachment, Exhibit 3, American Library Association 1973–74 Executive Board Minutes, July 7–11, 1974, New York City, mimeographed, p. 3.

5. This statement was made in a phone conversation with the writer in June 1974.

6. Howard Zinn, "The American Archivist and Radical Reform" (corrected title), unpublished typescript provided by Mr. Zinn, p. 3.

7. Philip P. Mason, "The Society of American Archivists in the Seventies: Report of the Committee for the 1970's," *American Archivist* 35 (1972): 193–217.

8. David C. Duniway, "Conflicts in Collecting," *American Archivist* 24 (1961): 55–63.

FOUR

SHARED CONCERNS

PUBLIC RELATIONS AND FUND RAISING

Alexis de Tocqueville claimed that "a public officer in the United States is uniformly simple in his manners, accessible to all the world, attentive to all requests, and obliging in his replies."[1] These attributes are also desirable in the staff and officers of institutions devoted to public service, such as libraries, archives, and manuscript repositories. If they are present, half of the public relations battle has been won, because almost every activity of a public institution is a manifestation of public relations. A poorly arranged catalog, a cluttered reading room, bad lighting, uncomfortable furniture, poorly designed publications, amateurish exhibits, and a surly or aloof staff can leave a lasting unfavorable impression on visitors to the institution. Because of the quirks of human nature, some negative impressions will adversely affect fund raising, while others can actually aid it. An unfriendly or inefficient staff may pique a prospective donor or legislator controlling funds, while a pleasant staff in run-down quarters may arouse their sympathies and loosen their purses. On a recent visit to the Ford Foundation's magnificent building in Manhattan, I heard a child ask her mother for a penny to toss into the small but well-tended pond in the garden court. The mother responded that she did not think that the Ford Foundation needed it. There were few, if any, coins in the pond.

Public relations, in the broadest sense, is a full-time task that must be practiced by all of the staff, both on and off the job, and cannot be confined to one or two experts during working hours. It is true, however, that the staff cannot carry out the full range of the task of public relations alone, and when management does establish some formalized program to supplement the staff effort, it has to pose three questions: what does it

111

wish to relate to the public; to what public does it wish to relate; and how does it wish to relate its message to the public?

These questions cannot be answered in a manual. "Public relations is an art—the art of winning over people so that they like an organization— (in this case a library). People who like a library try to help it. It is as simple as that."[2] This does not imply, however, that an institution cannot set out a statement of its own goals in relating to the public that it serves and regularly informing its staff what the aims of the institution are in performing its services.[3] Each institution has to make its own determination of those goals. Public relations for a branch library in Jamaica, New York, will not be the same as those at the Massachusetts Historical Society.

Many public relations methods are universally applicable, however. They will be either internal or external. Internal methods consist of service effectiveness, activities, and attractions at the institution. External methods are extensions of the institution, either in print, film, exhibits, professional activities, or related manifestations of the institution's programs. Unfortunately, most of the literature in the field deals with the mechanics instead of the meaning behind public relations in a public institution.[4] The mechanics described over the range of the literature include the role of publications, pamphlets, and brochures;[5] working through the newspaper and other media;[6] and even the use of department store techniques.[7] External public relations activities are discussed in handling special programs,[8] exhibits,[9] conferences, film festivals, ceremonies, receptions, and openings.

In addition, there is considerable literature on the use of organizations—labeled "friends," "associates," "docents," or just plain "volunteers"—that assist the institution in relating to the public and that are sometimes the bodies of public to which the institution wishes to relate. The labels are usually used to describe three distinct groups: contributors of funds or goods (furnishings, decorative art, rare books, etc.) who may or may not actively participate in the institution's programs; the group that pays an annual membership so that it may receive the publications and be invited to activities sponsored by the institution; and the group that volunteers to give tours, staff the sales and information desk, and generally provide free services for the benefit of the institution.

In many respects there is little difference between the public relations methods of libraries, manuscript collections, and archival institutions. The public to which each wishes to deliver its message might be different depending on the wealth and prestige of the institution, but the basic methods will not be different. Except in tone, there will even be little difference from the methods used by businesses or corporations (except for the full-page ad and the sponsored Christmas TV special). It is not the medium that is important to understand, but the message, and that message should spell SERVICE in capital letters, whether the service is in the area of specialized holdings, broad research collections, cultural offerings, community activities, or as a citizen information center. Unlike commercial advertising, which attempts to get people to buy a product, library public relations is usually aimed at informing the public about something the public (through taxes) has already bought, and explaining how useful it can be.

The public library probably bears the brunt of the public relations imperative in the information area. It, above others, has the biggest job of convincing an amorphous constituency of the need for its offerings. School and university libraries have built-in hucksters in the classrooms, sending their wards to the library to do specified research in specified sources, often during specified time periods. Corporate or special libraries have some selling to do, but they have a defined and delimited body of users to whom they can send messages through highly organized communications channels. Manuscript repositories and archives have unique sources to which scholars will beat a path if the material is worth it, although there is a continuing need to get out the word of new acquisitions. But what is the imperative in a public library to attract readers, and, indeed, are readers attracted by art exhibits, musical performances, and Buster Keaton movies? If not, is it really the library's aim to attract readers to books, or to attract people to the library? Is the intelligence or awareness of a community measured by the number of library cards issued to its members? Are circulation figures dramatically increased by library public-service programs? In the answers to these questions are the rationale for the library's public relations program.

The public library is also faced with other problems that many other information centers hardly need consider. In an urban environment there are alternatives to using a single library source—other branches, school libraries, book stores where items can be purchased instead of borrowed, and even commercial lending libraries operated out of book stores or novelty shops. But if the librarian's sole concern is the intellectual development and public awareness of the community, the librarian should not mind the availability of other sources in the community.

Unfortunately, if one probes deeply enough, and sometimes not even deeply at all, one frequently finds that the ulterior motive of public relations program is financial—an attempt to raise more funds or gifts of goods for the library through public sympathy for, and awareness of, its programs. At this stage, public relations and fund raising become handmaidens, and, since many libraries are supported by public funds, i.e., taxes—and taxes and budgets are controlled by a ruling body of managers, board of directors, or legislature—public relations often translates into "lobbying." As such, much of the effort of public relations is aimed at the legislators or corporate managers, and if the general public or user of the library benefits from these efforts, through courteous service, efficiency, and interesting public-service programs, it is a side effect of the true purpose for such activities. There is really nothing inappropriate about such an approach if the end justifies the means, and if the means are quite acceptable to the community. It is not unusual for an institution to schedule a major exhibit with a big opening and the trustees and cultural community invited in black tie to a champagne buffet with the ulterior motive of shaming the buildings and grounds department into applying a fresh coat of paint to the reading room and sanding and waxing the floors. That may be an example of Machiavellian P.R., but it is often necessary when an institution is competing with others for dollars and services.

In short, the institution wishes to attract attention to itself and show how culturally important it is to the community. The revelation of that importance may or may not increase the use of the institution, but that is in some ways irrelevant, since fund raising is often needed to support present services and help reduce whatever backlog of work there is. More money is needed, not to service more people, but rather to service properly the people already using the institution.

Not only is it important for an institution to determine what its public relations policy should be, and at whom to aim it, but also the basic purpose for it as well as the desired goal. Goodwill of the community is not always an end in itself, but it is sometimes important in that it can be called upon when needed to assist in providing resources to the institution or to assist in lobbying for the institution's point of view when confronted with proposed legislative action or inaction. This does not imply that when the institution has no immediate needs for outside assistance, it ignores public activities or the pleasing of its clientele. Basic responsibilities as a cultural institution, public or private, include an obligation for efficient and courteous service at all times.

The assumption to this point has been that the institution—library, archives, or manuscript repository—was acting independently in the public relations area. This is true for certain portions of the public relations spectrum, such as personnel activities and direct services, but most institutions using these programs are part of a larger parent body. They are university libraries, or corporate libraries, or state archives, church archives, manuscript collections within a department of special collections, or a division within a department within a major library, such as in the Library of Congress. In these cases the external and media-oriented public relations are not always under the administration and control of the lesser unit. Being a unit within a larger corporate or institutional body can have its advantages and disadvantages. One advantage is that there is usually a professional public relations staff that functions for the parent organization and which is available to service the corporate units without a concurrent drain on that unit's limited budget. In these circumstances the librarian, archivist, or curator should cultivate the friendship and understanding of the public relations staff, who will normally reciprocate by providing the services that are wanted. In most cases, especially with manuscript collections, and to a lesser degree with archives, the curator will find that the collection has public relations appeal to a greater degree than many of the other units of the parent body. It has cultural prestige, and it contains the papers and books of the great people to whom the organization owes its name and its reputation. It contains the record of the institution's accomplishments (not to mention its failures—and nobody mentions them), and it usually has quarters and an ambience that provide a showplace for visiting dignitaries at high-level ceremonies. Its exhibits may provide the only museum function that the institution can muster, and a well-organized and well-designed museum shouts "culture." The curator or librarian must not ignore these positive attributes, and must use them to the unit's advantage when appropriate.

The disadvantage of being a unit within a corporate body is the competition for funds and services, lack of full control over policy and the decision-making process, and the possibility that the parent organization may see the unit as so much window dressing—a pleasant place to hold cocktail parties and entertain dignitaries, but not a place to be taken seriously in the daily affairs of the organization. The unit then becomes a showpiece to be used from time to time, but relegated to an inferior position during business hours. The unit, therefore, must prove daily that its functions and activities are important to the functioning of the parent organization.

All of these remarks about public relations also relate to fund raising, whether it is in-house or external. Efficient and relevant service should be rewarded with appropriate budget increases from the appropriating authority. Good public-service programs will attract friends, if not users, and the friends can be a base for fund raising during special campaigns to supplement the budget. Good relations with the parent organization and the establishment of mutual respect will provide the best atmosphere for the parent and the unit to cooperate in showing off the collection and its quarters at receptions and other events, especially if those events are part of general fund raising drives. The unit can justifiably request a certain percentage of the funds derived from such activities, if only to keep the collection and the quarters presentable and in good repair for future affairs. A good rare book room, manuscript collection, or other special collections department are parts of the fund raising mechanisms of many institutions, and they should, therefore, be maintained accordingly. By contrast, rarely does one see soft lighting, plush carpets, fine furnishings, drapes, and perhaps even tapestries and fine prints in the cataloging or government documents departments. Special librarians and curators should recognize the role that these departments play and act accordingly when it comes to allocation of corporate resources.

In fund raising, as in public relations, there is little difference between the approach taken by libraries, archives, and manuscript collections. The methods are so obvious that they need not be dwelled on here. Private gifts and endowments, named or unnamed, are a key source of funds for many institutions, followed closely by continuing or ad hoc grants from public foundations.

The tendency to consider fund raising as an extramural activity, however, causes most librarians and curators to forget that the most essential source of fund raising for all institutions is the basic appropriation or budget allocation from the parent or controlling body. After this, many public institutions, mostly those with a strong museum function, depend on income from admissions and the sale of publications or special items in the gift shop. In order to influence these two sources, the basic requirements are to provide good service and to operate efficiently—administrators and tourists are rarely influenced by cocktail parties.

For some institutions the private endowment is the foundation of the budget. In times of inflation old endowments are often found wanting, and the institution finds itself letting down the barriers on certain fund raising techniques by sponsoring pop concerts, raffles, or many of the other techniques most often associated with church societies or fraternal organizations. Fund raising at endowed institutions naturally involves wooing new endowments, and in these instances, the celebration of an anniversary, a reception to mark the acquisition of a fine item or to commemorate the memory of a great person may well be aimed at attracting additional funds from relatives or others associated with the item or person.

The present role of foundations in institutional fund raising has been supplemented by the entry into the field of increasingly well-endowed federal funding units: the National Foundation on the Arts and Humanities, consisting of the National Endowment for the Arts (NEA), and the National Endowment for the Humanities (NEH); and the National Historical Publications and Records Commission (NHPRC). Added to the National Science Foundation, the Rockefeller and Ford Foundations and the latter's subsidiary, the Council on Library Resources, and hundreds of other private and public foundations, federal acts, such as the Library Services and Construction Act, plus granting agencies of the federal and state governments, libraries, and to a lesser extent manuscript and archival institutions, have available to them sums of money undreamed of earlier in this century. But it is not money that can be won by smiling faces in the reading room and at intimate cocktail parties. In almost all cases, foundations and granting agencies have two limitations on their largess: they will support specific projects, but not long-term basic programs; and they want to see a well-conceived and developed plan as well as the ultimate product. Thus, there may be grant money available to put into shape a major collection of books and documents within an institution (the Schomberg Collection in the New York Public Library comes to mind), but there might not be money to support an entire cataloging department in its routine chores. Grants may support research and experimentation in automation applications, but may not be provided to implement automation throughout the system. Grants, therefore, are shots of Adrenalin, not lifeblood, to an institution, and the applications that are most well received are those that indicate normal budgetary funding once the proposed project has been launched.

In the search for grant funds it is extremely helpful, if not absolutely necessary, to be aware of the Foundation Center in Washington, D.C., where there is assembled a vast amount of mostly current information about hundreds of public and private foundations, their areas of specialization, amount of grant money available, average grant awarded, and a brief analysis of recent grants awarded by the foundation.

Grantsmanship is a process in which one studies the habits of foundations, the timing of grant applications, and the proper preparation of a proposal. More important than all of these actions, however, is the value of the project for which funds are being sought. Most funding agencies will overlook errors in application techniques but will easily discern phony projects because grant requests are circulated to specialists or other professionals in the same discipline, who are asked to evaluate them on their merits.

In summary, fund raising is not a single process but must be approached with different techniques depending on the source from which an institution wishes to raise funds. In some cases it must be preceded by posing the question as to whether the institution's charter permits it to receive private money, and, if so, if there are limitations on what it can be used for, or how much of it can be applied to the ultimate product. Universities invariably take a large chunk off the top of any grant received in their name, for any project, using administrative expenses as their justification. Grant requests must therefore take into account the indirect costs deduction to be made and increase the requested amount accordingly.

Many government organizations have no authority to receive outside funds and would have no account in which to deposit money if received. Others have limited trust fund or gift fund accounts which permit the expenditure of private funds for cultural purposes but not for financing cocktail parties, luncheons, or other social events. It is also the custom that one government agency cannot receive a grant from another agency of the same government—state from state, federal from federal. Legislatures have long recognized that permitting one agency to provide grant funds to another could easily short-circuit the budgetary process and the role of the appropriations committees to oversee the financing of programs. The legislature would indirectly be financing projects which were not placed before it by the program agency, but for which an executive agency with grant powers would make the decisions on project validity and funding levels. A fund raiser must take the time to study whatever limitations apply to the case before plotting out an institutional campaign.

The one great difference between libraries, manuscript repositories, and archives in the whole field of public relations and fund raising is that archives are more commonly an arm of the administration of an institution, and, although they may contain rare and valuable items, they are not usually concerned with them per se. The operation of an archives is considered a normal administrative cost, much like the operation of the personnel department or the accounting and payroll office. In this respect, corporate archives are not as likely to get into the areas of public relations in order to draw attention to themselves or fund raising in order to support themselves, as are libraries and manuscript repositories.

After all things are considered, one should not become too paranoid about the prospect of public neglect of a worthwhile institution and the resultant necessity for big public relations campaigns.

> The fact remains that no one is against the library; it is accepted that a library is surely one of the things you just have in a community, even if it isn't always fully understood why. No one really can argue against the coaxing thought that the library stoutly stands as an investment in the intelligence of a community. The point is that libraries have a positive, noncommercial story to tell that presumes greater acceptance in the telling. And it is self-evident that the message should be planted on the noses of those who can and should use the library and to those on whom [sic] the library depends for its support.[10]

NOTES

1. Alexis de Tocqueville, *Democracy in America*, vol. 1, ed. by Phillips Bradley (New York: Vintage, 1954), p. 214.

2. Josephine Raburn, "Public Relations for a 'Special' Public," *Special Libraries* 60 (December 1969): 647.

3. Richard B. Harwell, "Public Relations in Librarianship," *Library Trends* 7 (October 1958): 249.

4. Two publications are basic to the subject of public relations and the library: the special issue of *Library Trends* 7 (October 1958); and the special issue of the *Wilson Library Bulletin* 42 (November 1967), both of which are devoted to the theme, cumulating some twenty articles on the subject. In addition, see recent works such as Allan Angoff, *Public Relations for Libraries* (Westport, Conn.: Greenwood Press, 1973).

5. Sarah Wallace, "Public Relations of the Public Library," *Library Trends* 7 (October 1958): 259.

6. Margaret Gignilliat, "Reaching Your Public through the Newspaper," AASLH *Technical Leaflet* No. 45, in *History News* 23 (April 1968).
7. Robert W. Rodger, "Borrowing Department Store Techniques to Promote Library Service," *Wilson Library Bulletin* 42 (November 1967): 304.
8. Barbara Hagist and Fred Neighbors, "Fine Arts Festival in Tulsa," *Wilson Library Bulletin* 42 (November 1967): 309.
9. S. Neil Fujita, "Design as a Public Relations Tool," *Wilson Library Bulletin* 42 (November 1967): 243–244.
10. Eugene F. Burke, "Organizing for Public Relations," *Wilson Library Bulletin* 42 (November 1967): 284.

COLLECTION BUILDING AND ACQUISITION POLICIES

LIBRARIES AND BOOK COLLECTIONS

If, as Milton wrote, "A good book is the precious life-blood of a master spirit, embalmed and treasured up on purpose to a life beyond life," then the selection of books for addition to a library's collections can contribute to the immortality of the author and the subject written about. Each book, however, has to prove itself over the long term before the decision is made to retain it in the permanent collection. Even so, we all recognize the need for temporary knowledge and expendable facts, and the ability of a librarian to recognize these needs and act properly upon them is probably just as important as aiming at the ages.

While book selection is perhaps the most professional act a librarian can perform, followed closely by providing excellent reference service, it is also, enigmatically, the easiest task to define but the one that, if carried out badly, can most quickly destroy a library's effectiveness. Definition is easy, because it is an axiom that librarians should select books that their patrons require. And what the patrons require is determined to a great extent by the nature and purpose of the library in question. If the library is technical, corporate, school, university, public, or special, the proper book selection will be geared to the public that uses that library, and no other. It should be an adage that if the patron or reader cannot find the book wanted, either it is charged out or the patron is in the wrong library. Most users do not realize this, and if the branch public library does not have the technical book wanted, the blame first goes on the librarians. The public should have learned by now that that is akin to blaming the local tavern keeper for not having size 10 dresses or a carburetor for a 1939 Plymouth.

The implication is that librarians understand the role of their institution and the requirements of the public. In order to have that understanding, they must analyze that public and know what it wants and needs, even in such seemingly obvious cases as universities, technical societies, and corporations. Librarians must therefore assemble all of their professional skills to keep a finger on the intellectual pulse of their readers, and to consult with them about new institutional, school, or community programs so that the library's collections can reflect them. Even more professionally, librarians must attempt to divine where the community—be it scholars, technicians, or neighbors—is going, and anticipate near future needs with perceptive book ordering and accessioning. It does not take a crystal ball for a public library to see that beginning in 1976 there will probably be an increased call for popular material on the American Revolution, as well as a run on the standard founding fathers' biographies, colonial map collections, and eighteenth-century reference works.

But perhaps that will not be true in all public library branches. The central library can concentrate on reinforcing its collection in those areas, while some of the urban branches may still be building in ethnic history, environmental popularizations, and what may generally be termed "consumer books" on real estate, auto repair, and home decorating. This implies that book selection for a branch library may be the most difficult of all library selection jobs, because it is not a simple matter to feel the intellectual pulse of a diverse community.

Almost any but a branch librarian has available a group of advisers who can effectively aid in selecting library materials. A college, university, or even school library has faculty and department people who will assist in book selection. A business, corporation, or government agency has specialized staff, division, branch, and section chiefs, and other members who can let the librarian know their needs, and if those needs fit within the general acquisition policy, the librarian can rely on them as a guide for purchasing. This procedure requires the existence of an acquisition policy, which should be the first order of business for any library, and which should be reviewed periodically for timeliness. An acquisition policy sets broad policy guidelines for a library and delineates the areas within which it will collect.[1]

Advisers obviously should be representative of the library's public, and not self-serving. There is always the prospect that faculty members will provide acquisition advice based on their own course requirements or special scholarly interests at the moment, while failing to see the overall needs of the department that they represent. A scientist working on a special project may emphasize literature dealing with that subject to the exclusion of almost all others, and the librarian should be perceptive enough to realize this when taking advice. The librarian's goal is to provide as many resources for as broad a range of users as possible within the confines of the book budget.

While the acquisition policy is important, it should not be confused with the process of book selection. The policy sets broad outlines—literature, science, history (modern and ancient), imprints in English only, all materials on a subject, etc. Book selection is made within the confines of the acquisition policy—if the policy calls for ignoring certain subject areas (such as Japanese history) no book selection is made in that field, no matter how popular or authoritative a publication might be.[2]

Neither a stated acquisition policy nor a well-defined book selection process is of any use to the library, however, if it is not known to the staff, and a misunderstanding of either can lessen the effect of the library's collection building practices. It would seem that the greatest problem of a major library's acquisition department would be the avoidance of duplication or obtaining books not really wanted. Procedures have been established to manage that problem so that they are not the threat that one would imagine. Rather, the true role of an acquisitions department is one of searching out titles that might not normally come to its attention, and the staff's knowledge of acquisition and selection policies can be important in eliminating the possibility of overlooking significant material because a staff member thought it was outside the library's sphere. In any one subject area or field, there may be only one staff member who is methodically perusing the offerings of publishers and dealers. If that staff member misunderstands the current acquisition policy, serious selection omissions may be made that will affect the patron's faith in the library's ability to provide needed services.

This brings up the question of selection methods. Every library has a procedure for selecting material. The most common method of assuring collection coverage is, of course, the specialist committee approach, where each selector is a specialist in one or more fields and is given the primary responsibility for studying bibliographies and making acquisition recommendations. These bibliographers are, in many institutions, faculty or corporate division chiefs, who are chosen because they should be the persons most aware of the current literature in their field. Until recently this criterion was a valid one, or so it seemed. Recent thinking in some circles is that it is as important to know the needs of the eventual user of the material as it is to know what material is available. In 1970 this hypothesis was tested in a rather limited way by surveying 4 institutions and analyzing the use of materials selected by three sets of bibliographers: librarians, faculty, and book jobbers. The result of the study indicated that there was a higher percentage of use of librarian-selected material than of the others. Presumably, one would want to have a larger sampling—50 to 100 institutions—before drawing any firm conclusions from this study, but there is merit in the hypothesis. One would also want to go back and reanalyze the use patterns after five, ten, and fifteen years in order to take into account the lasting value of some materials as opposed to others. There is always the danger of shallow acquisition policies responding to immediate contemporary needs but not building the collection for the future by the selection of seminal works that will grow in importance as there are further developments in the field. In order to make such prognoses, the depth of knowledge and intuitive reaction of a specialist is imperative.

Although purchase is probably the most common process for acquiring books, there are many other avenues open to the librarian building a collection. The copyright deposit procedure at the Library of Congress is one avenue, and while unique, it has some parallels in the government depository system. Many universities decree that all dissertations will be deposited in the library. Some institutions promote the idea of having staff who publish deposit in the institutional library one or two copies of each item published. Gifts and exchanges are common methods for both building collection strength and disposing of unwanted items, and most large libraries have a staff devoted just to that activity. The exchange process implies the existence of multiple copies of material but it may also indicate the ineffectiveness of an acquisition policy that brought in a considerable number of unwanted titles. However, there are instances where a library changes its acquisition policy or its subject-area thrust and decides to clear its shelves of old material that no longer fits the new policy.

Libraries are in continual flux. As the interests of the patrons change the library attempts to change with them. It strives to lay a foundation of classics while at the same time meeting short-lived current needs. When it adds material, the demands of space often require it to subtract other material. If it is an active institution, it is adding at a high rate and its book budget increases yearly. But at the same time it must make room for what is new and desirable by continually weeding out what is old and unneeded. The disposition of older materials is probably as important, therefore, as the acquisition of new, at least from the administrative viewpoint, and yet it is an area that is little stressed in the training of librarians. The systematic analysis and review of collections is an important library function that cannot be ignored by library administrators.

This balancing of collections is an area that is subject to the applications of modern technology, but such applications have been slight. In 1970 there was a report on experiments conducted at the Countway Library of Medicine at Harvard, the Yale Medical Library, and the Washington University School of Medicine Library to determine the feasibility of using the Library of Congress produced MARC tapes as a selection tool.[3] There is little evidence in current literature that any institution is using computer-controlled circulation statistics to determine the use patterns in a library, either by class or title. It is possible to gather such use figures, but they can be misleading and would have to be balanced with other considerations before being applied as a management tool for acquisitions and disposition. Books on such prominent women as Jane Addams, Carrie Chapman Catt, the Abbot sisters, or Julia Lathrop might have been consulted very little for three or four decades, and use figures alone could have warranted their removal a few years ago. It is probable that, though old, such books would now suddenly show considerable increase in use, and perhaps even lead the librarian to seek additional copies to meet demand. At any rate, any automated process, whether for selection or disposition, has to be tempered with human judgment.

In some areas the panacea for most of the collecting problems of a library—the problems of space, appropriateness, budget, and competition—is the establishment of spheres of cooperation. When a cluster of libraries (university, private, or public) determines that it is in their own best interest to cooperate in collecting and administering collections, the entire community benefits. In one city, two major private libraries had for years bid against each other in the rare book auctions where their collection policies overlapped. The librarians finally realized that they were driving the price up on each book eventually purchased at auction, so they moved from competition to cooperation, and prior to each auction the librarians compared bid sheets and split up the responsibility for going after the most wanted books. In the end, the community of scholars got more books, and the libraries' budgets were saved. The overriding consideration was the benefits to the research community, not the nebulous prestige of the individual libraries, each of which had enough prestige already.

From cooperative bidding and purchasing, one can go on to cooperative cataloging as a budget-saving device. The services of the Library of Congress, through its sale of catalog cards, have been basic to the standardization of cataloging systems in the United States, and have also been economically important to medium-sized libraries that cannot afford a large cataloging staff but must put most of their resources into acquisitions and reader services. The recent growth of commercial cataloging and classification services is evidence of the modern role of libraries as big business, and of the development of peripheral services living off, but also providing needed support to, them. If "agribusiness" is a product of the past few decades, we may see "bibliobusiness" booming in the next few. In the field of archives and manuscripts, entrepreneurial advances have been made in the supplying of acid-free document folders and boxes and in provision for commercial deacidification and lamination services. Bibliographic jobbers are becoming quite common in the library world, although there naturally should be caution about a library abrogating its right to determine its own acquisition policy. Manuscript and archival appraisal has not yet been farmed out, and such a movement is not on the horizon.

MANUSCRIPTS

The point is made elsewhere in this book (see Part Two, "Materials and Methodology") that the librarian and manuscript curator have something in common in their method for selecting new acquisitions. Both choose from a whole universe of material, and having chosen, care little about the residue left in the universe. They presume that some other institution will obtain the unselected items—another institution with a different acquisition policy from their own. Librarians and manuscript curators, therefore, select positively, whereas archivists select negatively, in that their role is to determine what shall be thrown away.

Since manuscript collections depend on the acquisition of material that is created by others, it is as important for them to have well-defined acquisition policies as it is for a library. But their policies generally are confined within narrower bounds. Since everything that they collect is, in theory at least, unique, there is no such thing as building a foundation on the basic classics, or establishing a general reference collection prior to specializing. Manuscript collections are most often limited by linguistic, chronological, or geographic restraints. They are devoted to collecting materials relating to a region, an ethnic group, a profession, discipline or specialized field (labor, science, agriculture), a person, or an institution. Even the Library of Congress Manuscript Division has its collecting bounds—it is not concerned with gathering original documents on all areas of human knowledge, but concentrates on the papers of individuals or corporate entities having *national* impact. There are the women's collection at Smith College, the Labor Archives at Wayne State, the regional history collection at Cornell, and the American scientists' collection at the Niels Bohr Library as other cases in point.

Dealing with unique materials puts tighter limitations on the manuscript curator than on the librarian and demands a different approach to acquiring materials. Two or more libraries, in different parts of the country, may independently decide to have the same acquisition policy—perhaps collecting books on art and architecture—without any difficulty. Staff at both will scan the lists of publishers looking for their latest offering, and they will prowl through bookstores in San Francisco, Boston, and London to pick up choice out-of-print items. They may compete in an auction and drive up the price of some offerings, but if they miss a chance to buy this year, it is possible that the item will appear on another list in future years.

Two manuscript repositories may have similar acquisition policies, but they can never be the same. Chicago and Berkeley cannot decide that they will collect the papers of all prominent atomic scientists. As soon as one acquires the papers and research notes of Fermi, Szilard, Compton, and Teller, all other institutions have effectively been kept out of the field. Berkeley may attempt to acquire the papers of all atomic scientists who worked at Berkeley, but Chicago would have cornered the market with the acquisition of the works of four key men of national stature.

This situation makes the establishment of an acquisition policy a tenuous thing. An institution may state that its policy is to collect everything on subject X, but there is no imperative for other institutions to stay out of the field, and if one institution is more aggressive or lucky, it can negate the acquisition policies of another. For this reason, manuscript acquisition policies are generally broad and vague. The State Historical Society of Wisconsin has major manuscript and archival holdings, but in a recent article discussing local history materials in libraries, where the Wisconsin collection policy was outlined, no mention was made of these types of materials. The policy as reported was to collect:

1. All materials of a monographic character of a descriptive or historical nature relating to the state or any of its regions or political subdivisions. This includes pamphlets of any content. We do not generally collect advertising materials unless they originated in the early history of the state.
2. All periodicals (magazines) issued by state organizations; religious, fraternal, political, etc. Also annual reports.
3. All newspapers published in Wisconsin.
4. The publications of government bodies, states, city, and county, if any.
5. We do not collect "Wisconsin authors," except for a small collection of outstanding ones that classify as literature.
6. We do collect intensively pre-1865 Wisconsin imprints.
7. In general we collect all state and local atlases.[4]

On the other hand, the Harry S. Truman Library, one of the six presidential libraries administered by the National Archives and Records Service of GSA, had a specific statement in its 1958 "Acquisition Policy of the Harry S. Truman Library" pamphlet relating to manuscript materials:

In acquiring papers and other historical materials under the above-cited provisions of law, the Harry S. Truman Library will concentrate on developing its holdings in those fields that relate to its principal collection—the papers and other historical materials of former President Truman—and that will be useful to scholars and others who are most likely to use that collection. In so doing, the library will be guided by the following principles:
1. [relates to the president's papers]
2. papers relating to national and international affairs during the period of Mr. Truman's service in the White House, including papers of members of his Cabinet and of his White House aides; of other officials of the Executive Branch of the Government who served under his leadership; of persons who were closely associated with his administration or exerted notable influence on national and international developments during that period; and records of national political and other organizations whose activities importantly affected the course of the domestic and foreign policies and programs of the United States during those years. Materials available for deposit in the Library will be thoroughly studied as to their appropriateness. They will not be sought by the Library if, in the opinion of the Director, they could be more appropriately preserved elsewhere.

Such a statement can be useful in indicating to whomever is interested that the library probably would not consider the papers of Samuel Clemens or some ancient Chinese scrolls. But one could read into it authority to accept the papers of Mao Tse-tung as one who exerted influence on international developments, or importantly affected the course of foreign policies and programs. The delineation of the policy permitted the library to amass 200 collections dealing with individuals or organizations associated with Truman.[5] It is appropriate that the library attempts to collect materials relating to the president and his actions, but it is in no sense an imperative that such papers go to the library instead of elsewhere.

Every individual, and more so every public individual, has a life or a career that touches many other individuals, spans many careers, spreads out over various geographic areas, and often encompasses more than one profession or avocation. It is this multidimensionality of man that makes the establishment of firm acquisition policy guidelines and cooperative collecting programs almost impossible. As a Canadian archivist explained:

> There is the matter, first of all, of conflicting interests. . . . I was for years archivist of the Federal Government, and we had a conflict of interest over the papers of such a man as Jimmy Gardiner. He was premier of the Province of Saskatchewan, and later, Minister of Agriculture for a long period of time, a very important Federal figure, a very important Provincial figure. Where should the Gardiner papers be? We both have interests.[6]

The Canadians have the Gardiners, the United States has its Adlai Stevensons, Averell Harrimans, and Nelson Rockefellers.

Attempts to establish boundaries for manuscript collecting have floundered on the rocks of multiple interests. The exceptions to a proposed, seemingly rational, collecting policy often negate the policy itself, and it is the abundance of exceptions that one can apply that has kept the archival profession from agreeing to anything that could be called a positive policy. Another Canadian archivist, agonizing over the method for dividing up the manuscript universe, devised a formula worse than the disease:

> For example, valid exceptions might include: documents relating directly to the institutions concerned or of interest solely to a local community; documents which the donor may be unwilling to give to an institution outside his municipality; documents which relate directly to a large collection already stored in a regional institution; or a large collection of documents which the central depository might be unwilling to preserve "in toto." Moreover, for the purpose of this brief exposition, I will not go into the question of what institutions should be building up specialized depositories, such as a centralized business Archives, scientific research Archives, literary Archives, architectural Archives, and so on. Neither will I attempt to go into the question of the federal versus provincial Archives' acquisition policies, which, in any case, is in my experience a matter of less urgency and more open to practical solutions and compromise.[7]

In sum, no collection of unique material, documenting an active career, can easily be categorized as suitable for deposit in only one institution, but since documents are unique, and can be physically located in only one place, conflict always arises about which institution will be the fortunate beneficiary. Occasionally the unfortunate choice is made to split up the collection, as was done with the Felix Frankfurter papers, which went to two institutions. Happily, photocopying has ameliorated many of the inherent ills in the system, and recent developments in the preparation and publication of national guides to documents, such as Philip M. Hamer's *Guide to Archives and Manuscripts in the United States*, and the Library of Congress publication of the multivolumed *National Union Catalog of Manuscript Collections*, have provided intellectual if not physical distribution of collections throughout the world.

The rationale for the deposit of manuscripts is largely a question of prestige and applying acquisition policy. The competitive factor has led to development of solicitation and acquisition techniques largely unknown in the general library world, except perhaps, in rare books and some other special collections.

Manuscript collections are invariably received from donors, most often as a gift. They are rarely bought, and there are no lists advertising their availability. Sometimes the donors are the creators of the collection, but quite often the donors are the heirs or assigns of the creator. Their existence is sniffed out by specialists at the concerned repository, scouts go out, courteous probing letters are written, visits are made, conditions are discussed, tax benefits are investigated, and the benefits of prestige are announced. The process compares best with that of college coaches wooing exemplary high school stars to their school. For these reasons manuscript people are very sensitive about the details of their solicitation lists, protecting them like an industrial secret and often even reluctant to discuss their existence. This is partly because of competition in the marketplace, but also because of the desire to keep negotiations elevated and untinged by any hint of crassness.

Manuscript solicitors rival the foreign service in the diplomatic arts. As professionals, they are quite ready to discuss old conquests with glee, recent acquisitions with circumspection, but planned campaigns or past failures not at all. They are also aware of the seriousness of their mission:

> It is well always for the uninitiated to keep in mind the fact that manuscripts are assembled not because they are autographs, but because they are historical evidence: It is as original sources for the reconstruction of the past, for the interpretation of parallel experience, for the impeachment of false or mistaken or perverted testimony, for the clarification of blurred report, for the detection, identification, and dismissal of fable, and the recovery of reality that they are sought and brought together.[8]

In order to accomplish this task, the staff of one manuscript institution for many years ate lunch together four or five days a week, with the composition changing slightly from day to day as one staff member was not available but another was. They discussed the news events of the day, the book reviews in the *Times*, and the obituary columns. Behind each discussion was the implied prospect that the newsworthy figure, the author, or the deceased must have produced documentary evidence of a contribution to society. The pros and cons of making a probing attempt to contact the person or the heirs were weighed. At least once a week the Grand Old Names were injected into the conversation, Marlene Dietrich, Al Capone, and others who had made a significant splash on the American scene. The strategy sessions often resulted in a probe letter and the establishment of a folder in the "Solicitation File." Sometimes the number of these folders ran into the hundreds, and it was a task just to keep up with when to send a follow-up or determine that the prospective donor had decided in favor of another institution. There was an urgency in some cases, even though the sought-after papers might have been moldering unwanted for a decade or more. Once the name was put forth as a prospective candidate for acquisition it was as if a premonition of fire, flood, or pestilence was about to come true. Some writings on manuscript collecting reflect this urgency:

> Get in touch with the widow or other relatives of an individual, with whose papers one is concerned. This step should be taken as promptly as good taste will permit after the death of the person with whom the collection deals; otherwise, it may be found that valuable records have been destroyed in housekeeping operations.[9]

Where general book collections have collection-development staff, or bibliographers, or faculty, or other staff assistance in selecting materials for addition to the collection, manuscript repositories rely on the expertise of their own staff, with occasional help from a friend of the subject. Whereas a library may accession thousands of books in a year, a manuscript repository may add fewer than a half-dozen significant collections. This allows the staff time to concentrate on handling all of the negotiations. Since modern collections are sometimes massive in bulk, with anywhere from 30 to 300 cubic feet of documents at stake, each institution must go for quality rather than quantity. The requirements for a good solicitation agent are diverse:

> He must have the skills of a public relations expert to spread the word that manuscripts are important and should be preserved, preferably in libraries; a genealogist, to identify descendants who may still have the papers of illustrious forebears; a tracer of lost persons, to find out where they moved from their last known address; a historian, to decide whether a collection is worth the space in the library; and a psychologist, to know whether to stress the benefits of a tax deduction for a gift, the risk of a collection being destroyed by fire or some other disaster while in private hands, the prestige of having family papers in an important library, or the satisfaction of having helped to preserve our country's historical heritage.[10]

The manuscript curator is caught in a continual dilemma. It is necessary that decisions on acquisitions be made without too much delay because of competition and the prospect that the documents sought after might begin to disappear through attrition or major loss due to carelessness on the part of the owner. On the other hand, the decision must be made deliberately because it is an unwritten axiom that once a collection has been solicited and received, it is never disposed of. There are some exceptions that one could cite, but they are rare, and it is always the option, though rarely exercised, to whittle down a collection through selection and weeding. Once received, a collection is expected to occupy shelf space for the remaining life of the institution. Manuscript collecting, like a marriage, should therefore not be a contract entered into lightly. The declaration that something is permanently valuable implies a permanent obligation.

ARCHIVES

Most archivists would shun the use of the terms "acquisition policy" or "collection policy" as related to archives. Their more familiar jargon includes such terms as "appraisal," "retention," and "disposition." It has been pointed out (see Part Two, "Materials and Methodology") that archivists already have technical possession of the universe of materials created by the corporate entity of which they are a part. Their role is to dispose of what is not wanted. Therefore, they do not solicit, they appraise; they do not acquire, they retain. If one is discussing the archives of the local Elks club, the PTA at the local school, a county political organization, or a small business, there is little merit in talking about collecting policies or collection building. If, however, one is discussing the state of New York, the University of California, IBM, or the federal government, there is some validity to using the terms collection building or acquisition policy, so long as it is understood that the terms are used loosely and rather unarchivally.

The archivist has an obligation to preserve, at the direction of the corporation, the permanently valuable records of the corporate body. Since these are generally the policy and major program documents, they obviously include such files as the correspondence of the chief executive, files relating to fiscal policy, material documenting corporate obligations, and similar records. But beyond that there are some gray areas—light gray and dark gray if you will. What about prefederal material? Modern payroll accounts are normally disposed of, but what of a payroll ledger from the government of a colony? Age makes a difference and redefines archival values. There is almost an unwritten axiom that equates age with retainability. But what of the tape recording of the governor's inaugural or the remarks of the pope at the Polo Grounds? Both of these events are available in documentary form, so what is the archival value of the recordings? Or if the recording is more evidentiary than the document, why keep the document of the speech? And what of the series of photographs of the destruction of the Long Island beaches by the hurricane of 1938? They are evidentiary, too, and they have nothing to do with the policy and procedures of the state government, but photographs take on a special archival meaning, as do sound recordings and motion pictures. It is in these areas that an archivist creates a special retention policy that is akin to a library or manuscript acquisition policy. But there is no competition if the corporate archives are protected by regulations on the disposition of corporate records. There is no scouting, or negotiating, or soliciting in the true sense, although in a large government or corporate structure there is the process of identifying the existence of special materials, discussion with administrative officers about their disposition, and appraisal of the material to determine if any or all of it should be kept. Retention schedules for archives are not only important, they are imperative. Unlike acquisition policies, retention schedules have the force of corporate regulation or governmental law behind them. But they, too, must be reviewed from time to time for validity.

> A. W. Mabbs referred to the appraiser's "elusive distillation of knowledge, wisdom, experience, common sense and whatever else . . . contributes to an understanding of the historical criterion for solving difficult appraisal problems." I do not even rule out, in addition, educated intuition although my predecessors claimed that "the old concept of intuitive judgment has been completely discredited." All of these qualities are necessary for the appraiser in determining whether he has difficult problems if he so plans to spend his time on obviously valuable or valueless records. When he lacks special knowledge about the subject matter of a body of records, the appraiser should seek the advice of experts.[11]

While the archivist is obviously concerned with evidential values, another consideration is that which leads to the retention of the audiovisual materials noted above. This is information value.

> The only thing that matters here is the amount of factual data records contain regarding persons, places, events, and subjects. . . . In appraising "information values" it is necessary to have a knowledge of research sources, needs, and methods as distinct from the knowledge of administrative history required to determine "evidential values."[12]

This reinforces the view that archives are not retained solely as evidence of the activity of the corporation, but may be retained with an eye to future research use by noncorporate inquirers. Tradition for this view comes from one of the most respected archival theoreticians, who might be expected to believe otherwise.

> The function of an archival institution, I believe, is not one of collecting and hoarding research materials, but one of serving the needs of scholars and other users; and these needs can be best served by having documentary resources preserved in the places to which they pertain, and where they are most likely to be used. It is not the function of an archivist to complicate the problems of research resources; it is his function to bring them together.[13]

Since World War II archivists have developed a method to assist them in making sure the good records do not get away. There is always the danger of an agency disposing of records because they are taking up too much space in the offices, or, what is almost as bad, storing the records in out-of-the-way places such as damp cellars, hot and dry attics, or old warehouse buildings that are rat-infested tinder boxes. All of these conditions can lead to destruction, but there are persuasive arguments for getting records out of expensive downtown office space. Archivists have at their disposal the tool to lessen these abuses, and it is called the records center. This is a safe, well-administered storage area for records in limbo. Not only does the records center serve as a convenience to the agency or office that wants to get rid of records without disposing of them for a number of years, but it is a convenience to the archivist, who can leisurely analyze the records in a records center for appraisal purposes and know that they are safe while he is deciding their eventual fate. It is a procedure not generally open to manuscript curators, and not needed by librarians, but is of great importance to archivists in carrying out their obligation to preserve that which is permanently valuable.

NOTES

1. An excellent place to start for anyone wishing to establish an acquisition policy is Calvin J. Boyer and Nancy L. Eaton, *Book Selection Policies in American Libraries* (Austin: Armadillo Press, 1971). As the subtitle states, it is "an anthology of policies from college, public and school libraries."

2. Mary Duncan Carter and Wallace J. Bonk, *Building Library Collections*, 3rd ed. (Metuchen, N.J.: The Scarecrow Press, 1969), p. 51.

3. Dohn H. Martin, "MARC Tape as a Selection Tool in the Medical Library," *Special Libraries* 61 (April 1970): 190.

4. Richard B. Sealock, "Acquisition and Organization of Local History Materials in Libraries," *Library Trends* 13 (April 1965): 184.

5. *Historical Materials in the Harry S. Truman Library* (Independence, Mo.: The Library, 1973).

6. W. Kaye Lamb, "Acquisition Policy: Competition or Cooperation?" *The Canadian Archivist* 2 (1970): 21.

7. Donald McQuat, "Acquisition Policy: Competition or Cooperation?" *The Canadian Archivist* 2 (1970): 24–25.

8. David C. Mearns, "Historical Manuscripts, Including Personal Papers," *Library Trends* 5 (January 1957): 316.

9. Robert B. Downs, "Collecting Manuscripts: By Libraries," *Library Trends* 5 (January 1957): 341.

10. Robert L. Brubaker, "Clio's Midwife: Collecting Manuscripts at a State Historical Library," *Illinois Libraries* 47 (June 1965): 599.

11. Meyer Fishbein, "Viewpoint on Appraisal of National Records," *American Archivist* 33 (April 1970): 186.

12. Dellene M. Tweedale, "Procurement and Evaluation of Materials for a University Archives," *College and Research Libraries* 26 (November 1965): 520–521.

13. T. R. Schellenberg, "The Future of the Archival Profession," *American Archivist* 22 (January 1959): 56.

STANDARDIZATION AND TECHNOLOGY

The issue of standardization for communication of information among and between institutions has never been more crucial. Attention given to the issue of technology in the archive-library world could not exist without standardization. The views of technology range from those of the visionaries who feel librarians, archivists, buildings, and materials are so out of step with the current advancements in technology that nothing short of complete automation of the communication of information will suffice, to the other extreme—a " . . . reactionary fear of the costly disruption of status quo."[1]

The issue is not whether there should be standardization and technology but to what extent services will be improved with their implementation. Libraries are facing a flood of publications, and archives are confronting mountains of paper. To what extent can archives and libraries be compatible in standardizing their techniques for control of their holdings? To what extent can user's needs be better satisfied and services improved?

Standards of one kind or another exist in virtually all areas of information handling. Because information is essential for communication of data between individuals, groups, and institutions, standards for format, communication, and retrieval are essential for the transfer of knowledge and mobility in and among professions. More important, standards are necessary for efficient service to users.

Standardization of techniques and methodology in archives and libraries has been used with great success. Witness the remarkable and reliable catalog card, a method of indexing used by archives and libraries. It is standardized in its unit size. If basic principles of cataloging and classification are used, it is standardized in its descriptive content. If these principles are not used, it is at least standardized to the extent that it contains basic descriptive data which lead to one document among millions or one book among thousands.

The card catalog is also standardized in its limitations. The user is required to search the catalog in the institution if its format is the traditional card, and cannot use it in a distant city or in his home. It is limited in its information retrieval capability, for the user must examine only a small portion of the catalog for a book or collection when the author or overall subject is known. The user cannot, however, use the card catalog for a search involving the entire catalog, such as for the appearance of a certain word in titles.

It is at this point that technology, based on standards, must interface with traditional methods. Archives and libraries, therefore, are concerned with the use of computer technology, microform technology, and the standards necessary for communication between institutions.

Changes in established standards are usually looked upon with suspicion, and implementation of standards where none exists is always tedious. It is not easy where one profession is involved (in 1972 there was a controversy over the International Standard for Bibliographic Description), and it is a complex task where many professions and interests are concerned. Technology, frequently the impetus for change in standardization, is not always compatible with existing standards and is ineffective in the absence of standards. Existing standards come under attack when technology demands change for more feasible and efficient communication of information.

How are standards adopted? Internationally, standards are implemented for the exchange of goods and services and the development of cooperation in intellectual, scientific, technological, and economic activity. The International Organization for Standardization (ISO), headquartered in Geneva, is the official carrier of international standardization. Each member country is allowed one national standards body for representation. The ISO maintains 145 technical committees, plus some 900 subcommittees and working groups to carry out its charge.

The American National Standards Institute (ANSI), founded in 1918, represents the United States in the ISO. The American National Standards Institute gives the official status of American National Standards to projects developed by agreement from all groups concerned in areas of definitions, terminology, symbols, testing, and procedures and methods of rating.

Professional experts operating as committees, employees within professional associations, and national and international organizations adopt the standards as guidelines. For example, ANSI Committee Z39 is concerned with library and information science and includes as representatives professionals from information associations, publishing companies, and the information industry. Standards adopted by these official committees form a complex interface for professional bodies, government, and industry. Recognized authorities create, experiment, test, and submit reports and recommendations concerning their specialities to appropriate groups.

In an economic system thriving on competition, the implementation of standards in the commercial environment is difficult. Problems in the use of commercial equipment and supplies—in the absence of strict standards protecting professional interests—make it imperative that the prospective purchaser of the goods and services think carefully before making a commitment to a system with inflexible requirements.

Of special interest to the library and archival community is the Library Technology Program (LTP), part of the American Library Association. The LTP represents the interests of the consumer and places a special emphasis on standards development, equipment research, and evaluation projects. The LTP is concerned with performance standards and coordinates efforts with ANSI for photographic systems, materials, apparatus, nomenclature, and test methods.

Also of interest is the National Microfilm Association (NMA), active in the development of methods of evaluation of microfilm to determine quality, uniformity, and life of materials used for this growing industry. Concerned archivists, on an individual basis, are involved in NMA standards committee activities, which emphasize the quality and durability of film and standards for filming public records.

The issue of standards to facilitate computer technology in archives and libraries is best described in a report presented to the National Advisory Commission on Libraries. It said:

> The most important changes in libraries will be (1) increasing interactions between them, which will reduce duplication of holdings, and (2) the growth of special-purpose collections dealing in depth with narrow fields. Effective interaction will be greatly facilitated through some of the automation procedures under discussion. . . .[2]

Bibliographic communication between libraries, between archives, or between archives and libraries, requires knowledge of what is in the collection of another. The obvious solution to this requirement is a union catalog. Also important is updating and distributing information on holdings. Computer applications to solve this latter requirement are well under way in the library-archive world. Already many applications exist that instantly make available information on holdings by on-line data bases or the use of Computer Output Microfilm to facilitate the distribution of microform catalogs.

What has aided these technological accomplishments? In 1971, ANSI Committee Z39 developed a standard for the communication of bibliographic information on magnetic tape. This standard will have far-reaching impact on the library and archival professions. The standard is called the "American National Standard for Bibliographic Information Interchange on Magnetic Tape." The standard is a machine readable format structure designed to accommodate records for all kinds of materials used by various groups of users, be they archive or library patrons.

This standard was influenced by a 1964 Council on Library Resources contract awarded to the Library of Congress for a study of methods of converting information on Library of Congress catalog cards to machine readable form for printing the products by computer. From this study evolved several conferences and the initiation of the Machine Readable

Cataloging (MARC) Pilot Project. In 1968, at the conclusion of the pilot project, Hennriette Avram, the MARC project director, wrote:

> The single most significant result of MARC has been the impetus to set standards . . . MARC accelerated standardization and still more important, the standards are being set and agreed to by a large segment of the library community. The cooperation among the producers and users of bibliographic description has been a rewarding experience.[3]

The success of the MARC pilot project has made possible a distribution service of centrally produced machine readable cataloging data from the Library of Congress. The Distribution Service began in March of 1969 and is based on the MARC II format, developed as a result of the pilot project.

What is the MARC format? Human beings are able to read and understand standardized descriptive bibliographic data as they would appear on a catalog card. The traditional catalog card, guide, calendar, or inventory is nonexplicit in its format, and as human beings we are able to recognize the author, title, record group, series, dates, spaces, punctuation, and an unlimited amount of other descriptive data. If we were machines, we would have to be told each time we looked at the descriptive record that it was bibliographic data, what it contained, how long it was, what language it was in, and much more. The problems become obvious. If libraries and archives are to utilize the machine to process bibliographic data, then there must be some standardization to prevent duplication and permit communication of the information from one institution to another.

This international standard is provided by MARC II. The MARC II format is precise in arrangement and consistency, just as the traditional methods and mediums of bibliographic description are precise. Compared to the standardization in descriptive cataloging procedures that already exist in the Anglo-American Cataloging Rules, the MARC format goes further into the content of the record by providing a structure for the content. It has been compared to an empty container, to which one adds the cataloging information.[4] As long as the information appears in machine readable form in the MARC format, the machine has no problem in manipulating the data by using the standardization imposed by the format. Different institutions have no difficulty in using machine readable cataloging data as long as they appear in the standardized format and standardized code. This permits ease and economy of the interchange and communication of bibliographic information. There are MARC formats developed for books, manuscripts, films, serials, and maps.

The Library of Congress had distributed over 600,000 MARC records to subscribing institutions as of June 1976. This represents the cataloging effort of the Library of Congress in English-language monographs since January of 1968. These records are distributed at the rate of approximately 2,500 a week. Several institutions have made economical and expedient use of the MARC Distribution Service. An internationally recognized application of the service is the Ohio College Library Center's (OCLC) online cataloging and locater service used by a network of 300 institutions in 28 states. The use of OCLC stretches from New England to New Mexico. Several regional networks use the OCLC data base, including the Southeastern Library Network and the New England Library Information Network.

A by-product of the MARC II format for books is the MARC format for manuscripts. This format, developed by the Library of Congress, was created cooperatively with the library's Information Systems Office, the MARC Development Office, the Manuscript Division, and the Descriptive Cataloging Division. The Library of Congress does not plan at this time to distribute MARC records for manuscripts but has developed this format for its own internal use and the use of other institutions wishing to convert descriptive data on their manuscript collections into machine readable form.

Unlike the MARC format for books, the MARC manuscript format is designed to describe items that are unique to a particular institution. The format includes ample space for local control information. The need for local information reflects the uniqueness of the material and hints at the problem of standardization for archives and manuscripts.

Examples of information included in the MARC format for manuscripts are codes which allow for retrieval by control numbers, dates, country, repository, case files, form of reproduction, processing status, language, and shelf location. In addition, it follows Anglo-American Cataloging Rules for the description of manuscripts for main entry, title, imprint, physical description (including item counts, linear footage, and value), series notations, restrictions, scope and contents, repository information, literary rights, provenance, user records, biographical tracings, finding aids available, subject heading assignments, and added entries.[5]

In addition to the above, there is a chronological coverage code which will enable users of MARC to isolate material covering a particular time span. For example, a reference request for all material on Tennessee at the time of the Civil War could be filled by searching the geographic area code field for Tennessee and the chronological coverage code field for the appropriate century and decade.

The development of the MARC format for manuscripts was an evolutionary process. In 1961 a study of the possibilities of automation application at the Library of Congress concluded:

> The Manuscript Division, Map Division, Music Division, and Prints and Photographs Division were considered outside the scope of this report because their collections involve materials which differ markedly from the central library collections.[6]

The MARC format has changed this conclusion, but the development of automated techniques in the Manuscript Division gives insight into the unique problems facing standardization and applied technology in the control of original material.

In considering automated techniques, the Manuscript Division considered the nature of the finding aids, the indexes to the collections, and the size of the holdings. Questions asked by researchers ranged from the custody of a collection to questions on provenance, subject content, and the relation of one collection to another. Answers to these questions were scattered throughout the division's supporting files. In 1966 Frank Burke, then with the Manuscript Division, wrote:

> The question facing the Manuscript Division is essentially the same question facing librarians, archivists, and others interested in retrieving information: how does one convert many massive data files into one active one? In library terms, the problem could be solved by the conversion of all the information on a catalog card into rapidly retrievable data. In manuscript terms the problem entails the conversion of information from catalogs, guides, registers, case files, and accession records into a single record with retrievable elements.[7]

The National Union Catalog of Manuscript Collections was the impetus for automating essential information about a collection. The evolution of machine application began with a sort-and-list program developed over a six-year period. This program was standardized to provide physical characteristics of the collection but did not provide for retrieval of subjects or names. In order to alleviate this shortcoming, a modified Key-Word-in-Context (KWIC) program was applied and given the name SPIN-DEX (Selective Permutation Index).[8]

This index is able to manipulate descriptive information on collections and produce various lists by name or subject, or reformat the information to conform to Library of Congress rules for cataloging manuscript collections. Although SPINDEX is a workable approach to control of massive files, it lacks the standardization of international usage the MARC format for manuscripts can lend (through the ANSI standards) for communication among repositories.

The development of SPINDEX and the MARC II format for manuscripts reveals an attempt to find a solution to control that provides reasonable in-depth analysis of material that works internally and that can provide the basis for communication in standardized codes and formats so various institutions can use the information. Books, films, serials, and maps lend themselves more to standardization and have a longer history of standardization for control than do manuscripts and archives. The demand for standardization is strongest when the material is distributable, or when uniqueness is absent.

As important as computer applications is microform technology. Reduction of the bulk of information to easily manageable proportions has been a method widely used by archives and libraries for many years. Its use by libraries and archives dates back to about 1935. Despite copyright problems, libraries are increasingly aware of the benefits derived by purchasing periodicals, books, and special materials on microform. Archives use microform for preservation, security, and distribution purposes for original source material. The practice of forming an interface with computer technology is being applied in an increasing number of institutions concerned with records management and distribution of catalogs and union lists. Reader's resistance to microforms is lowered by the capability of converting film to hard copy.

Computer Output Microfilm (COM) technology is able to display and film at great speeds data taken directly from magnetic tape. Archival institutions, especially those with records management responsibilities, are aware of the benefits the reduction in space and the economy COM can afford. Libraries are increasingly using COM for production and distribution of microfilm catalogs and union lists, or using commercial bibliographic services derived through COM technology.

Coordination of efforts at standardization for the microform field has been partially realized by a U.S. Office of Education grant under the aegis of the Association of Research Libraries. Representatives from interested organizations took on the task of doing systematic and solid planning for the microform field, keeping in mind the interests of libraries and archives as distinguished from the needs of the business world. A well-balanced plan of action has been devised, and the representation of archives and libraries is in good hands.

Questions still remain to be answered before any widespread use of micromaterials is undertaken. What are the obstacles to standards agreements now? What organization or governmental agency could act to influence acceptance of basic standards? Will the user accept microforms if standards and equipment are improved? Are computer storage of micro-images and the transmission of the image materials practical? How much will early standardization influence networking among archives and libraries? Will archives and libraries take advantage of cable television for direct service to a community by microform transmission?

This chapter has attempted to present the pragmatic issues confronting both the archival and library worlds. Nothing has been mentioned of our technical capability to create, store, and transmit data via microwave or satellite carriers. Communications among and between archives and libraries can use these technological accomplishments for optimum service. The major question before implementation is funding. How much is optimum informational service worth? How much is the public willing to pay?

The uniqueness of manuscripts and archives, or the special problems of technology as applied to library service, cannot be an excuse to prohibit standardization and application of technology where warranted. Nothing can take the place of the researcher or user in determining needs and digesting from a universe of information that small part which fulfills those needs. It is the responsibility of the librarian and archivist to efficiently serve the user. Through standardization and intelligent applications of technology, the librarian, the archivist, and the user will do a better job.

NOTES

1. Douglas M. Knight and E. Shepley Nourse, eds., *Libraries at Large: Tradition, Innovation, and the National Interest* (New York: R. R. Bowker, 1969), p. 264.
2. Max V. Matthews and W. Stanley Brown, "Research Libraries and the New Technology," in *Libraries at Large: Tradition, Innovation, and the National Interest*, ed. by Douglas M. Knight and E. Shepley Nourse (New York: R. R. Bowker, 1969), p. 270.
3. Hennriette D. Avram, ed., *The MARC Pilot Project: Final Report Sponsored by the Council on Library Resources* (Washington, D.C.: Library of Congress, 1968), p. 1.
4. *MARC Manuals Used by the Library of Congress*, 2nd ed. (Chicago: American Library Association, 1970), p. 2.
5. "Manuscripts: A MARC Format" (unpublished working document developed by the Library of Congress, 1971), pp. 2–32.
6. Frank G. Burke, "The Application of Automated Techniques in the Management and Control of Source Materials," *American Archivist* 30 (April 1967): 256.
7. Ibid., p. 262.
8. Ibid., p. 268.

PRESERVATION

For reasons not altogether clear, archivists have generally appeared to have a deeper interest in the care and preservation of their collections than have librarians. One reason may well be that archival records are typically unique documents. The loss of any one document may be significant, whereas most books are produced in multiple copies and thus are often considered expendable. Whatever the reasons, this situation shows signs of changing. Librarians are becoming increasingly aware that the volumes which are now deteriorating on their own shelves are also deteriorating on the shelves of their colleagues. Thus, for archivists and librarians alike, the conservation of their collections has indeed become a shared concern.

The present chapter does not presume to be exhaustive as this is a complex and rapidly changing field. It does aim to place the problems of conserving collections, whether they be library or archival collections, in some perspective; to outline certain major aspects of the problem; to suggest some preservation guidelines which may be useful to both librarians and archivists; to review briefly some important trends in conservation; and to indicate sources which can provide detailed information and assistance on problems of particular importance or interest.

DEFINITIONS

It will be useful to begin this chapter with a definition of terms, and if the terminology of conservation is not always consistent, there is progress in this direction. *Conservation*, as defined by Webster's *Third New International Dictionary—Unabridged*, is: "deliberate, planned, or thoughtful preserving, guarding, or protecting: a keeping in a safe or entire state: preservation: . . . the repair and preservation of works of art." Thus, conservation is an inclusive term, encompassing those actions which retard and control deterioration (e.g., maintenance of the proper environment, fumigation, control of ultraviolet radiation, and the physical protection of the collection); as well as repair, which returns damaged materials to sound and usable condition; and restoration, which returns damaged or deteriorated materials to near original condition. It should be noted that restoration often involves ethical considerations, since curators and conservators do not ordinarily wish to have a book or document so treated that the restoration cannot be detected. Since preservation attempts to control the physical and chemical condition of artifacts, it emphasizes the scientific aspects of conservation, while restoration tends to emphasize the craft aspects.

Persons with a broad and comprehensive knowledge of the many aspects of conservation are generally called conservators. Such individuals have both the theoretical knowledge of chemistry, paper technology, and the nature of library and archival materials necessary to give them a fundamental understanding of preservation problems and their solutions, as well as the craft skills required to treat, repair, and restore damaged materials.

NATURE OF LIBRARY AND ARCHIVAL MATERIALS

With few exceptions, libraries and archives acquire, store, service, and preserve the same basic kinds of materials. Thus, the two types of institutions differ not so much in kind but rather in the proportion of each class of material they hold in their collections. The great bulk of the materials held by archives and libraries are paper documents: books, manuscripts, maps, prints, drawings, photographs, and the like. Both archives and libraries, however, collect and must preserve microfilm and microfiche, as well as motion picture films, phonograph records, and magnetic tapes. As for such a contemporary medium as videotape, it seems likely that this, too, will ultimately find its way into the collections of both archives and libraries.

As noted above, the basic difference between archival and library collections rests not so much on the types of materials in the library or the archive but on the relative quantities of each class held by the two types of institutions. Thus, in libraries, the preponderant format of the collections is usually the bound volume, while in archives the principal format is the single sheet. There are many exceptions to this general distribution, however. Maps exist in single sheets in both institutions, although large map collections are perhaps more characteristic of libraries than of archives. In general, of course, the same is true with regard to prints and drawings. Photographs are common to both library and archival collections; so are microfilms. As regards single sheets, there was a period when archivists tended to preserve their manuscripts in bound volumes, although this practice often did more to damage valuable documents than to preserve them. Today, most manuscripts and other records in single sheet form are stored in special acid-free manuscript boxes. Preferably, such materials are stored flat, although the majority of archives and libraries use vertical storage boxes.

Because the materials of archives and library collections exhibit so many basic similarities and almost no fundamental differences, the preservation problems of the one are also the preservation problems of the other, and the present discussion is based on this fact.

FUNDAMENTAL CAUSES OF DETERIORATION

Deterioration of paper poses the major problem for the conservator simply because the great bulk of the printed materials is of this substance, a substance used as a medium for the written and printed word for nearly two thousand years.

Relatively few libraries and archives in the United States contain large collections of materials older than the fifteenth century, although there are scattered examples from earlier years in many libraries and notable collections in a few. In any case, enough examples of early papermaking have been handed down from the past to demonstrate that, fragile though it may be under some conditions, paper which is properly made and properly cared for has an amazingly long life. Thus, the paper made for the *Gutenberg Bible* must have been some of the finest ever produced, for today the paper in those copies of the *Gutenberg* still in existence is in nearly perfect condition. Many other volumes from the same period attest to the excellence of early paper. At the opposite end of the scale is modern book paper, most of which will endure only a few years, even when given normal care. In fact, research by the late William J. Barrow led him to conclude that 97 percent of nonfiction books printed between 1900 and 1939 had a useful life of less than 50 years. What is true for books is also true for many other paper documents of the same vintage in the nation's archives—their useful life is limited.

During the long period in which paper was made from rags, or from flax, cotton, or other strong fibers; had not been treated with bleaching agents; and contained no whiteners, beater sizes, and the like, it was a permanent and durable substance possessing both long life (permanence) in the chemical sense, and the physical strength (durability) necessary to resist the wear and tear of the ages. Scholars can be grateful that this was so; otherwise a considerably smaller number of books printed during the fifteenth, sixteenth, and seventeenth centuries would have survived in library collections.

As printing spread and the demand for paper increased, papermakers began a search for cheaper and faster ways to make paper—a search which continues to the present day. Other factors, especially the shortage of rags which began early in the eighteenth century, also contributed to cheapening the end product. It was, in fact, the shortage of clean rags and the necessity of using colored and dirty rags for papermaking which led to bleaching paper pulp, and it was the German chemist, Karl Scheele, who, in 1774, discovered chlorine. This chemical was quickly adopted by papermakers as a means of bleaching used rags so that they could be used for producing "fine" paper. This development in papermaking, and the papermakers' failure to remove the residual chlorine after bleaching, resulted in the deterioration of many late eighteenth- and early nineteenth-century volumes now on library shelves.

The cheapening process, once started, never stopped. As rags and other sources of more durable fibers became scarcer and more expensive, papermakers looked for substitutes. Wood fibers were both abundant and relatively cheap. Once papermakers learned how to use them, such fibers came into common use for book papers, newsprint, and other papers in which cost was a major factor. At about the same time, alum, which had been used for hardening gelatin size as early as the latter part of the sixteenth century, was combined with rosin to produce a new kind of size which could be added to the pulp in the beater. Although the result was cheaper paper, the use of alum rosin sizing and wood fibers brought trouble for librarians and archivists. In combination with the moisture in the air, alum rosin produces acid which leads, in turn, to the deterioration, discoloration, and embrittlement of paper. Groundwood pulp contains lignin, a complex organic compound which breaks down into acid components and causes darkening and embrittlement of the paper. Acid derived from pollutants in the atmosphere, notably sulfur dioxide, also attacks paper and causes its deterioration.

In this connection, it is interesting to note that acid paper deteriorates much more rapidly in a humid environment than in a dry environment. If librarians could segregate their collections (an impracticable procedure), it would be well to store those volumes published since about 1850—when alum rosin sizing and wood pulp came into common use—at a lower humidity than volumes published before that date.

The acid hydrolysis which results in weakening the cellulose molecule to the point that embrittlement occurs is a chemical reaction retarded by low temperatures and accelerated by high temperatures. This reaction follows what chemists call the Arrhenius equation, which is simply a statement of the relationship between temperature and the rate at which a chemical reaction takes place.

In the absence of specific data, the Arrhenius equation enables chemists to use a rule of thumb which predicts that for every 10° F. decrease in temperature, the life of paper will be increased more than twofold. Conversely, for every 10° F. increase in temperature, the useful life of acid paper will be reduced 50 percent or more. It is this relationship between temperature and the longevity of paper which leads to the recommendation that storage temperatures for library and archival materials be as low as practical. Thus, for libraries and archives with closed stacks, the effective life of the collections could be approximately doubled by reducing stack temperatures from the 75° F. so commonly used to 65° F. In England and other northern European countries where lower temperatures are more frequently encountered in libraries, this would pose no problem. In American libraries, stack attendants and others would probably find it desirable to wear sweaters under such conditions.

Light, too, plays an important role in paper deterioration by setting up photochemical or oxidation reactions. It should be emphasized that nearly all wavelengths of light are involved to some degree in the deterioration of cellulose. However, those at the lower end of the spectrum—particularly the invisible rays of ultraviolet—are most damaging.

Of the three common sources of light—sunlight, fluorescent, and incandescent—sunlight emits four to five times as much ultraviolet as does fluorescent, while fluorescent lighting, on the average, emits two to three times as much as does incandescent. Incandescent lighting, in fact, contains so little ultraviolet that ordinarily it need not be of concern. Fluorescent lighting, on the other hand, can be damaging, especially to manuscripts, open books, and any other documents which may be fully exposed when displayed in exhibit cases. In the general book collection on open shelves in libraries with fluorescent lighting, the attendant ultraviolet radiation results in faded bindings, but it probably has only a slight effect on the paper in books because of the shielding effect of shelves, bindings, and other volumes. In rare book collections, however, stacks should have canopy tops, and fluorescent tubes should be shielded with Arm-A-Lite or UF-3 Plexiglas sleeves which remove some 95 percent of the ultraviolet rays. Very delicate materials on exhibit require the added protection of Kodagraph yellow filters.

It goes without saying that because of its powerful ultraviolet emissions, no paper materials, either in stacks or exhibit cases, should ever be exposed to the direct rays of the sun. Since even indirect sunlight from a clear sky causes serious damage to paper, textiles, and other cellulosic materials, sunlight should be taken into account in planning buildings designed to house such collections.

In an earlier day, pollution of the atmosphere was largely restricted to ozone created by thunderstorms; combustion by-products from fires in homes or forests; and emissions of active volcanoes. Such pollutants included sulfur dioxide, the oxides of nitrogen, sulfides, and others. Where present in high concentrations they were undoubtedly damaging to paper, although their total effect was probably limited. The industrial revolution, however, brought the increased use of fuels in factory operations and, still later, the use of methane gas for lighting. With these developments man began to pollute the atmosphere to such a degree that the deterioration of paper was significantly increased. Today, it is well known that such common atmospheric pollutants as sulfur dioxide, ozone, nitrogen oxides, and hydrogen sulfide are contributing factors in the deterioration of paper.

The mechanism by which this takes place, using sulfur dioxide as an example, is the conversion of SO_2 to SO_3, at which point the SO_3 unites with atmospheric moisture to form H_2SO_4—sulfuric acid.

There is, finally, paper deterioration caused by living organisms: molds or fungi, bacteria, insects, and rodents. Mildew, mold, and fungus are no more than different words for the same form of primitive life which is often classed as part of the plant kingdom, but is considered by some scientists to be of a different order because it lacks chlorophyll, the green coloring found in higher plants. Whatever their classification, molds are of interest to librarians and archivists because they may attack and destroy paper, or may leave it badly stained and discolored. The familiar reddish brown spots called foxing, so characteristic of paper of the late nineteenth and early twentieth centuries, are caused by the reaction of acids produced by certain molds on particles of iron in the paper. Molds not only thrive on cellulose, they also feed on other nutrients in books and documents such as gelatin, starch, glue, paste, and leather.

It is not always realized that mold spores are always present in the air, both indoors and outdoors. These spores settle on furniture, floors, books, and other objects. Fortunately, mold can be controlled by maintaining temperature and humidity so that spores cannot develop. Certain types of bacteria, too, can damage paper, but this is so infrequent that it will not be considered further here.

Insects of many kinds attack paper and books. These pests can be especially troublesome in the tropics. In the United States, insect attacks on books are more common in the South Atlantic and Gulf Coast states, but cause problems elsewhere as well. Termites, book beetles, silver fish, firebrats, and a long list of other species have been known to attack books and other paper documents.

Rodents are ordinarily not a problem in libraries and archives, but they will eat paper, and if other food is scarce, books and other materials may suffer.

Last but by no means least as a factor in the deterioration of books and documents is man himself. Unfortunately, librarians and archivists as well as users and readers are among those who far too often destroy or damage the very items they are expected to protect. Improper storage and handling, resulting from indifference, ignorance, carelessness, or neglect, are responsible for far more damage than most of us would care to admit.

SOME ALTERNATIVES IN CONSERVATION

At some point, most librarians and archivists, faced with the responsibility of preserving their collections for future generations, come to the realization that not all materials can be preserved indefinitely in their original format. Thus, the great majority of American books printed between

1850 and 1950 will probably not last out the century. Of some 17 million volumes in the collections of the Library of Congress, for example, it is estimated that nearly 6 million are so seriously embrittled that they cannot be given to a user, because to turn a leaf is to break it off. Similarly, archival documents on cheap bond papers, and carbon copies on acid second sheets or onionskin, will become so embrittled in 25 to 50 years that they cannot be used without damage. Some manuscript and typewriter inks will fade to the point of illegibility within the same length of time.

Under these circumstances, the question of how to preserve such documents is a crucial one. Silking was once thought to be the final answer. Later, it was recognized that silked documents continued to undergo deterioration so that in 25 or 30 years such documents were again in seriously deteriorated condition. The researches of William J. Barrow led to the use of what has become widely known as "Barrow lamination." In this process a document is first deacidified and alkaline buffered, then sandwiched between sheets of thin cellulose acetate film and strong, neutral or slightly alkaline tissue, and passed between heated platens which melt the acetate film so that it acts as an adhesive and adheres the tissue to the document. Finally, the document is passed between rollers which remove air bubbles and insure good contact between tissue and document.

In theory, deacidification neutralizes the acid and chemically stabilizes the paper, while the tissue gives physical strength to the document. If properly carried out, the deacidification treatment also acts as an alkaline buffer to protect the document against acid produced by atmospheric pollutants or against acid which may develop in the paper as a result of lignin deterioration or other causes. In practice, many institutions neglect to deacidify their documents before laminating them, or fail to deacidify and buffer them properly. Under these circumstances treated documents continue to deteriorate within the laminate. Lamination, perhaps because it seems so simple and because it permits the treatment of large numbers of documents and thus makes "big" statistics, has tended to become a sort of panacea for many of the preservation problems of archives. In most libraries, with the exception of its use in protecting manuscripts and maps, lamination is of limited usefulness, since deacidifying and laminating a book is many times as costly as laminating a single sheet. Today, many of the major national archives and state archives make extensive use of lamination as a means of preserving manuscripts and similar documents, while in both Central and South America the use of this process appears to be increasing.

It should be noted that although this discussion refers to lamination with cellulose acetate and tissue produced in accordance with the specifications established by Barrow, untested materials such as polyethylene and polyvinyl chloride (PVC) are often used for the lamination of valuable documents. For example, PVC, used to some extent in Western Europe, is known to give off hydrochloric acid as it ages. This can result in significant damage to documents so laminated.

Lamination without deacidification and buffering is worthless, generally doing more harm than good, although too often this is unrecognized or ignored. Cellulose acetate film melts at about 340° F. The curator need only stand at the laminator and observe the darkening of many documents as they are subjected to this heat to be aware that some degree of damage is taking place. Further, the undeacidified, unbuffered document continues to deteriorate and embrittle within the lamination, so that within a span of 20 to 75 years it has deteriorated, just as it would if not laminated.

A further objection to lamination (with or without deacidification and alkaline buffering) is the fact that although theoretically the tissue and acetate are removable, in practice this is very difficult, and often impossible. Lamination, in other words, should not be considered an archival treatment, and valuable documents should not be so treated if they are expected to last indefinitely. For these reasons, archivists, in particular, should reconsider the value of lamination, with or without deacidification, for those documents which they believe should last indefinitely (i.e., documents with archival value) and begin to examine the alternatives.

One new technique, polyester film encapsulation, now in general use at the Library of Congress, offers substantially better physical protection than traditional lamination; provides the added advantage of immediate accessibility; does not result in changing the nature of the document; and can be undone if necessary by simply cutting open the envelope. However, proper deacidification and buffering which will leave an alkaline reserve equivalent to 3 percent calcium carbonate in the sheet is as important in this technique as it is in cellulose acetate lamination.

One striking phenomenon in polyester film encapsulation is the fact that most embrittled paper can withstand the roughest treatment without fracturing when protected by a four-edge-sealed polyester envelope. At the Library of Congress, the polyester film and the two-sided acrylic tape used to fabricate the envelopes have been subjected to accelerated aging for an approximate life of 500 years with no observable adverse effects.

However, polyester film encapsulation should not be considered a panacea either, although it offers several distinct advantages over lamination. The truth is that different problems demand different solutions and the knowledgeable conservator or curator will have available as many methods and techniques as possible. For those documents with a fair degree of initial strength and not likely to receive a significant degree of use, deacidification and alkaline buffering are essential, but neither lamination nor encapsulation is necessary. It is the indiscriminate use of any process without careful consideration of the document to be treated and the desired end result against which curators and conservators should be on their guard.

For most archival and library materials, and certainly for all such materials on paper, the most satisfactory method of preserving collections for the future, and the least expensive on a per item basis, is low temperature storage, i.e., 60° F. or below. The fact that this method usually requires a major capital outlay means that few institutions can afford it. For collections of significant importance and value and of relatively small size, however, the creation of special low temperature vaults or rooms can provide long-term preservation at minimum cost.

For those materials not of sufficient importance to justify low temperature storage, preservation of the intellectual content by reduction to microformat, followed by destruction of the brittle originals, is one option. Although this is not an alternative to be taken lightly, the increasing cost of storage space—a cost which could be significantly reduced by the use of microfilming—makes it an option to be considered seriously. Further, there are thousands of items in both archival and library collections which cannot economically or practically be preserved indefinitely in any case. Such materials include, for example, twentieth-century carbon copies which make up large segments of many archival collections, either as letter books or as loose materials. Not only will the paper of such documents deteriorate to the point of becoming unusable in a measurable period of time, some typescripts, too, may fade to the point of illegibility in the same period of time. Millions of late nineteenth- and twentieth-century books and pamphlets in the nation's libraries will become similarly embrittled. Short of low temperature storage, microfilming to preserve the intellectual content is the only economically feasible means by which such materials can be preserved indefinitely.

CURRENT DIRECTIONS IN CONSERVATION

As librarians and archivists look more closely at their collections, the sheer magnitude of the preservation problem becomes increasingly apparent. In part this has been caused by decades of neglect, in part by unfavorable environmental conditions often beyond the control of the custodian, and in part by the paper manufacturer's lack of concern for the permanence and durability of the product as sold to the publishers and printer. The result has been the deterioration of our collections in such quantities that the numbers sometimes boggle the mind. The estimated 6 million brittle volumes in the collections of the Library of Congress have already been noted. Similarly at the Library of Congress, required restoration work on the rare book collections is estimated at more than 5,000 man-years. No other American library has collections as large as the Library of Congress, but in proportion to the size and the resources of the institution the preservation problems of most libraries and archives are comparable.

As a result, both librarians and archivists are faced with increasing numbers of items requiring some type of conservation work, while the conservator and the research chemist are faced with the necessity of finding better and more effective solutions to the complex problems of preservation.

Two general approaches to these massive problems are currently being tried and are under continuing investigation: (1) phased preservation and (2) mass treatment. Phased preservation, a concept developed at the Library of Congress, relies on variant techniques, each different, but each designed to provide rapid stabilization of deteriorating materials pending the development of effective mass treatments or the acquisition of the highly trained staff necessary to perform work for which no mass treatment is likely to be possible. For some materials and for some problems, stabilization procedures short of ultimate restoration do not exist, and phased preservation is not possible. Where it is possible, phased preservation buys time; time in which to develop, perfect, and apply new conservation techniques, or time in which to acquire the funds, the staff, and the equipment necessary to undertake full conservation treatment.

The second approach is the development of suitable and effective mass treatment methods. Where thousands, hundreds of thousands, and even millions of items must be dealt with, treatment on an item-by-item basis is economically unsound and practically impossible. The truth is that those who control library-archive budgets will not accept the cost of item-by-item conservation wherever mass treatment methods are technically possible. Thus, what today's librarian hopes for and today's conservator is actively seeking are methods by which deteriorating materials can be effectively treated in large numbers. The ongoing search for an economical and effective means of gaseous deacidification which would permit gas chamber treatment of thousands of brittle books at one time is an example. A utopian solution, but one currently being researched, is a gaseous treatment which would restore lost strength to brittle paper.

The developing technique of leafcasting makes possible repairs to mutilated or damaged documents which are as good as, or better than, hand mending, and ten times more rapid. Leafcasting replaces missing margins or fills voids in the sheet by the deposition of new pulp from a fiber slurry which can be formulated to match the paper being repaired. Special equipment and a high degree of skill are required, but the technique has now been developed to the point where it is superior in many instances to methods of hand repair. At the Library of Congress, which purchased the first commercial equipment of its kind from the Yissum Research Institute of the Hebrew National Library in Jerusalem, further studies have led to the design of more refined and sophisticated equipment capable of mending and backlining large maps and posters up to 3½ by 5 feet.

Initially, one of the major problems in the successful application of this technique was the precise computation of the area to be filled and the use of this measurement to determine the fiber content of the slurry. At the Library of Congress this problem has been solved by a photoelectric cell scanning device used with a computer so that the area to be filled is determined electronically and the resulting data fed to the computer which reads back the quantities for the pulp required. This equipment is used in conjunction with a pulp catalog giving formulas for more than one thousand papers of different types.

Other mass treatment techniques are under investigation both in the United States and in conservation centers abroad. Hopefully, many of these studies will be successful. Indeed, preservation of the nation's library and archival collections depends on the ultimate success of such investigations.

Even successful mass treatment techniques will not solve all the problems, however, since the necessary equipment will require capital outlays well beyond the financial resources of many institutions. Thus, in many cases, the preservation of archival and library collections will depend on yet undeveloped regional conservation centers supported initially by foundation or government grants-in-aid. That such regional centers are economically viable enterprises, given adequate initial funding, a proper location, and sound management, has been demonstrated by the New England Regional Conservation Center which has become entirely self-supporting in two years.

Although there has been some discussion of establishing a series of national conservation centers in the United States, such as is being tried in Canada, we believe that conservation centers should be the outgrowth of demonstrated need and regional willingness to undertake such ventures. Indeed, consortia of interested libraries, archives, and local historical societies might well be formed for this special purpose. With sound planning and carefully developed programs, private and foundation funding would undoubtedly become available. The primary deterrent to the development of new regional conservation centers at the present time is the lack of trained staff. Unfortunately, despite the increase in conservation training programs, this is a problem which is not likely to be alleviated in the near future.

SOURCES OF HELP

A decade ago conservation was the concern of a comparative few. Today it is the shared concern of all who hold responsibility for collections of books, manuscripts, historical documents, art on paper, and related materials which have value for future generations. Conservation, however, is a field with as many questions as answers, although expanding research programs in many parts of the world give promise of producing better answers and better techniques.

Meanwhile, archivists and librarians with only a limited knowledge of conservation need sources to which they can turn for sound, accurate, practical information. Unfortunately, such sources are still limited. The Office of the Assistant Director for Preservation, Library of Congress, provides a special reference service for conservation inquiries from institutions and individuals. The conservator of the Newberry Library in Chicago also provides a reference service on the conservation of library materials. In the northeast, the New England Document Conservation Center not only answers general inquiries but undertakes conservation treatment of artifacts on paper for institutions and individuals in the region.

CONSERVATION ORGANIZATIONS AND PUBLICATIONS

An increasing awareness of the major problems of conserving museum, library, and archival collections has led, in recent years, to more interest in conservation by major research libraries, archives, state and local historical societies, and other institutions. In turn, this has led to a demand for more trained conservators and to an awakened interest in conservation as a profession.

For many years the chief professional organization in the field was the International Institute for Conservation of Historic and Artistic Works (IIC), headquartered in London. In the United States, American conservators formed a subsidiary organization known as the IIC–American Group. The growing number of conservators in the United States, however, led, in 1972–1973, to the formation of a separate organization formally designated as the American Institute of Conservation.

Still more recently, an additional organization has come into being. This group, known as the National Conservation Advisory Council, was formed in November 1973, with two-year funding from the National Museum Act. The basic assignment of the NCAC is to assess the broad preservation needs of the United States in all fields, and to make recommendations for their solution.

Increased interest in conservation problems has also led to some increase in the literature of the profession. Since 1955, IIC has published its *Studies in Conservation*. The *AIC Bulletin* has been published since 1960, having been initiated by the IIC-American Group. Both journals address themselves to the conservation problems of museum objects and paintings more than to those of books and manuscripts.

Restaurator, an international journal for the preservation of library and archival material, is one of the few journals to cover this more restricted field. Published in Copenhagen, *Restaurator* has an international board of editors and covers a full range of conservation problems of interest to librarians and archivists. Although a small editorial staff in the main office results in irregular publication dates, the journal contains much information of special interest to conservators.

Encompassing somewhat the same field is the *Bollettino Dell'Istituto di Patologia Del Libro*. The Istituto, founded in Rome in 1941, and largely supported by the Italian government, undertakes a variety of research problems in the field of book and paper conservation. The *Bollettino* has long been one of the most respected journals in the field.

Art and Archeology Technical Abstracts, published semiannually for the IIC by the Institute of Fine Arts, New York University, should also be noted. These abstracts, which include items on the conservation of paper and related subjects, constitute an excellent reference source to the literature in the field.

Of special interest to librarians and archivists is the preservation leaflet series recently initiated by the Library of Congress. This series will cover a wide range of topics: from the treatment of leather bindings to the use of manuscript marking inks. These leaflets are available without charge from the Office of the Assistant Director for Preservation, Administrative Department, Library of Congress, Washington, D.C. 20540.

TRAINING IN CONSERVATION

Despite the greatly increased interest in the conservation of library-archive collections, the dearth of trained paper conservators continues to be a barrier to progress in the establishment of sound conservation programs in both types of institutions. There are, however, some hopeful signs. Persons interested in paper conservation as a career can now obtain advanced degrees in conservation through the Conservation Center of the Institute of Fine Arts of New York University, the Cooperstown Graduate Programs of New York State University, and the Winterthur Program in the Conservation of Artistic and Historic Objects, a program conducted jointly with the University of Delaware. The conservation programs of these three institutions are not only outstanding, they are probably unparalleled anywhere else in the world.

SUMMARY

Conservation of archives-library collections is a matter of growing concern to those charged with the custody of such materials. However, significant obstacles remain before archivists and librarians can be assured of the ultimate preservation of their collections. A large number of technical problems must be resolved; funding for preservation must be increased; pooling of resources must be undertaken; and, most important, training programs for conservators must be improved and expanded.

There are, at the same time, encouraging indications. New organizations are being formed to survey these problems and to identify means of resolving them; research into the technical problems of conservation is increasing; technical assistance and information is available from an increasing number of sources; new conservation training programs are being initiated; and a number of new conservation treatments superior to previous methods are being developed.

LIBRARY MANAGEMENT OF ARCHIVES

Much has been written concerning the perennial dilemma of archives administered by libraries. The arguments are many and may leave confusion for the answer seeker, but library control and management of archives and manuscripts exist on a large scale and will continue. This basic fact overshadows the dilemma as to whether the appropriate institution is administering some archive and manuscript collections, but it is still a question where new archival programs are contemplated.

The most common argument against library control of archives is based on a fear that unqualified personnel may be appointed to administer the programs. Archivists become uneasy since different training, standards, and methodology are required for archival programs.

Examples exist in libraries of funding discrimination and inadequate personnel appointments for archival programs, but smooth arrangements also exist where strong programs are under way, administered by an able library director. Any gap in communication and understanding of the archival program is bridged by such a person.

Sometimes implied in library management of archives is that the archivist's job is a subordinate position in the library hierarchy, but this argument is not often used because in many organizations the archivist is on a par with other department heads such as technical services, reference, and acquisitions.

Meager library support of archival endeavors, although a sound argument against library control, leaves the question as to whether there would be any archives if it were not for the library assuming some responsibility. Any library responsive to its clientele will place funding emphasis on the services most in demand. Barring outright funding discrimination, the library must support those services in proportion to the available resources according to the purpose of the institution.

Much progress has resulted from educating library administrators to the distinctness of the archival program and the results are seen in cases where library administrators demand more highly qualified archivists. Many administrators demand library skills as well as archival training.

In a society where archival institutions, except for the very largest, are comparatively unknown, archival survival may be strongest under the wing of a powerful and well-established library. The integrated library-archive program benefits in indirect administrative costs which are borne by the parent library agency. Costs such as housing, accounting, top level administration, supplies, ordering, and in-service training may not be reflected in the archives' operating budget but are nevertheless advantages if funded by the parent agency. Under the wing of a strong library, the archives' staff has direct access to the immense book collections for back-

155

ground reading and research. Users benefit from the parent library agency when they are able to supplement the original sources with other media in the library.

The fact remains that some strong and well-developed programs flourish when independent of a library operating within the same jurisdiction. Those jurisdictions fortunate enough to support a separate archives can usually boast of adequate buildings, salaries, and recognized authority over the collection of certain records. Where independent archives and library situations exist, there is a need to maintain a close relationship.

It is in the area of the systematic collection of archival materials that library control is sometimes a disadvantage. Problems tend to exist in areas of unnecessary competition for materials and in duplication of programs. The situation is complicated where agencies strictly archival in nature are legally designated as a repository for records within the same state, region, or locale as a library possessing an archive and manuscript program.

The collection and competition problems must be faced on an individual basis. This is also the prescription for deciding whether or not an integrated library-archive is preferable to an independent library and an independent archives operating in the same jurisdiction. The answer to the dilemma over library control of archives is neither black nor white, but definitely gray.

At the state level, the two situations confront the management of archives and libraries. A variety of specific management organizations cause variations of these two basic situations, depending on the extent of differences in state legislation. Where independent state archives and state libraries exist in the same jurisdiction, there is often a tradition of administrative and funding history which impedes competition and duplication of programs. Each agency has its own legislative responsibilities, and money for new programs is difficult to obtain. There is still a need for duplicative research collections on state and local history and government documents to support both the state library and the state archival programs.

State archives independent of library control usually have other management situations with which to contend. Where archival programs are managed by a combined archives and history department (e.g., a historical society), there are other activities (such as historic sites, archeology, and museums) conducted by the agency in addition to special historical libraries. Generally, in situations where archives are independent of historical agencies, the archives may have a records management function. In fact, some state archives are justified in part by the records management responsibility. For statutory reasons, archival arrangements which include records management programs are compelled to develop close relations with current records management at the expense of its relations with library endeavors. There is often an archives and records commission or board to oversee the disposition of state records, but this body may not be the same as the governing board of the parent agency.

The fully integrated library-archives situation, managed by state library agencies, has recently ranged from 8 to 11 states depending on periodic changes in legislation. A survey, conducted for the purpose of sampling library management of archival programs, sheds some light on the current management policies of these state libraries. A questionnaire designed to elicit such information was sent to all state libraries listed in Philip Hamer's *Guide to Archives and Manuscripts in the United States* (1961) as having archives and/or manuscripts. It was found that three of these state libraries no longer assumed archival responsibility. They were Massachusetts, Maine, and Oregon. Legislative action accounted for these changes. Of the agencies reporting, 50 percent acquired the responsibility of archives and/or manuscripts during the period from 1850 to 1900. The other 50 percent assumed the responsibility between 1900 and 1950. Of the eight reporting, 50 percent possessed both archive and manuscript responsibility while the remainder were divided between only manuscript responsibility and only archives responsibility. As expected, 87.5 percent of the reporting state agencies had a legal basis for their activities in the area of archives (see Tables 1 and 2).

There is no evidence that the state library-archives arrangement is working to the detriment of library responsibilities or the archival program. Professional personnel assigned to archives and manuscripts are well-qualified educationally. Among those with higher educational degrees 47.8 percent hold B.A. degrees, 27.8 percent hold an M.A. in history, 21.1 percent hold M.L.S. degrees, and 3.3 percent possess a Ph.D. Most archives and manuscripts personnel (73 percent) working in the library organization attended state and regional meetings of their profession. While 20 percent of the group attended the Society of American Archivists' annual meeting, interestingly, no institution reported that their archives personnel attended the annual meeting of the ALA. Other national meetings accounted for the remaining 7 percent. The average percentage of total agency employees assigned to archives and/or manuscripts was a significant 9.5 percent.

Three of the state library-archive agencies reported the percentage of the parent agency's budget allocated to archives and manuscripts. These were Texas, Virginia, and New Jersey. The average percentage among these states was 24 percent, with Virginia leading the field with 40 percent.

The administrative status of the archives-manuscript function within the state library organization varies. The administrative archivist an-

Table 1. Questionnaire on Library Management of Archive and/or Manuscript Function

1. Library name _____
2. Name of person completing questionnaire _____
3. Title of person completing questionnaire_____
4. Is an archive and/or manuscript function part of your library organization? _____ yes _____ no*
5. Approximately when did the library acquire this responsibility? _____ year
6. Does the archive and/or manuscript function have
   _____ only private manuscripts and collections?
   _____ only university archives or government archives?
   _____ both of the above?
7. If the archive function contains university or government records, is there a legal basis (statute, charter, etc.) for the existence of the function in the library? _____ yes _____ no
8. What percent of the total number of persons employed by the library is assigned to archives and/or manuscripts? _____ (percent)
9. Of the total number of persons employed in the archive and/or manuscript function, how many have (exclude student employees):
   _____ BA degree   _____ Ph.D—history
   _____ MA—history   _____ Ph.D—other
   _____ MLS or MALS   _____ other (specify)
   _____ MA—other   _____
10. How many employees of the archive and/or manuscript function regularly attend meetings of the:
    _____ American Library Association
    _____ Society of American Archivists
    _____ other national meetings
    _____ other state or regional meetings
11. In the 1973–1974 fiscal year, what percent of the library's total operating budget was assigned to the archive and/or manuscript function?
12. For purposes of defining the organizational status of the archive or manuscript function, a department reports to the director; a division reports to a department; and a branch reports to a division. Please check the organizational status of your archive and/or manuscript function.
    _____ department   _____ division   _____ branch
    If your organization does not fall into the above definition, please explain your organizational hierarchy as relating to the archive or manuscript function. _____
    _____
13. Additional comments _____
    _____

*If the answer is "no" you have completed the questionnaire.

Table 2.   State Library Management of Archives and Manuscripts
(Eight Reporting Institutions)

Questionnaire Item	*No.*	*Percent*
1. Date of acquiring archives and/or manuscript responsibility		
a. 1800–1850	4	50
b. 1850–1900	0	0
c. 1900–1950	4	50
d. 1950–	0	0
2. Repositories having		
a. only manuscript responsibility	2	25
b. only archival responsibility	2	25
c. both archival and manuscript responsibility	4	50
3. Institutions having legal basis for archives (charter, statute)	7	87.5
4. Average percentage of library agency operating budget allocated to archives and manuscripts (three reporting)		24
5. Administrative status of archives or manuscript function (a department reports to the director of libraries; a division reports to a department; and a branch reports to a division)		
a. department status	3	50
b. division status	1	16.66
c. branch status	2	33.33
6. Average percentage of total library employees assigned to archives and/or manuscripts		9.5
7. Archive and manuscript personnel holding		
a. Bachelor of Arts	43	47.8
b. Master of Arts—history	25	27.8
c. Master of Library Science	19	21.1
d. Doctor of Philosophy	3	3.3
e. Master of Arts—other	0	0
8. Archive and manuscript employees attending meetings of		
a. American Library Association	0	0
b. Society of American Archivists	9	20.4
c. other national meetings	3	6.8
d. other state and regional meetings	32	72.8

swered directly to the director of the parent agency in 50 percent of the reporting states. Only one state reported that its administrative archivist held division status (once removed) under the director of the agency. Two states, or 33.33 percent, reported that the archives administrators held branch status (twice removed) under the administrative head of the library agency.

Today, 8 states combine state library and archive responsibilities. Looking at the benefits of this arrangement objectively, there is flexibility in staff assignment and budget allocation. These 8 states are able to share facilities of reproduction and restoration as well as staff expertise in specialities for maximum visibility. It is left only to speculation as to whether or not activities purely library or purely archival in nature would benefit more if independent of each other. The state libraries responding to the questionnaire were: Arizona, Washington, Texas, Virginia, New Jersey, New York, Connecticut, California, Massachusetts, Maine, and Oregon.

In a university setting, the archives and manuscript collections are very much at home in the library. Circumstance may make the above statement contradictory, but, theoretically, archival placement within the university library is a natural union. Obviously, the main reason for this union is the supplementary research materials provided only by the library. Also, in the area of special collections, increasingly being viewed as learning laboratories, archival endeavors are becoming integrated with a variety of academic departments in providing resources which have not been heavily used by the students of certain disciplines in the past.[1]

Archives and special collections, as part of the university library, are undergoing changes in management techniques, budgeting, and personnel. These changes are due to several factors indicative of the changes universities as a whole are experiencing. First, there is the decline of enrollments and the general stabilization of financial support. Add this to frequent changes in the presidency of universities, changes in academic disciplines, staff attitudes, and increasing control by state boards of regents and you have a changing university library.[2] All departments of a university library are affected when changes in collection policies require more selectivity in purchases, and these changes directly affect the working capital.

There are varieties of administrative arrangements for archives and manuscripts within universities. The great majority fall under university library management, and the success of this arrangement depends to a large extent on the attitude of the library administrator. The director can do much in fund raising, aid in acquiring manuscripts, and generally be sympathetic to the growth of the archives and manuscripts. Perhaps the most important duty of such a person is selecting a competent staff and structuring the archives and manuscript function within the library organization. Because of the particular nature of original source material, an idealized structure would have a head of the repository who would report to the director of libraries without the necessity of going through various administrative channels. The repository, in the utopian state, would be organized along the lines of an academic department with faculty responsible for reference, administration, development, publication, and processing.[3]

In managing the repository, the director of libraries obviously has the prerogative of formulating policy in regard to use, accessibility, and loan of material in the repository. In spite of cordial relations between the researcher and custodian, the access problem persists as a management issue unique to archives and libraries.[4] Walter Rundell, Jr., in "The Survey on the Use of Original Sources in Graduate History Training," identified access to original sources as a major problem preventing research in U.S. history. It is a management matter because access is a policy decision which can limit open, free access to information in terms of facilities, personnel, and attitudes, except when donor restrictions demand otherwise.[5]

For sampling purposes, 30 university libraries listed in Hamer's *Guide* as tax supported and holding over one million volumes responded to a survey by the author. The survey was designed to shed light on university library management of archives and manuscripts, and the questionnaire used was the same as for the state library management arena previously reported. It revealed that university archives and manuscript functions in libraries are of relatively recent vintage. During the period from 1900 to 1949, 46.7 percent acquired responsibility for archives/manuscripts. Another 40 percent acquired the responsibility since 1950 (see Table 3).

Possession of both archives and manuscripts was claimed by 93.3 percent of reporting institutions, but only 40 percent of the libraries had a legal base (charter, statute, etc.) for archival activity. Compared to state library support of archives/manuscripts, university libraries offered meager funding, revealing an average of only 3.6 percent of the total library operating budget. It must be noted, however, that the university libraries sampled in this survey often had larger operating budgets than the state libraries queried. The educational level of the professional staff assigned to archives/manuscripts was comparable to that of state library staff, except that university library staff held more Ph.D.s. Most repository staff in university libraries attended meetings of state and regional groups (49.2 percent), 29.5 percent attended meetings of the Society of American Archivists, and 7.4 percent attended ALA annual meetings.

In 53.3 percent of the cases, the archives/manuscript function reported directly to the director of university libraries. Another 35.7 percent were once removed, and 11 percent found it necessary to wade through

Table 3. University Library Management of Archives and Manuscripts

(Thirty Reporting Institutions)

Questionnaire Item	No.	Percent
1. Date of acquiring archives and/or manuscript responsibility		
a. 1800–1850	1	3.3
b. 1850–1900	3	10
c. 1900–1950	14	46.7
d. 1950–	12	40
2. Repositories having		
a. only manuscript responsibility	1	3.3
b. only archival responsibility	1	3.3
c. both archival and manuscript responsibility	28	93.3
3. Institutions having legal basis for archives (charter, statute)	12	40
4. Average percentage of library agency operating budget allocated to archives and manuscripts (twelve reporting)		3.6
5. Administrative status of archives or manuscript function (a department reports to the director of libraries; a division reports to a department; and a branch reports to a division)		
a. department status	15	53.3
b. division status	10	35.7
c. branch status	3	11
6. Average percentage of total library employees assigned to archives and/or manuscripts		3.24
7. Archive and manuscript personnel holding		
a. Bachelor of Arts	85	45.8
b. Master of Arts—history	41	22.2
c. Master of Library Science	34	18.7
d. Doctor of Philosophy	9	4.7
e. Master of Arts—other	16	8.6
8. Archive and manuscript employees attending meetings of		
a. American Library Association	9	7.4
b. Society of American Archivists	36	29.5
c. other national meetings	17	13.9
d. other state and regional meetings	60	49.2

Table 4. Public Library Management of Archives and Manuscripts
(Six Reporting Institutions)

Questionnaire Item	No.	Percent
1. Date of acquiring archives and/or manuscript responsibility		
a. 1800–1850	0	0
b. 1850–1900	1	20
c. 1900–1950	3	60
d. 1950–	1	20
2. Repositories having		
a. only manuscript responsibility	2	33.3
b. only archival responsibility	0	0
c. both archival and manuscript responsibility	4	66.7
3. Institutions having legal basis for archives (charter, statute)	0	
4. Average percentage of library agency operating budget allocated to archives and manuscripts (four reporting)		0.755
5. Administrative status of archives or manuscript function (a department reports to the director of libraries; a division reports to a department; and a branch reports to a division)		
a. department status	1	20
b. division status	4	80
c. branch status	0	
6. Average percentage of total library employees assigned to archives and/or manuscripts		0.650
7. Archive and manuscript personnel holding		
a. Bachelor of Arts	10	40
b. Master of Arts—history	3	12
c. Master of Library Science	7	28
d. Doctor of Philosophy	1	4
e. Master of Arts—other	4	16
8. Archive and manuscript employees attending meetings of		
a. American Library Association	2	18.1
b. Society of American Archivists	2	18.1
c. other national meetings	3	27.4
d. other state and regional	4	36.4

two individuals before receiving top level administrative recognition. The libraries reporting were the universities of: Minnesota, Georgia, Iowa, New Mexico, Arizona, Illinois at Urbana, Hawaii, Kentucky, South Carolina, Virginia, Mississippi, Rhode Island, Vermont, Oregon, Arkansas, Texas, Missouri, Tennessee at Knoxville, Colorado, Idaho, Kansas, Pennsylvania, and Washington. In addition, the University of California at Los Angeles, the Bancroft Library, Oklahoma State University, Louisiana State University, Mississippi State University, Pennsylvania State University, Southern Illinois University, and Northwestern University responded to the questionnaire.

The importance of public libraries as resource centers for research materials should not be considered lightly. In questionnaire responses to Walter Rundell's study of graduate history training in the United States, public libraries ranked only third to state libraries and university libraries as places where students went for research materials.[6]

For sampling purposes, the same questionnaire sent to state and university libraries by the author was sent to large public libraries listed in Hamer's *Guide*. Understandably, no public library reported having only archival responsibility, but four libraries reported possessing both archives and manuscripts. No library had a charter or statute as a legal basis for its archival activities (see Table 4).

A low 0.650 percent of total library employees was assigned to archives/manuscripts and a low 0.755 percent of library operating budget was allocated to this function. These low figures reflect the different purpose of public libraries and their priorities are obviously not in the archive/manuscript area. Large public libraries, like those reporting, usually have large staffs and operating budgets, compared to the average size of the university and state libraries queried, and this accounts for the low percentage figures for staff and funds which may not be reflective of the actual amount of support within the institution.

An indication of the size of the reporting public libraries staff is that a total of 25 professional personnel in the six reporting libraries were assigned to archives and manuscripts. Forty percent of these held Bachelor of Arts degrees, 28 percent held M.L.S. degrees, 12 percent held M.A. degrees in history, 16 percent held other master's degrees, and there was only one Ph.D. Most of the archives/manuscript staff attended meetings of state and regional groups (36.4 percent). National meetings attracted 27.4 percent of the staff while the Society of American Archivists annual convention was attended by 18.1 percent. The ALA also attracted 18.1 percent of the staff.

It is important to note that the return on the questionnaire from state, university, and public libraries was 66.2 percent.

NOTES

1. Barbara Fisher, "The University Chain of Being: A Look at the Library Link" (paper presented at the 34th annual meeting of the Society of American Archivists, Washington, D.C., September 1970), p. 4.

2. Arthur McNally and Robert Downs, "The Changing Role of Directors of University Libraries," *College and Research Libraries* 34 (March 1973): 103–110.

3. Herbert Finch, "Administrative Relationships in a Large Manuscript Repository," *American Archivist* 34 (January 1971): 23.

4. Walter Rundell, Jr., *In Pursuit of American History: Research and Training in the United States* (Norman: University of Oklahoma Press, 1970), p. 285.

5. Ibid.

6. Ibid., p. 398.

FIVE

PROFESSIONAL COMMUNICATION

THE NEED FOR COMMUNICATION

Librarians, archivists and manuscript curators, and historians have all developed their own channels of professional communication. Each profession has established international, national, regional, and state associations. Other associations have been established which are devoted to special aspects of a discipline or field. The associations hold meetings once or twice a year at which papers are read and discussed, issues are debated, friendships are renewed, and information about recent activities is exchanged in informal conversations. The associations also appoint committees whose members converse, correspond, disseminate circular letters and questionnaires, conduct surveys, compile reports and recommendations, and plan programs. Journals and newsletters containing articles, reviews, and other features are issued by libraries and archives, associations, and other agencies. Individuals correspond with colleagues, converse in faculty centers and staff rooms, visit other institutions, and telephone to inquire about policies and practices elsewhere.

For archivists and manuscript curators, the major professional organization in the United States is the Society of American Archivists (SAA), organized in 1936. The SAA publishes a quarterly journal, the *American Archivist*, and the *SAA Newsletter*.

Numerous regional, state, and local archival associations have been established since 1966. In the East, these include the New England Archivists, the Mid-Atlantic Regional Archives Conference, the New York State Manuscripts Curators Conference, and the Long Island Archives Conference. Midwestern associations include the Midwest Archives Conference, the Society of Ohio Archivists, the Society of Indiana Archivists, the Michigan Archival Association, and the Association of St. Louis Area

169

Archivists. The South has the South Atlantic Archives and Records Conference, the Tennessee Archivists, and the Society of Georgia Archivists. Western associations include the Northwest Archivists, the Society of Southwest Archivists, and the Society of California Archivists.[1]

Librarians have organized a much more complex structure of professional associations.[2] The association with the largest and most diversified membership, the American Library Association, organized in 1876, has an almost bewildering array of divisions, sections, committees, subcommittees, joint committees, round tables, and affiliated organizations. All members receive *American Libraries*, published monthly since 1970, which contains brief news articles on libraries, ALA activities, other library associations, personalities, pending legislation, recent publications, and other matters. Journals are also published by some of the 13 ALA divisions, notably *College & Research Libraries*, issued by the Association of College and Research Libraries, the Resource and Technical Service Division's *Library Resources & Technical Services*, the Reference and Adult Services Division's *RQ*, and the Information Science and Automation Division's *Journal of Library Automation*.

Most of the other national library associations facilitate communication among librarians who work in special libraries or divisions of libraries devoted to a particular subject or type of material. The Special Libraries Association, established in 1909, publishes *Special Libraries*, a journal received by all members, and other journals or newsletters issued by divisions, such as the Geography and Map Division's *Bulletin* and the Picture Division's *Picturescope*. Other national associations include the Medical Library Association, the American Association of Law Libraries, the Music Library Association, the Theatre Library Association, the American Theological Library Association, the Catholic Library Association, and the Association of Jewish Libraries. All issue journals and a variety of other publications.

State library associations now exist in 44 states, and regional associations have been organized in New England, the Middle Atlantic states, the Southeast, the Southwest, the Mountain Plains states, and the Pacific Northwest. Almost all of the state and regional library associations issue journals, such as the *California Librarian*, the *Nebraska Library Association Quarterly*, *Connecticut Libraries*, and variations on these titles.

A great many historical associations have been established in the United States.[3] The largest professional associations are the American Historical Association and the Organization of American Historians. The American Historical Association, founded in 1884, has published the *American Historical Review* since 1895 and the *AHA Newsletter* since 1962, and includes scholars in all fields of history. The Organization of American Historians was organized in 1907 as a regional association—the

Mississippi Valley Historical Association, which began publishing the *Mississippi Valley Historical Review* in 1914—but the focus had become national long before 1964, when the association changed its name to the Organization of American Historians and the review became the *Journal of American History*.

Other professional historical associations are devoted to specific aspects of history. Some of the more important are the Agricultural History Society, the Forest History Society, the Economic History Association, the Society for the History of Technology, the History of Science Society, and the Society of Architectural Historians. There are several regional associations, notably the Southern Historical Association and the Western History Association. All publish important journals.

Most states have a state historical society or a major independent historical society. Membership is generally open to anyone interested in the history of a state or area, but most of the societies have a substantial proportion of professional historians among their members, and many are dominated by them. All of the societies publish journals, such as the *Massachusetts Historical Society Proceedings*, the Ohio Historical Society's *Ohio History*, the *Journal of the Illinois State Historical Society*, and the California Historical Society's *California Historical Quarterly*.

Means of communication among historical society directors and staff are provided by the American Association for State and Local History, founded in 1940 after an earlier series of conferences of state and local historical societies held at annual meetings of the American Historical Association since 1904. The AASLH published a popular history journal, *American Heritage*, from 1947 to 1954, and continued as a sponsor after publication was shifted to a separate firm. Since 1941 the AASLH has also published *History News*, a monthly concerning the activities of historical societies.

A substantial amount of interprofessional communication occurs among archivists, librarians, and historians due to blurring of lines between the three professions. Many individuals are active in at least two and sometimes all three types of professional associations. Of the members of the Society of American Archivists who responded to a 1971 survey, for instance, 21 percent were also members of the American Historical Association, 18 percent belonged to the Organization of American Historians, 33 percent belonged to a state historical association, 12 percent belonged to the American Library Association, 5 percent belonged to the Special Libraries Association, and 19 percent belonged to a state library association.[4]

Most professional communication, nevertheless, undoubtedly takes place within a particular profession. Few historians attend meetings of archival or library associations unless they are invited as speakers. Few librarians attend meetings of historical or archival associations unless they are responsible for manuscripts and need to learn something about practices in manuscript departments. Archivists rarely attend meetings of library associations, although many archivists are active in historical associations.

Means of effective interprofessional communication among archivists, librarians, and historians are vitally important for a number of reasons:

1. Joint or concerted action by associations in all three professions can be much more effective than action by a single association when it is necessary to attempt to influence decisions by federal, state, and local governments concerning legislation, appropriations, and other matters. Many issues affecting all three professions could be cited, and some have been discussed in previous chapters: copyright revision proposals concerning photocopying and literary rights in unpublished materials; attempts to amend the Tax Reform Act of 1969, which ended tax deductions for donations of personal papers and drastically reduced the flow of such materials to libraries; proposals for a National Historic Records Commission which would provide grants to public and private institutions throughout the United States for collecting and making available documentary sources; and adequate funding for archives, libraries, and agencies such as the National Historical Publications Commission and the National Endowments for the Arts and Humanities.

2. Other issues involving institutional policies affect all three professional groups. Examples are: policies on access, restrictions on use of classified or sensitive materials, library use fees, and policies on whether manuscripts and other unique or rare materials can be photocopied for researchers or published in microform or reprint editions. An exchange of viewpoints is essential to ensure that policies adopted by institutions and that statements on professional standards issued by associations are reasonable and desirable.

3. Archivists and librarians need to keep informed about the changing interests of historians, the state of research in different fields of history, and changing methodologies—such as increased reliance on statistics, computer processing of data, content analysis, and an interest in the visual evidence provided by photographs—that have an impact on the types of materials that historians want to examine.

4. Historians, as well as archivists and librarians, need to keep informed about new collecting programs and specialties of archives

and libraries, recent acquisitions, new bibliographies, and other guides to records.

5. Budgets for staff, equipment, and space for work with manuscripts in libraries with special collections, rare book, or manuscript departments depend upon recommendations by library administrators. If administrators do not fully understand the importance of manuscripts in research, or if they are unaware of the special problems posed by manuscripts, then budgets are likely to be insufficient for adequate programs of acquisition, processing, and description.

6. Many staff members in both archives and libraries lack part of the appropriate professional or graduate training, so the information they can obtain by attending professional meetings and institutes or by reading journals and other literature is a necessary part of their continuing education. This is true, for instance, when librarians or historians without archival training take positions in archival institutions or manuscript departments.

Archivists, librarians, and historians have made many attempts to improve interprofessional communication through joint programs, joint committees, and other means. The record is far from blank, although much remains to be done, as spokesmen for all three professions have stressed in recent years. The remainder of this part will discuss accomplishments and needs on the national, regional, and state levels.

NOTES

1. "Archival Organizations," *American Archivist* 37 (1974): 505–510. [See also similar sections in subsequent issues, which provide information on publications, meetings, other activities, and officers.]

2. The *Bowker Annual of Library and Book Trade Information*, 21st ed. (New York: R. R. Bowker, 1976), pp. 493–578. [Information on objectives, officers, committee chairmen, and publications of national and state library associations.]

3. American Association for State and Local History, *Directory of Historical Societies and Agencies in the United States and Canada, 1975–1976* (Nashville, Tenn.: AASLH, 1975).

4. Frank B. Evans and Robert M. Warner, "American Archivists and Their Society: A Composite View," *American Archivist* 34 (1971): 168–169.

HISTORIANS AND THE INFORMATION PROFESSIONS

To a greater extent than in most disciplines, historians must depend on libraries and archives for the great variety of sources needed for research. Almost any type of material on any subject may be grist for the historian's mill, but the total production of records is so immense that it is neither economically feasible nor desirable for everything to be retained, even in a national network of libraries and archives. Decisions on acquisition must be made, and although advice is often sought from scholars either individually or in advisory committees, most of the decisions must be made by librarians and archivists. If there is a single area in which communication is most important, therefore, it is communication concerning changing research interests, the nature of the sources likely to be needed both now and in the future, and guidelines for selection.

Almost equally important is the production of the complex array of catalogs, indexes, bibliographies, guides, and other finding aids that are necessary if research materials are to become fully accessible. Because of the variety of sources that historians use, the many time periods that they study, the range of subjects in which they are interested, and the lack of computer-based bibliographic retrieval services comparable to those available in the sciences, historians must consult a large number of general and specialized bibliographic tools. Many are produced by historians themselves, but most are the products of librarians, archivists, associations, and firms such as the American Bibliographical Center. Awareness of new bibliographic tools is important to historians, archivists, and librarians who must acquire these tools and utilize them in reference services.

The historical profession's concern about the adequacy of resources for research and bibliography has been evident from the earliest years of the American Historical Association. The first AHA standing committee was the Historical Manuscripts Commission, created in 1895, which made a preliminary survey of manuscripts and archives in American libraries, historical societies, and other institutions; published a list of printed guides to collections; sent circular letters to libraries urging them to use "the broadest possible construction in determining what manuscript accumulations are worthy of deposit"; and published the texts of many important documents in successive volumes of the AHA Annual Report.[1]

The work of the Historical Manuscripts Commission was supplemented after 1899 by the Public Archives Commission, which published a series of reports, generally prepared by historians, describing the public records of most states and several cities. These reports and other attempts to persuade state governments that reforms were long overdue helped bring about the creation of a number of state archival agencies. The American Historical Association was also active in the movement to establish a national archives, from 1908 until the National Archives Act was passed in 1934.[2]

An AHA Committee on Historical Source Materials, appointed in 1939, and subsequent special committees, were concerned with a broader range of research materials: archives, manuscripts, business records, newspapers, library holdings, documentary reproduction, and historical objects. Members of these committees included archivists and librarians as well as historians.[3]

A thorough examination of the adequacy of bibliographic services to history and means of improvement was conducted by the Joint Committee on Bibliographical Services to History, established in 1966, and consisted of representatives of the American Historical Association, the Organization of American Historians, American Association for State and Local History, Southern Historical Association, Western Historical Association, Agricultural History Society, National Historical Publications Commission, the Library of Congress, the American Biographical Center, and several other associations. The work of the committee culminated in a conference in 1967 held at the Belmont Conference Center of the Smithsonian Institution. Staff reports, working papers, reports concerning the conference, and recommendations for improved bibliographic services were published in *Bibliography and the Historian*. The American Historical Association subsequently established a Committee on Information Services to implement the conference's recommendations.[4]

The American Historical Association and the Organization of American Historians both publish some news concerning libraries and archival institutions in their journals. The news predominantly concerns recent acquisitions of manuscripts and archives or guides to such materials, but occasionally information is included about conferences, new collecting programs, bibliographies, appointments, and other matters. Before 1957 the *American Historical Review* included occasional notes on libraries and archives in a section on "Other Historical Activities," and between 1957 and 1966 there was a separate section on "Archives and Libraries." Subsequently, such news was transferred to a section on "Research and Publication" in the *AHA Newsletter*. The *Journal of American History* includes notes concerning libraries and archives in a section on "Historical News and Comments."[5]

Although historians are vitally interested in the adequacy of resources for research and bibliography, they generally show little or no interest in either library or archival methodology. Historians often take a condescending attitude not only toward librarians and archivists but also toward other historians engaged in bibliographic work or documentary editing rather than substantive research. This has changed somewhat in recent years because of the job crisis for historians. At the 1971 annual meeting of the American Historical Association, for instance, one historian, commenting on the restricted job market, objected to "a hierarchical structure that relegates archivists, junior college faculty and non-academically affiliated historians to the status of second-class citizens."[5]

A report on a session on The Historian and the Archivist held at Ohio State University during the 1972 annual meeting of the Society of American Archivists reflects the general attitude of disinterest. Attendance was outstanding, but few historians were present, despite the fact that one of the speakers was Thomas D. Clark, secretary of the Organization of American Historians. "The fact that no one from campus came to the afternoon session was particularly disappointing, although I had been warned that historians were not at all interested in learning about the archival profession," wrote the chairman of the program committee. "Nevertheless, I believed that this time we had all the necessary ingredients, including prominent speakers and advance publicity. The only mingling of historians and archivists on the Ohio State campus, however, occurred at the open-bar reception at the faculty club following the session."[6]

Important exceptions can be cited through the years. Some historians, realizing that the practices and policies of archives and libraries can either facilitate or impede research, have tried to exert influence by joining in a dialogue with archivists and librarians.

Beginning in 1909, for instance, a Conference of Archivists, held at annual meetings of the American Historical Association, was attended by historians as well as staff members of the new state archival agencies and libraries containing historical manuscripts. The Conference of Archivists, unlike the Historical Manuscripts Commission and the Public Archives Commission, focused primarily on aspects of archival management.[7]

Historians exerted great influence in the Society of American Archivists during the early years after it was founded in 1936. The impetus for the organization came largely from staff members of the newly established National Archives, but among the founding members were at least 20 academic historians, including the first president of the society, the first editor of the *American Archivist*, and the chairman of the important Committee on the Training of Archivists. In his presidential address on the "Objectives of the Society of American Archivists," historian A. R. Newsome called on the society "to foster a wider and more intensive interest in archives among the national organizations of historians, economists, sociologists, political scientists, statisticians, lawyers, and other learned professions."[8]

The Ad Hoc Committee on Manuscripts appointed by the American Historical Association in 1948 provides another example of the interest of historians in archival methodology. This committee, which consisted of three historians and three archivists or manuscript curators, was primarily concerned with the problems posed by large twentieth-century collections and made recommendations concerning acquisition policies, competition in collecting, arrangement, finding aids, procedures for safeguarding materials against theft, policies on the qualifications of users, restrictions on the use of manuscripts, and the adequacy of facilities for use.[9]

The communication gap between historians and archivists or librarians, nevertheless, seems to have widened during the next two decades. Philip C. Brooks commented in the *American Archivist* in 1951 that archivists had "gradually grown apart from the close relation with the historians that we had when this Society was established as an offshoot from the American Historical Association."[10] Walter Rundell, Jr., in a 1970 report on the use of documentary source materials in graduate training in history, concluded that a "major problem affecting research in United States history is the poor communication between professors of history and persons with other historical and curatorial vocations."[11]

A major step toward improving communication among historians and archivists was taken in 1972 with the creation of a Joint AHA–OAH–SAA Committee on Historians and Archives, which consists of three representatives from each association.

This joint committee was a salutary result of a major dispute between historians and archivists touched off in 1968 by charges from Professor Francis L. Loewenheim of Rice University that he had been a victim of unfair and discriminatory treatment. Among other things, Loewenheim charged that the Franklin D. Roosevelt Library had denied him access to some Roosevelt letters so that they could be published first in one of the library's documentary publications. Other historians joined the fray, including 20 who signed a letter published in the *New York Times* stating that the work of many scholars had been seriously affected because documents had been withheld from them. The final report of the Joint AHA–OAH Ad Hoc Committee, issued in August 1970, was a massive 448-page examination of the charges, countercharges, evidence, and conclusions.[12]

To provide a continuing forum for dealing with problems related to the impact of government policies and procedures on historical research, the American Historical Association and the Organization of American Historians established a Joint Committee on the Historian and Federal Government in the fall of 1969. During the next three years, the joint committee worked out some procedures for dealing with complaints; recommended that all federal records be transferred to the control of the archivist of the United States no more than 20 years after creation and, with clearly defined exceptions, be automatically declassified and made available for scholarly use at that time; and recommended changes in the publication of the Foreign Relations Series.[13]

Meanwhile, the Society of American Archivists protested the failure of both the Joint Ad Hoc Committee on the Roosevelt Library and the Joint Committee on the Historian and Federal Government to include any representatives of the archival profession. It seemed obvious that the SAA should have a role in the settlement of disputes between archivists and historians, and that recommendations on archival policies and practices would be more realistic if historians had an opportunity to hear comments by archivists on some of the problems that were involved. As a result, the Society of American Archivists was invited to become an equal sponsor of the committee, and at the October 1972 meeting, the committee's name was changed to include the SAA.[14]

The statement of purpose of the Joint AHA–OAH–SAA Committee on Historians and Archives, approved at a meeting on September 15, 1973, acknowledges that "the health of historical scholarship in this country depends to a very considerable extent on mutual confidence and goodwill between historians and archivists and a close and cordial working relationship between these two disciplines," and states that one objective of the committee is to eliminate sources of friction and misunderstanding. "The committee is especially concerned with working out means whereby historians will be better able to appreciate the methods, techniques, and policies used in administering archives and manuscript repositories and thus gain a better understanding of their needs. Archivists, on the other hand, must become thoroughly familiar with the needs and viewpoints of scholars who are dependent on access to manuscripts and archives collections in order to conduct their research."[15]

Since 1973 the Joint AHA–OAH–SAA Committee on Historians and Archives has issued guidelines for adjudicating disputes between historians and archivists, has issued a statement on user fees and access, has worked on a resolution concerning automatic declassification of national security documents, and has appointed subcommittees to consider such matters as the appraisal of papers for tax purposes. The committee has also made plans to study problems of access to other types of research materials.[16]

Some sessions at annual meetings during recent years have been especially designed to promote interprofessional communication. The Society of American Archivists has had sessions on Documenting Urban Society, Documenting Working Class History, Quantitative Approaches to History: Implications for Archivists, and similar topics. These focused on historical methodology as well as on the needed sources, and included both historians and archivists as speakers.

The American Library Association held similar sessions sponsored by the Rare Books and Manuscripts Section of the Association of College and Research Libraries or the Reference Service Division's History Section. Among these were sessions on problems of access to manuscript materials and preconference institutes on research collections in the Midwest and on the Pacific coast.

Programs at recent meetings of the Organization of American Historians also provided evidence of a desire to promote communication among archivists and historians. Archivists have appeared at sessions on topics such as Archival and Manuscripts Sources for the Study of Women's History, Archives of Public Programs for Social Welfare, and the Historian's Use of Illustrative Material. The American Historical Association has done less, but sessions have been held on topics such as Access to Government Documents and Sources for American Indian Historiography.

There have been increased opportunities for interprofessional communication among historians and the information professions during recent years. Attendance by historians at meetings of archival and library associations, nevertheless, will probably continue to be sparse. It is highly desirable for historical associations to schedule more sessions concerning archival and library aspects of research with panels consisting of representatives from all three professions. And archival institutions and libraries should encourage their staff members to attend meetings of historical associations, especially sessions concerning changing research interests, methodology, and needed sources.

NOTES

1. J. Franklin Jameson et al., "Report of the Historical Manuscripts Commission," *Annual Report of the American Historical Association for the Year 1896*, Vol. 1 (Washington, D.C.: U.S. Govt. Printing Office, 1897), pp. 467–512 (hereinafter cited as *Annual Report of the AHA for . . .*); see also subsequent reports of the commission in AHA annual reports.

2. Ernst Posner, *American State Archives* (Chicago: University of Chicago Press, 1964), pp. 18–19; H. G. Jones, *The Records of a Nation: Their Management, Preservation, and Use* (New York: Atheneum, 1969), pp. 6–8.

3. Herbert A. Kellar, "The Committee on Historical Source Materials," *Annual Report of the AHA for 1939*, Vol. 1 (Washington, D.C.: U.S. Govt. Printing Office, 1941), pp. 71–82; see also subsequent reports of the committee in AHA annual reports.

4. Oron J. Hale, "Joint Committee on Bibliographical Services to History," *Annual Report of the AHA for 1966*, Vol. 1 (Washington, D.C.: Smithsonian Institution Press, n.d.), pp. 76–77; Dagmar Horna Perman, ed., *Bibliography and the Historian: The Conference at Belmont of the Joint Committee on Bibliographical Services to History, May 1967* (Santa Barbara, Cal.: Clio Press, 1968); Aubrey C. Land, "Committee on Information Services," *Annual Re-*

port of the AHA for 1968, Vol. 1 (Washington, D.C.: Smithsonian Institution Press, n.d.), pp. 130–131.

5. "Jobs for Historians and the Role of the AHA: Two Comments Delivered at the Annual Meeting," *AHA Newsletter* 10 (1972): 21.

6. Herman J. Viola. " 'Come to Columbus!' The SAA 36th Annual Meeting Revisited," *American Archivist* 36 (1973): 235.

7. Waldo Gifford Leland, "The First Conference of Archivists, December 1909: The Beginnings of a Profession," *American Archivist* 13 (1950): 109–120; "Proceedings of the First Annual Conference of Archivists," *Annual Report of the AHA for 1909*, Vol. 1 (Washington, D.C.: U.S. Govt. Printing Office, 1911), pp. 339–490.

8. Philip C. Brooks, "The First Decade of the Society of American Archivists," *American Archivist* 10 (1947): 117–119; Lester J. Cappon, "The Archival Profession and the Society of American Archivists," *American Archivist* 15 (1952): 197; Society of American Archivists, *Proceedings, Providence, R.I., December 29–30, 1936 and Washington, D.C., June 18–19, 1937* (Urbana, Ill.: SAA, 1937), pp. 5, 61–64.

9. Thomas C. Cochran et al., "Report of the Ad Hoc Committee on Manuscripts," *Annual Report of the AHA for 1950*, Vol. 1 (Washington, D.C.: U.S. Govt. Printing Office, n.d.), pp. 64–71.

10. Philip C. Brooks, "Archivists and Their Colleagues: Common Denominators," *American Archivist* 14 (1951): 44.

11. Walter Rundell, Jr., *In Pursuit of American History: Research and Training in the United States* (Norman: University of Oklahoma Press, 1970), pp. 326–327.

12. "Final Report of the Joint AHA–OAH Ad Hoc Committee to Investigate the Charges Against the Franklin D. Roosevelt Library and Related Matters, August 24, 1970" (American Historical Association and Organization of American Historians, n.p.).

13. Reports of the Joint Committee (AHA–OAH) on the Historian and the Federal Government, *Annual Report of the AHA for 1970* (Washington, D.C.: Smithsonian Institution Press, n.d.), pp. 135–137; *Annual Report of the AHA for 1971* (Washington, D.C.: Smithsonian Institution Press, n.d.), pp. 142–143.

14. Report of SAA Council Meeting, October 31, 1972, *American Archivist* 36 (1973): 308; Report of the Joint Committee (AHA–OAH) on the Historian and the Federal Government, *Annual Report of the AHA for 1972* (Washington, D.C.: Smithsonian Institution Press, n.d.), p. 119.

15. "Statement of Objectives by the Joint Committee on Historians and Archives," *AHA Newsletter* 11 (1973): 39–40.

16. *American Archivist* 36 (1973): 303, 474; 37 (1974): 159–160, 171, 370; "Statement on User Fees and Access by the Joint Committee on Historians and Archives," *AHA Newsletter* 12 (1974): 3.

THE SOCIETY OF AMERICAN ARCHIVISTS
AND THE AMERICAN LIBRARY ASSOCIATION

For 40 years, the Society of American Archivists has sought, with considerable success, to promote communication and cooperation among individuals and institutions concerned with archives, manuscripts, and current records. Its constitution states that the objectives of the SAA include the adoption of sound principles and standards by all agencies that have responsibility for the preservation and administration of records; the stimulation of research on archival administration and records management and publication of the results; and the development of standards and facilities for training archivists, records managers, and custodians of private papers. The constitution also states that the SAA was established "to maintain and strengthen relations with historians, librarians, educators, public administrators, and others in allied disciplines; and to cooperate with other professional organizations, cultural and educational institutions, and international organizations having mutual interests in the preservation and use of man's recorded heritage."[1]

The composition of the membership has changed somewhat through the years as new types of collecting agencies were established or became more widespread. At first most members worked for state archival agencies and the National Archives. Gradually more and more members came from university archives, special collections departments, regional history collections, manuscript departments in colleges and universities, public and other libraries, historical societies, and archives established by businesses, churches, and other organizations. More SAA members now work for colleges and universities than for any other single type of agency.[2] Until recently the work of the organization was carried out entirely through the voluntary efforts of the officers, council, and committees.

By the late 1960s it was increasingly apparent that a full-time professional staff was sorely needed. The Committee of the 1970s, appointed in 1970 to study the structure, objectives, and program of the society, strongly recommended that an executive director be employed to meet the growing needs and demands of the membership, initiate and supervise new programs, maintain effective liaison with other professional organizations, monitor state and federal legislation affecting the archival profession, and seek grants and other necessary funds.[3] At the annual meeting in Columbus in 1972, the membership voted to change the position of an elected secretary to an executive director appointed by the council. The office was filled on a voluntary basis until 1974, when a dues increase made sufficient funds available to employ the society's first full-time, paid executive director and an assistant.[4]

181

SAA members have an opportunity to participate in approximately 28 committees. Specific types of institutions or subjects are the focus of committees such as those on archives of science, labor archives, business archives, urban archives, and college and university archives. Some committees are concerned with special forms of materials: aural and graphic records, data archives, and oral history. Procedures and other special aspects of work with archives and manuscripts are dealt with by committees on collecting personal papers and manuscripts, finding aids, reference and access policies, and preservation methods. Among the other committees are those on education and professional development, status of women, professional standards, paper research, international archival affairs, and archives-library relationships.[5]

Annual meetings of the SAA try to provide a diversified program to meet the needs of both experienced and beginning archivists and manuscript curators in all types of institutions. An annual meeting now includes 30 or more sessions and workshops over a four-day period, plus luncheon and dinner meetings, meetings of the council and committees, a business meeting, mixers, and tours of libraries and archival institutions.

Sessions at recent annual meetings have been devoted to such topics as restrictions on access to manuscripts and archives, literary rights, problems of confidentiality in personal case records, and ethical responsibilities of researchers. Conservation was discussed in sessions on breakthroughs in paper research, the rehabilitation of water-damaged records, and in workshops on paper conservation techniques and the conservation of visual materials. There were sessions on film, still pictures, and information retrieval from audiovisual archives. Oral history was touched on in several sessions, including one on tape recording black history. A session on archival security discussed major incidents of theft during recent years and suggested means of preventing further losses. Other workshops and sessions were devoted to such topics as finding aids, reference, exhibits, publications, microphotography, automation, and records management. ·

The *American Archivist*, a quarterly published by the SAA since 1938, is the major professional journal in the United States concerning archives and manuscripts. Most issues contain articles on a variety of subjects as well as news notes and reviews. Some issues contain a group of articles focused on a particular aspect of archival administration, such as automation in archives and manuscript collections, archives of the arts, archival training, and women in archives.

The *American Archivist* provides a means of learning about other archival literature—not only through book reviews but also through a selective bibliography (published annually since 1943), "Writings on Archives, Historical Manuscripts, and Current Records." The bibliography includes periodical articles, books, and other publications, arranged by topic in nine major categories and subdivisions. It is international in scope, including some articles in French, Italian, Spanish, German, Russian, and other languages, although most are in English. There is a time lag of about 18 months between the period covered and publication of the bibliography, so *Library Literature* must be consulted for more recent citations.

The "News Notes" present "comprehensive news about recent accessions and openings; published finding aids and documentary materials, both letterpress and microform; administrative and program changes at archival institutions; activities of state and regional archival associations; and education and training opportunities in the fields of archives administration and records management."[6] The *American Archivist* provides much more news on these subjects than similar departments in historical journals or *College & Research Libraries News*.

Other types of news are provided by three other departments of the *American Archivist*. "Technical Notes" contains information concerning new equipment and supplies, innovations in conservation, microreproduction, automation, and similar processes. "The International Scene: News and Abstracts" provides extensive coverage of international news about archives and abstracts from foreign periodicals. A section entitled "The Society of American Archivists" contains minutes of council meetings; reports of officers, the executive director, and committees; statements on standards; and other news concerning the society.

The *American Archivist* is supplemented by a newsletter issued six times annually. This began in 1967 as a *Placement Newsletter*, listing job vacancies and applicants. In 1973 the council decided to expand the scope of the newsletter and change the name to the *SAA Newsletter*. In addition to placement information, the eight-page newsletter now contains announcements concerning such matters as SAA elections, candidates, proposed amendments to the constitution and bylaws, suggested standards of archival procedures, recent publications of interest to archivists, archival courses, and professional meetings.

The SAA also has a small but important program to publish or sponsor monographs and occasional publications. *American State Archives*, Ernst Posner's thorough study of agencies and their programs, was sponsored by the SAA with funds provided by the Council on Library Resources and published by the University of Chicago Press in 1964. *Archives & the Public Interest*, a collection of essays by Posner, who taught archival courses and summer institutes at American University in Washington, D.C., was published for the SAA by Public Affairs Press. H. G. Jones' *The Records of a Nation*, published by Atheneum in 1969, was commissioned by a joint committee established by the SAA, the American Historical Association, and the Organization of American Historians to study the organization, programs, and progress of the National Archives and Records Service. Other publications include a *Reader for Archives and Records Center Buildings*, a *Forms Manual*, and directories of *College and University Archives*, *State and Provincial Archivists*, *Business Archives*, and *Individual and Institutional Members*.

Regional symposia on archival administration sponsored by the SAA and held throughout the United States since 1964 have been another important means of professional communication. Seventy-six symposia were held by 1972, attended by almost six thousand people, and cosponsored by the National Archives and Records Service, 22 state libraries or archives, 6 historical societies, and 48 educational institutions. In 1969 the secretary reported that "these meetings have been extremely useful in interpreting the work of the society and in providing professional assistance to organizations and institutions in the early stages of inaugurating archival programs."[7]

Although the Society of American Archivists is the major professional organization in the United States for archivists and manuscript curators, the American Library Association also provides means of communication in this area. The Rare Books and Manuscripts Section of the Association of College and Research Libraries (a division of ALA) sponsors an important series of preconferences and sessions at ALA annual meetings. These programs are especially useful for staff members of the many colleges and universities, public libraries, and other research libraries in which manuscripts are administered as part of a special collections or rare books department. The policies and problems of such departments, and the many interrelationships between rare books and manuscripts, cannot always be explored adequately in a professional association devoted solely to manuscripts and archives.

The ALA's interest in archives and manuscripts goes back at least to 1935, when the ALA established a Committee on Archives and Libraries.[8] This was not, however, the first such committee established by a library association. In 1910 the National Association of State Libraries (NASL) formed a Committee on Public Archives, which published annual reports during the following decade on legal provisions for state and local archives and activities of archival agencies, and continued to sponsor occasional sessions on archives at annual meetings until the late 1930s.[9]

The ALA Committee on Archives and Libraries (CAL) was active until 1956 and was an important means of communication among librarians, archivists, manuscript curators, and staff of special collections departments. This was especially true during its first decade, when programs at annual meetings generally included eight or nine papers on archival topics that were subsequently published. The membership included representatives of both the library and archival professions, such as A. F.

Kuhlman of the Joint University Libraries in Nashville, who served as chairman during the first five years; R. D. W. Connor, archivist of the United States; David C. Mearns, chief of the Division of Manuscripts at the Library of Congress, and chairman during the early 1950s; and Jacqueline P. Bull, head of the Department of Special Collections at the University of Kentucky Library, the last chairman before the committee was discontinued.[10]

The CAL's first report conceded that some "problems peculiar to the organization and administration of public archives" could be dealt with more effectively by the Society of American Archivists, but the committee believed that "archivists and librarians have certain common problems" that the committee should explore.[11] Margaret C. Norton of the Illinois State Archives, the chairman during the early 1940s, later wrote that the objective of the committee was "to act as a medium for exchange of information between librarians and archivists in those fields in which their techniques overlap," and that during the first five years "the programs were devoted largely to enlightening librarians as to the purpose, scope of work, and problems of archivists in the interest of more effective cooperation. This information was eagerly sought by librarians, many of whom, especially state librarians, are administrative heads over archival agencies and manuscript collections."[12]

For some years the ALA published an annual volume containing papers presented at programs sponsored by the CAL, at first as part of an earlier annual containing proceedings of the Committee on Public Documents. In 1939 a separate volume entitled *Archives and Libraries* was published, containing papers presented at a joint meeting of the CAL, Pacific coast members of the SAA, and the Historical Records Survey. A similar volume was published in 1940 for a joint meeting of the CAL, Midwest members of the SAA, the Conference on Historical Societies, and an ALA Committee on Bibliography. World War II subsequently brought about the demise of the annual and curtailment of the programs. There were still occasional sessions on archives at annual meetings, but proceedings were no longer published, and reports of the committee in the *ALA Bulletin* shrank to little more than lists of members.[13]

The present Rare Books and Manuscripts Section evolved from a Committee on Rare Books, Manuscripts, and Special Collections formed within the Association of College and Research Libraries in 1955. The programs at ALA annual meetings sponsored by the committee during the first few years all included some discussion of manuscripts: the purchase of rare books and manuscripts, the project to publish the Adams Papers, and conservation. The committee also formulated plans for a manual on rare books, eventually published in 1965 as an ACRL monograph edited by H. Richard Archer, *Rare Book Collections*, which included incidental references to manuscripts. A proposal to reorganize the committee and give it section status was introduced at the 1957 annual meeting and effected at the next midwinter meeting.[14]

The Rare Books Section, at its first meeting in 1958, began planning a conference to precede the ALA annual meetings that would provide more extensive opportunities for discussion of rare books. The first ACRL Rare Books Conference, held at the University of Virginia in 1959, focused largely on the subjects to be covered in the rare book manual, but it also included an address by David C. Mearns on the need to support the National Union Catalog of Manuscript Collections. A few of the subsequent conferences—held annually beginning in 1961 and called preconference institutes beginning in 1963—devoted some attention to manuscripts. The preconference institute on Western Americana in 1963, for instance, brought together historians—who discussed current trends in their disciplines—and librarians or archivists, such as Delores C. Renze, director of the Colorado State Archives, who discussed available resources, gaps, and problems. Most preconference institutes, however, had little or nothing to do with manuscripts.[15]

The impetus for the transformation of the Rare Books Section into the Rare Books and Manuscripts Section came from Richard C. Berner of the University of Washington and other manuscript curators who met at the San Francisco Conference in 1967 to consider organizing a separate group within ALA concerned with manuscripts. Berner, an active member of SAA who believed that librarians needed more opportunities to learn about the special problems involved in processing and describing manuscripts, presented the results of a survey indicating that many ALA members would like to join such a group. Arline Custer, editor of the National Union Catalog of Manuscript Collections, pointed out that many collections were located in libraries that did not have full-time manuscript curators, and she strongly supported creation of a group within ALA that could assist librarians assigned responsibility for manuscripts. Objections were posed by Herman Kahn of the National Archives, who believed that the SAA was sufficient for both manuscript curators and archivists and that fragmentation was undesirable. Thereupon, William H. Runge of the University of Virginia invited the group to join the Rare Books Section. After further negotiations, the Rare Books Section established a Committee on Manuscript Collections in 1969, and, at a business meeting in 1971 following a preconference institute on the Interdependence of Rare Books and Manuscripts, the name of the section was changed to the Rare Books and Manuscripts Section.[16]

Preconference institutes, sponsored by the ACRL Rare Books and Manuscripts Section (RBMS) since 1972, have included few sessions devoted exclusively to manuscripts, but the institutes do devote a great deal of attention to interrelationships among manuscripts, rare books, and other research materials. Other ALA programs concerning manuscripts have included a series on access sponsored by the RBMS Committee on Manuscript Collections as part of its work on an ACRL standards statement concerning access to manuscripts.[17] The RBMS programs are by no means a substitute for those offered by the SAA, which generally explore issues related to manuscripts in much greater depth. But the RBMS programs are extremely valuable to librarians responsible for both manuscripts and other research materials.

Programs concerning archives and manuscripts are occasionally sponsored by other units of ALA, especially the History Section of the Reference and Adult Services Division. The History Section was organized in 1961 to "represent librarians, archivists, bibliographers, documentalists, and others who may be interested in reference and research in the history field" and to be "concerned with the problems of history departments of large municipal and university libraries, archives and history departments of state agencies, historical societies and special historical collections, and the local history interests of small public, school, and business libraries." Programs have focused on such topics as audiovisual materials as historical archives, with Philip P. Mason, then secretary of the SAA, as one of the speakers; and on automation and historical research, with Frank G. Burke of the National Archives discussing automated finding aids for archives and manuscripts.[18]

A great deal of interprofessional communication took place between librarians and archivists during the late 1930s. Many archivists and manuscript curators spoke at ALA meetings, and some librarians spoke at SAA meetings. The founding members of the SAA included a few librarians, and the ALA Committee on Archives and Libraries included archivists.

Relations between the two professions deteriorated during the 1940s. The widening gap was noted in 1951 by Philip C. Brooks who stated that librarians and archivists had grown "unduly far apart." Brooks believed that this resulted in part from a controversy at a joint ALA–SAA meeting in the late 1930s over whether librarians or historians should train archivists and from statements by library leaders that archival work was merely a subordinate branch of library science.[19] Randolph W. Church of the Virginia State Library, for instance, in a 1943 article on "The Relationship between Archival Agencies and Libraries," contended that a subject arrangement should be used for archives and that the archival principle of "respect pour les fonds" could be "a serious impediment to the use" of records.[20] In a rebuttal published the next year, entitled "Librarians and Archivists—Some Aspects of Their Partnership," Herman Kahn replied that "no one can doubt that libraries and archival institutions must of necessity work closely together," but there was "no need to jump from such a premise to the conclusion that archival agencies and libraries ought to be governed by the same principles, and that techniques which are sound in the one agency are equally sound in the other."[21]

By 1951 Brooks believed that the situation had improved. Citing examples of archives-library cooperation, he stated that he thought that "we have now gone past the stage of misunderstanding with most leaders of the library profession, and that we mutually appreciate our interests in many common problems."[22]

Relations were further strained in 1956, nevertheless, by the publication of a report by the National Association of State Libraries on *The Role of the State Library*. The SAA sent a formal protest to the NASL against the proposed inclusion of archival services among the responsibilities of state libraries, stating that the "study of librarianship and library work experience, while pertinent, cannot provide adequately professional training and work experience for effective archival administration, disproving the library's exclusive right to jurisdiction in matters archival."[23]

The movement to establish an ALA manuscript group also caused concern within the SAA. Philip P. Mason's report as secretary for 1967–1968 regarded the new group as one more example of an alarming tendency to splinter the archival profession. There was, he contended, "no basis for a separate organization of manuscript custodians. The charge by a few of the individuals who formed this new association that the Society was not concerned or interested in the problems of manuscript curators is ridiculous and should be exposed." Mason pointed out that recent annual meetings had devoted considerable attention to manuscripts. "Regardless of the motives of the sponsors of such competing organizations," he urged, "the Society must take strong action to discourage such splintering of the profession."[24]

As a result of this concern, the SAA took steps that eventually led to the creation of a Joint SAA–ALA Committee on Archives–Library Relationships. At meetings in October 1969 the SAA council decided that the SAA should devote more attention to manuscript operations administered by research libraries and staffed by librarians, discussed the feasibility of establishing closer ties with the library profession, and authorized SAA President Herman Kahn to try to arrange a joint meeting with the ACRL Rare Books Section at its next preconference.[25]

Subsequent negotiations between the SAA and ALA resulted in the creation of the Joint SAA–ALA Committee on Archives–Library Relationships in 1970. A Committee on Archives–Library Relationships was created within the SAA in January, and the SAA and ALA agreed to jointly sponsor a program at the ALA meeting in July. Shortly thereafter, ALA Executive Director David H. Clift wrote to SAA President Herman Kahn to propose a joint SAA–ALA committee that would be composed of five members: two appointed by the SAA and three—including the chairman—by the ALA. After an agreement was reached that the SAA and ALA would alternate each year in appointing the chairman, the creation of the joint committee was formally approved by both organizations. The membership was subsequently increased from five to seven, with one additional member appointed by each organization.[26]

Each year at ALA and SAA meetings, the Joint SAA–ALA Committee on Archives–Library Relationships has sponsored programs such as a session at an ALA meeting on the place of archival training in library education and a session at an SAA meeting on the handling of ephemeral materials such as pamphlets found in manuscript collections. Potentially even more important, the joint committee's meetings have provided a forum for discussion of mutual needs, problems, objectives, and issues. The SAA Committee on Archives–Library Relationships has also been continued, enabling other SAA members to participate in such discussions.

Another important means of developing a better understanding of archives and manuscripts among librarians is the publication of articles on this subject in library periodicals. Librarians who are especially interested in archives and manuscripts, of course, are likely to read the *American Archivist* or other archival journals or attend meetings of archival associations. But more librarians might develop a broader appreciation of this specialty if more articles on archives and manuscripts appeared in the periodicals that librarians customarily read.

The number of such articles through the years has been small. In connection with recommendations to the SAA Committee on Archives–Library Relationships in 1972, Miriam I. Crawford analyzed the items listed in *Library Literature* under "archival," "archives," and "archivists" but not "manuscripts" for the period 1961–1971. During those years, there were five articles in *College & Research Libraries*, two in *Library Resources & Technical Services*, none in *RQ*, one in *Library Quarterly*, one in *Library Trends*, seven in *Special Libraries*, thirteen—mostly news notes—in *Library Journal*, and a few in other periodicals. Crawford found only one item in the official ALA journal, *American Libraries*, and none in its predecessor, the *ALA Bulletin*.[27] A check of the indexes to the *ALA Bulletin* reveals that it included no articles on archives or manuscripts during the preceding decade, 1950–1960, although there were about 20 notes concerning the Committee on Archives and Libraries.

Crawford urged the SAA Committee on Archives–Library Relationships to encourage archivists to contribute articles to library periodicals. During the 1970s a few additional articles have appeared, some of which may have been sparked by committee discussions, but it is too early to know whether the quantity of such articles will be larger in the 1970s than in the 1960s.

If relatively little concerning archives and manuscripts has appeared in library periodicals, even less concerning library operations—other than those involving manuscripts—has appeared in the *American Archivist* or other archival journals. Now that archival leaders have acknowledged that important benefits can be obtained from joint exploration of common problems, it is time for archival journals to include occasional articles that comment on recent developments in librarianship and their potential value to archivists.

NOTES

1. "Constitution and Bylaws of the Society of American Archivists," *American Archivist* 33 (1970): 263–268.
2. Frank B. Evans and Robert M. Warner, "American Archivists and Their Society: A Composite View," *American Archivist* 34 (1971): 159, 163.
3. Philip P. Mason, "The Society of American Archivists in the Seventies: Report of the Committee for the 1970's," *American Archivist* 35 (1972): 195–196.
4. *American Archivist* 36 (1973): 133; 37 (1974): 511–512.
5. "Committees for 1973–74," *American Archivist* 37 (1974): 179–182.
6. Daniel T. Goggin and Carmen R. Delle Donne, eds., "News Notes," *American Archivist* 37 (1974): 487.
7. A. K. Johnson, Jr., "Report of the Committee on Membership Development," *American Archivist* 28 (1965): 150; Paul A. Kohl, "Report of the Committee on Symposia and Regional Activities," *American Archivist* 37 (1974): 148; Philip P. Mason, "Secretary's Annual Report, 1967–68," *American Archivist* 32 (1969): 61.
8. *ALA Bulletin* 30 (1936): 88; 50 (1956): 712.
9. Ernst Posner, *American State Archives* (Chicago: University of Chicago Press, 1964), pp. 24–25.
10. See reports of the Committee on Archives and Libraries in issues of the *ALA Bulletin* for the years 1937–1957.
11. A. F. Kuhlman, "Report of the Committee on Archives and Libraries," *ALA Bulletin* 31 (1937): 550–551.
12. Margaret C. Norton, "Report of the Committee on Archives and Libraries," *ALA Bulletin* 36 (1942): 699–700.
13. American Library Association, Committee on Public Documents, "Public Documents," ed. by J. K. Wilcox (papers presented in 1937 and 1938 at the Conference of the American Library Association, n.p.); American Library Association, Committee on Archives and Libraries, "Archives and Libraries," ed. by A. F. Kuhlman (papers presented in 1939 and 1940 at the Conference of the American Library Association, n.p.).
14. ALA Annual Conference Proceedings, 1955, p. 33; 1956, p. 15; 1957, p. 19.
15. ALA Annual Conference Proceedings, 1958, p. 21; 1959, p. 12; Marjorie Gray Wynne, "The First ACRL Rare Books Conference," *College & Research Libraries* 20 (1959): 320.
16. ALA Annual Conference Proceedings, 1967, p. 166; 1968, p. 40; 1969, p. 124; 1971, p. 109.

17. ALA Annual Conference Programs, 1972, pp. 53–55; 1973, pp. 53–55; 1974, p. 57; Clyde C. Walton, "Access Denied? The Use of Manuscript Material," *College & Research Libraries* 35 (1974): 285; "ACRL RBMS Manuscripts Collections Committee," *Library of Congress Information Bulletin* 33 (1974): A-189.

18. American Library Association, News Release, September 6, 1961, in ALA Headquarters Library; ALA Annual Conference Programs, 1961–1974.

19. Philip C. Brooks, "Archivists and Their Colleagues: Common Denominators," *American Archivist* 14 (1951): 40.

20. Randolph W. Church, "The Relationship between Archival Agencies and Libraries," *American Archivist* 6 (1943): 145–150.

21. Herman Kahn, "Librarians and Archivists—Some Aspects of Their Partnership," *American Archivist* 7 (1944): 243.

22. Brooks, "Archivists and Their Colleagues," pp. 40–41.

23. "Minutes of the Council, December 29, 1958," *American Archivist* 22 (1959): 351; Dan M. Robison, "Archival Services of State Libraries," *American Archivist* 22 (1959): 197–198.

24. Philip P. Mason, "Secretary's Annual Report, 1967–68," *American Archivist* 32 (1969): 62–63.

25. "Minutes of the Council, October 7 and 10, 1969," *American Archivist* 33 (1970): 113, 125.

26. Elizabeth Hamer Kegan, "Report of the Joint SAA–ALA Committee on Archives–Library Relationships," *American Archivist* 36 (1973): 324–325; "Minutes of the Council, September 29, 1970," *American Archivist* 34 (1971): 88; "Minutes of the Council, December 29, 1970," *American Archivist* 34 (1971): 217.

27. Letter, Miriam I. Crawford to Robert L. Brubaker, October 14, 1974, enclosing copy of letter, Miriam I. Crawford to Elizabeth E. Hamer, February 7, 1972; and unpublished list, "Archives References in 'Library Literature,' 1961–1971 (August), to Periodicals Most Used by Librarians," August 1972.

REGIONAL AND STATE ASSOCIATIONS

The regional and state archival associations established since 1966 have taken an increasingly important role in professional communication. Discussions at meetings of the new associations and elsewhere make it clear that they can perform some functions better than a national organization.

Many archivists and librarians are unable to attend meetings of national associations because of the expense of travel to distant cities. This is especially true for junior staff members who have neither the funds nor freedom to attend a four- or five-day meeting. The regional and state archival associations, whose meetings are shorter and require much less travel, make it possible for those who cannot attend SAA meetings to participate in a meaningful way in a professional association.

Many staff members responsible for archives and manuscripts—the experienced as well as novices, and those who attend SAA meetings as well as those who cannot—feel a need for more opportunities to become acquainted with other archivists and manuscript curators in their state and region, to learn about the holdings and practices of other institutions in the surrounding area, and to discuss common problems. Archivists and manuscript curators in smaller and medium-sized institutions—which frequently have only one or two staff members in this specialty, but numerous librarians—are especially likely to feel isolated. Consequently, the provision of additional opportunities to become acquainted has become one of the most important functions of the new associations. "Our members want desperately to meet their peers in neighboring institutions," reported the *Mid-Atlantic Archivist*, "and found they could afford to come to Wilmington for two days when they could not make it to Columbus for five."[1]

Another need was frequently cited by those who organized the regional and state archival associations—basic training. Newcomers to the archival profession—especially those who have never taken any courses concerning archives—sometimes find that SAA sessions assume too much prior knowledge and fail to provide the basic information that paraprofessionals or junior staff members need. Conversely, experienced archivists dislike attending sessions that cover familiar ground. Because the regional and state archival associations are especially interested in attracting junior staff members and paraprofessionals, it has seemed logical for these associations to concentrate heavily—though not exclusively—on introductory sessions and workshops. "The regionals," wrote one of the founders of the Mid-Atlantic Regional Archives Conference, "have a clear mission to basic training in a field without training standards or certification, which they have correctly seized on."[2] (The SAA, nevertheless, continues to include some introductory sessions and workshops at annual meetings. And even though the advanced sessions seek to avoid repetition of basic information, they are usually quite intelligible to those who do not have prior archival training.)

The regional and state archival associations were organized as separate groups with no formal ties to the SAA, although the founders of the new associations included some of the most active members of the SAA, and at least three groups received funds for initial expenses from the SAA council.[3] The creation of separate associations aroused anxiety and opposition within the SAA. Some SAA members viewed the new associations as competing groups that would drain away members from the SAA and make it difficult for the SAA to raise sufficient funds to hire a full-time professional staff. SAA President Clifford K. Shipton, for instance, argued in 1968 that it was a mistake to establish separate associations when the SAA was not yet large enough to support a full-time secretary-treasurer.[4] And a newsletter issued by one of the regional associations commented in 1973 that some SAA members were "uneasy lest newcomers undermine, circumvent, and even destroy the existing structure of the SAA."[5]

Some apprehension was evident even among those who acknowledged that the new associations were needed. In a statement in the program for the 1972 annual meeting, SAA Secretary Robert M. Warner supported the creation of state and regional associations, but stressed the need for a vigorous national organization that could "present a voice strong enough to merit attention" from other professional groups such as historians and librarians, monitor legislation, develop professional standards, provide job placement programs, and publish an effective national archival journal and other materials. It is "healthy and hopeful" that regional and state archival associations are emerging, Warner wrote. "But we must not foster the mistaken premise that these new associations will replace the SAA. If there is to be a separate archival profession, there must be a national society."[6]

Many SAA members urged that some type of formal affiliation between the SAA and the state and regional associations should be negotiated. "As they succeed without our assistance, I fear they will tend to think they can do very nicely without us," wrote F. Gerald Ham in his report as SAA secretary for 1970–1971.[7] The Committee for the 1970s recommended either chapter affiliation in which all members of state and regional organizations would automatically be members of the SAA or some looser form of affiliation in which state and regional organizations would state in their publications and promotional material that they were affiliated with the SAA.[8]

The state and regional associations, however, generally opposed affiliation. The issue was discussed during the SAA annual meeting in Columbus in 1972 at a session on the emergence and functions of the state and regional associations and relationships between them and the SAA. Most of the participants agreed that the state and regional associations should cooperate with the SAA and work together toward common goals, but they were not in favor of affiliation.[9]

The functions and respective roles of the SAA and the state and regional associations were further explored at a symposium in Chicago on April 12, 1973, attended by most SAA officers and council members and representatives of the state and regional associations. The symposium emphasized cooperation: SAA council members affirmed that the SAA would do all it could to assist the regional and state associations through the SAA speakers bureau and other services, and representatives of the associations agreed that they should promote voluntary membership in the SAA.[10]

All but five of the regional and state archival associations publish newsletters or journals. *Georgia Archive*, published by the Society of Georgia Archivists, is a journal with longer articles as well as news notes, and contains about 60 pages per issue. The *Mid-Atlantic Archivist* grew to 24 pages per issue by 1974, when the Mid-Atlantic Regional Archives Conference began discussing the possibility of dividing it into a shorter newsletter and a journal similar to *Georgia Archive*.[11] The *Newsletter of the Midwest Archives Conference* contained approximately 36 pages per issue by 1974, when this association also began discussing plans for a journal, possibly entitled the *Midwestern Archivist*, and a shorter newsletter.[12] Shorter newsletters are issued by the New England Archivists, the Michigan Archival Association (*Open Entry*, published twice a year), the Society of Indiana Archivists (quarterly), the Northwest Archivists (quarterly), the Society of California Archivists (quarterly), and the Society of Ohio Archivists (*Ohio Archivist*). The Society of Southwest Archivists planned a bimonthly newsletter, but only one issue has appeared. The Long Island Archives Conference was offered space in a newsletter published by the Long Island Library Resources Council, but is considering publication of a newsletter of its own.[13]

All of the newsletters contain notes concerning the associations themselves and institutions within the particular state or region. Some newsletters also contain short articles that discuss a current issue or provide an overview of the holdings, development, and policies of a particular institution. *Georgia Archive* usually contains at least one major article concerning a particular institution. Shorter articles with a similar focus appear as a continuing feature under the heading "Institutional Spotlight" in the *Mid-Atlantic Archivist* and the *Newsletter of the Midwest Archives*

Conference. Institutional acquisitions are described regularly in newsletters issued by four associations. Several newsletters contain book reviews.

A few associations also issue other publications. The Society of Ohio Archivists, with the assistance of the Ohio Historical Society and the Ohio Network of American History Research Centers, published a 300-page *Guide to Manuscript Collections & Institutional Records in Ohio*. The Michigan Archival Association published a *Directory of Archival and Cultural Associations in Michigan* and has in progress a bibliography of manuscripts on microfilm in Michigan repositories. The Society of California Archivists announced in 1973 that a *Directory of California Archival Repositories* was in progress.[14] By 1974 the Midwest Archives Conference was also discussing plans for a more extensive publications program.[15]

The state and regional library associations have a much longer history and a larger membership than the state and regional archival associations. Through their meetings and journals, the library associations meet the needs of most public and academic librarians for communication on a state and regional level. These associations, however, rarely devote much attention to archives and manuscripts.

Articles on these subjects do appear infrequently in state library journals. Between 1961 and 1971, at least 78 articles concerning archives appeared in 22 state and regional library periodicals.[16] But 30 of the articles appeared in one journal, *Illinois Libraries*, which each year devotes an Archives Issue to the Illinois State Archives and other archival and manuscript repositories in the state. Most of the other state library journals published no more than one or two articles concerning archives during the decade.

Neither the archival nor the library associations appear to have given any thought to the possibility of promoting communication and cooperation among librarians and archivists on the state and regional levels similar to the efforts on the national level. Several archival associations have established relationships with historical associations: the Northwest Archivists holds a joint meeting each spring with the Pacific Northwest History Conference; and the Society of Ohio Archivists has joint committees with the Ohio Academy of History and with the Ohio Genealogical Society. But none of the regional and state archival associations has established any joint committees or holds joint meetings with library associations.

Occasional joint sessions or meetings could probably be mutually beneficial. At the very least, a session on archives and manuscripts at a meeting of a library association could alert librarians to the fact that the regional and state archival associations exist and that they can provide some basic training through their workshops. An exchange of viewpoints on collecting policies as they relate to different types of materials in a region could be useful. And there are other mutual problems on the state and local levels as well as on the national level that might better be explored together rather than separately.

NOTES

1. Don Harrison, "SAA and the Regionals," *Mid-Atlantic Archivist* 2 (February 1973): 2.
2. Elsie Freivogel, "Regarding 'SAA and the Regionals,' " *Mid-Atlantic Archivist* 2 (April 1973): 10.
3. Harrison, "SAA and the Regionals," pp. 2, 9.
4. Clifford K. Shipton, "President's Page," *American Archivist* 31 (1968): 67.
5. Harrison, "SAA and the Regionals," p. 2.
6. Robert M. Warner, "Secretary's Notes," *36th Annual Meeting, Society of American Archivists, October 31–November 3, 1972, Columbus, Ohio*, pp. 34–36.
7. F. Gerald Ham, "Report of the Secretary, 1970–71," *American Archivist* 35 (1972): 110.
8. Philip P. Mason, "The Society of American Archivists in the Seventies: Report of the Committee for the 1970's," *American Archivist* 35 (1972): 199.
9. *Newsletter of the Midwest Archives Conference* 1 (January 1973): 10; *Mid-Atlantic Archivist* 1 (October 1972): 2.
10. Tom Elliott and Archie Motley, "SAA and Regional Groups Meet in Chicago," *Newsletter of the Midwest Archives Conference* 1 (July 1973): 9–10; *Mid-Atlantic Archivist* 2 (June 1973): 9.
11. *Mid-Atlantic Archivist* 3 (April 1974): 5.
12. J. Frank Cook, "Editor's Note," *Newsletter of the Midwest Archives Conference* 2 (October 1974): 3.
13. Letter, Evert Volkers to Archie Motley, June 27, 1974.
14. *American Archivist* 37 (1974): 506; 36 (1973): 127.
15. "Publications Program for MAC?" *Newsletter of the Midwest Archives Conference* 2 (January 1974): 34–35.
16. Miriam I. Crawford, unpublished list, "Archives References in 'Library Literature,' 1961–1971 (August)," August 1972.

ANNOTATED BIBLIOGRAPHY

WRITINGS ON ARCHIVE–LIBRARY RELATED TOPICS

A survey of the literature dealing with the relationship between libraries and archives shows a strong evolutionary trend from differentiation toward cooperation. The 1930s were for the archival profession in the United States what the 1870s had been for librarianship, which today is a well-articulated, systematized discipline. American archivy is, by comparison, a relatively young profession, and the period covered by the comparative literature on archive–library relations comprises its formative years.

The archivists' early attempts at differentiation were more than just a search for identity or a struggle for status. They were the concomitant of conscious efforts to develop a methodology clearly derived from the nature of archives and the archival function. The factors influencing archival methodology are described by Dr. Schellenberg in the second chapter of *The Management of Archives*, and include the role played by libraries in this development (33).*

The theme of differentiation and cooperation is clearly discernible in articles dealing with archival training. The consensus seems to be that professional training for archivists must take an interdisciplinary approach. Probably the most interesting view is that of John C. Colson, who feels that recent technological and social changes demand stringent modifications in library school curricula to meet contemporary information and communication needs of an increasingly complex and interdependent society. Such modifications would make the study of archival methods and

*Numbers in parentheses refer to listings in the bibliography, which follows.

199

administration one of several specialized programs within the library school curriculum (12).

Librarians constitute a large group of records custodians, in many instances having statutory archival duties. Others, notably public librarians, have responsibilities for the preservation of local history sources. Their recognition of the need for adopting a separate methodology for archives, dictated by the difference in the nature of these primary source materials, forms a large part of the literature on archives–library relationships. In 1939 Margaret C. Norton, one of the pioneers of the profession, articulated the differences between archives and libraries, as well as the complementary nature of many of their activities (27); while Joseph M. Scammell, writing during the same period, urged librarians and historians to take an active interest in the development of archival methods (31).

The literature of the relationship between archives and historical manuscripts has undergone considerable change. Robert L. Brubaker points out that in the early days of the profession a sharp distinction was made between archives and historical manuscripts, requiring library techniques for the organization of manuscripts. The difference, it was argued, stemmed from the fact that manuscripts are collected, while archives accumulate, making the first an artificial and the second a natural or organic aggregate (8). Gradually the archival characteristics of historical manuscripts were recognized. Richard Berner, himself a manuscript curator, summed up contemporary practice in his 1965 article on "Manuscript Collections and Archives—A Unitary Approach" (4).

It would be surprising if the process of differentiation had proceeded without generating some conflicts. In 1943 Randolph W. Church told archivists bluntly that their principles were an impediment to research, and that libraries, with their subject orientation, were far better sources of government history (10). The following year Herman Kahn showed that subject orientation is detrimental to archives because it destroys their evidential value (21). Other discussions included the arguments for and against the inclusion of archival services among the duties of state librarians. Dan Robison believed that archives had much to gain from such inclusion (30), while Peter Biskup considered that it would retard archival development (5).

More recently James B. Rhoads, the archivist of the United States, writing about the role of archives in the 1970s, reaffirmed the common purpose of librarians and archivists to preserve and render accessible the collective recorded knowledge of the human race (28). L. Quincy Mumford, former librarian of Congress, took a new look at the two professions in 1970. He believes that archivists and librarians are increasingly drawn closer together, as a result of electronic media, by a greater similarity in the materials with which each must deal, by a common concern for the physical and intellectual control of rapidly escalating holdings, and by their relationship to their clientele (25).

BIBLIOGRAPHY

1. Ander, O. Fritiof. "Are Our Libraries Obligated to Collect and Preserve the Historical Records of the Community?" *Illinois Libraries* 34 (December 1952): 442–447.

It is widely acknowledged in the library and historical professions that public libraries have an obligation to assemble and preserve local historical material in manuscript, documentary, and published form. Leaving records of broader and more general significance to national, state, and academic institutions, and to large public libraries, libraries in small communities can contribute greatly by concentrating on local history, which is after all an indispensable complement to general history. Based on a survey of small libraries in one region of Illinois, this article outlines the scope of local history material that small libraries might attempt to acquire, and stresses the need for the establishment of a collection policy, and a fund for this purpose. In spite of the difficulties inherent in the collection and preservation of such materials, libraries will find they benefit from the public interest that local history generates.

2. Bahmer, Robert H. "Archives." In *Encyclopedia of Library and Information Science*, Vol. 1, compiled by Allen Kent and Harold Lancour (New York: Marcel Dekker, 1968), pp. 515–519.

This article clearly and concisely defines what archives are and gives a brief outline of institutional development. While archives administration shares a common purpose with library and information science, the basic character of archives as natural accumulations of documentary material requires different methods and techniques from those used by librarians. Unlike book selection where decisions are not necessarily final, the appraisal of unique archival records for retention or destruction involves making irrevocable decisions. The establishment of administrative and intellectual control over these primary sources links the archivist to the librarian and other information specialists. The article also lists areas of study needed by professional archivists and gives the names of the institutions currently providing the pertinent courses.

— 3. Benjamin, Mary A. "The Manuscript Market and the Librarian." *College and Research Libraries* 17 (March 1956): 119–126.

Librarians collecting manuscripts should specialize. While cultivating potential donors, they should work in close cooperation with dealers in order to purchase material. For a small fee the dealer will evaluate the authenticity of manuscripts, and appraise gifts for tax deduction, and private collections considered for purchase. Since manuscripts have a monetary as well as a research value, librarians must be concerned with the ethical questions involved in copying, and with tax assessment. The author, an experienced manuscript dealer, explains the process of acquisition of historical documents and, along with some caveats, also reminds librarians of their ethical obligations to both donors and dealers.

4. Berner, Richard. "Manuscript Collections and Archives—A Unitary Approach." *Library Resources and Technical Services* 9 (Spring 1965): 213–220.
The author treats archives and manuscripts as a unit on the premise that they have the same basic bibliographic characteristics, which differ considerably, however, from those of publications. His purpose is to provide librarians with theoretical guidelines for the arrangement and description of archives and manuscripts. To enable users to analyze the activities of persons or organizations in the context in which they took place, related groups of manuscripts and archives must be kept together, and not merged with other groups. Examples illustrate cases where internal rearrangement of the series within the groups was considered necessary and show alternatives of organization. The arrangement also determines the extent of the description needed for each group. Description should be in the form of inventories, supplemented by subject, name, and chronological indexes.

5. Biskup, Peter. "The Case against Library Control of Archives." *Australian Library Journal* 10 (January 1961): 40–41.
In rebuttal to an article by R. C. Sharman which appeared in the July 1960 issue of the same journal (36), the author argues that, except in the initial embryonic stages, library control prevents archives from achieving a separate identity, recognizable by the government agencies which they serve, as well as by the public, and that library control thereby retards the growth and hampers the effectiveness of archives. The article also contends that library control is detrimental to archives because, aside from some similarities in terminology, the approach of one profession differs fundamentally from that of the other. Though dealing with archival development in Australia, the issues can readily be generalized.

6. Born, Lester K. "International Cooperation to Preserve Historical Source Material." *American Archivist* 15 (July 1952): 219–230.
Though somewhat dated, this article gives a fascinating glimpse into the problems of international archives. It argues for the need to protect the cultural heritage of civilized societies in the form of archives, which ultimately are the "repositories of the object-lessons of life itself . . . ." Given the apparent inevitability of war and other disasters, protection must come in the form of international agreements for microfilm projects and for exchange of information. The author cites various efforts of this type, such as the ACLS British Manuscript Project and programs planned by the American Historical Association and UNESCO, and discusses the scope and costs involved. He also urges the establishment of emergency plans within the United States armed forces for the protection of international libraries and archives in case of war, to be implemented by experts placed at a high level within the table of organization of the armed services.

7. Brooks, Philip C. "Archivists and Their Colleagues: Common Denominators." *American Archivist* 14 (January 1951): 33–45.
This presidential address, delivered to the annual meeting of the Society of American Archivists, examines the work of archivists and its relationship to allied professions by asking how it fits into the whole process of recording human activities. The author concludes that the real basis of common interest among archivists, librarians, and other related disciplines is a concern for the control of information. Thus the archivist functions beyond the narrow scope of custodianship and shares

the administrator's concern for records creation and management, the manuscript curator's concern for criteria of appraisal, the librarian's concern for the organization and retrieval of material, and the historian's concern for historical method and for history itself.

8. Brubaker, Robert L. "Archival Principles and the Curator of Manuscripts." *American Archivist* 29 (October 1966): 505–514.

The literature of the relationship between archives and historical manuscripts has undergone an evolution from the early days of the profession, when a sharp distinction was made between archives and historical manuscripts, requiring library methods of organization for manuscript collections. Gradually the archival characteristics of manuscripts were recognized, particularly since many collections are really "fugitive archives," governmental or organizational records that have been acquired by private collectors and libraries, which are best administered according to archival principles. This recognition was further reinforced by the growing number and size of collections, and by the advent of automated indexing. The author discusses the dichotomy of card catalogs versus inventories and indexes for the control of manuscript collections, and recommends a modified card catalog, reflecting groups of manuscripts, as well as names of correspondents and subjects, and referring researchers to the appropriate inventories for greater detail.

9. Cappon, Lester J. "Historical Manuscripts as Archives: Some Definitions and Their Application." *American Archivist* 19 (April 1956): 101–110.

An analysis of the attributes of historical manuscripts leads the author to the conclusion that many are really types of archives, while others are often complementary in content. These archival characteristics greatly enhance the value of historical manuscripts. The value of imprints also increases by such archival association. Research libraries of all kinds are essential for the preservation of historical manuscripts, but to do this well, the curator must be an archivist at heart.

10. Church, Randolph W. "Relationships between Archival Agencies and Libraries." *American Archivist* 6 (July 1943): 145–150.

Archival agencies, to function properly, need to be supplemented by libraries; a connection between the two is vital. In addition, the author asserts, contrary to archivists' contentions, archives consist largely of noncurrent records of purely educational value to posterity and are generally approached for specific subject information. The dual approach to research topics via primary and secondary sources makes the principle of *respects pour les fonds* an impediment. Instead, the author thinks, libraries, with their subject orientation, where documents are fully cataloged, are a better source of governmental history than archives, where cataloging has not been developed. He therefore suggests that professional education for archivists should include courses in records management, cataloging, and bibliography, as well as a broad basis of general education.

11. Clark, Robert L. "Preserving Local History: The Public Library's Responsibility." *Oklahoma Librarian* 20 (January 1970): 14–16.

In 1960 a survey of the archival and manuscript holdings in Oklahoma public, college, and special libraries was attempted. The results were largely negative. A few years later a symposium on archives administration, held in Oklahoma by the Society of American Archivists, the National Archives, and the Oklahoma Department of Libraries, was also largely ignored by public libraries. Mr. Clark finds this apparent lack of interest regrettable because public libraries have a crucial role in the preservation of local history, the loss of which is irreversible. Because local historical societies often emphasize museum objects and historical sites, the author feels that public libraries must assume the responsibility for other historical records, if local history sources are to be preserved in a systematic way. The lack of courses on archives in Oklahoma library schools leaves librarians unprepared to initiate such collections. The article makes a number of practical suggestions for the acquisition and preservation of local archives and manuscripts.

— **12.** Colson, John C. "Archivists and Education: Modifying Library School Curricula." *RQ* 12 (Spring 1973): 267–272.

Recent meetings of the Society of American Archivists and the American Library Association have been concerned with the issue of expanding library school curricula to include archival education. The author rejects the approach of grafting archives administration courses to existing library school programs. Instead he urges a fundamental reorganization of library school curricula to prepare librarians to give more adequate service to a society in which individualism has been superseded by a complex and highly organized interdependence, resulting in crucial needs for information and communication. Rather than clinging to the traditional cultural and historical emphases of their respective professions, librarians and archivists have the mission to facilitate communication among persons and groups to enable them to establish better relations with each other. Accordingly, library schools should redesign their curricula to offer three-part programs consisting of general theory, specialized studies such as archival courses, and internship programs. The focus should be less on professional traditions and institutions, and more on the contemporary social environment in which librarians and archivists must function.

13. Colson, John C. "On the Education of Archivists and Librarians." *American Archivist* 31 (April 1968): 167–174.

This article argues that both archivists and librarians are in the business of making information available for use; that the emphasis on their separateness is derived from a struggle for professional status; and that the differences in the materials dealt with by each group are becoming increasingly blurred by the rapid development of electronic devices for recording knowledge. What is needed, according to the author, is the development of new educational programs that will meet the needs of both professions as information specialists.

14. Crittenden, Christopher C. "The Public Library and Local History Sources." *History News* 12 (July 1957): 69–70.

Based on the premise that local history materials ought to be preserved because they are of vital interest to the members of a community, this article points out that unless public libraries take on the task, it will most probably not be done. Collections should consist of both primary and secondary sources and should include all forms and media. The author also discusses the establishment of special collections around persons and topics of particular local significance. Librarians should also be prepared to refer people to other local, state, and other historical sources, and to advise persons interested in writing and publishing local history.

15. Duboscq, Guy. "The Educational Role of Archives." *UNESCO Library Bulletin* 24 (July/August 1970): 205–210.

Just as education is no longer an elite privilege but embraces all of society and the entire life span of individuals, so the use of archives is no longer confined to the intellectual elite of scholars and administrative authorities. It is increasingly becoming a tool for the extension and democratization of education through the use of archival exhibits, the establishment of school services, and the publication of reproductions of historical documents, texts, and commentaries. The author describes such services in France and England and urges archival institutions throughout the world to make efforts in that direction.

16. Duniway, David C. "Conflicts in Collecting." *American Archivist* 24 (January 1961): 55–63.

Competition is not necessarily the basis of all conflicts in collecting historical and archival records. Such conflicts, according to the author, frequently are inherent in the nature of personal papers or arise as a result of the legal mandates of historical and archival agencies tied to geographic areas, but with subject orientation in collecting running counter to such limits. The author analyzes such materials and proposes a number of ethical guidelines designed to diminish conflicts and enable archivists in various types of institutions to get on with their task of satisfying research needs.

17. Duniway, David C. "Where Do Public Records Belong?" *American Archivist* 31 (January 1968): 49–55.

Public records affecting individuals start at the grass roots and enter a system in which they are duplicated and new information is added. At the same time some data are abstracted from them and distributed to state and federal agencies. This elaborate record-keeping network creates problems of appraisal for the archivist in his effort to serve researchers, lawyers, government officials, and private individuals. The author urges archivists, records managers, systems designers, and programmers to cooperate in appraisal, in the establishment of responsibility for the retention of records that are used at various jurisdictional levels, and in the planning of retrieval systems. Failure to do so could result in the loss of essential records, or in the creation of retrieval systems incompatible with each other. The author further urges adoption of systems that make it possible to retain basic records of primary evidence at the local level, where they were created, and where they are most likely to be needed.

18. Hobbs, John L. *Local History and the Library.* Completely revised and partly rewritten by George A. Carter. London: Andre Deutsch, 1973.

This thoughtful work is based on the rationale that librarians, committed to providing literature of potential interest to their communities, have the duty of collecting local history materials which are a vital part of such literature. Such collections are complementary to government archives and museums. This handbook for the preservation of local history sources in libraries is a complete revision and updating of the 1962 classic by J. L. Hobbs. Though primarily for British librarians and written from the librarian's rather than the archivist's point of view, its discussion of the nature of local materials, the philosophy guiding the administration of such collections, as well as the techniques for their preservation, arrangement, and use, can be helpful to librarians and students of local history everywhere.

\ **19.** Hyde, Dorsey W. "The National Archives and Our Libraries." *Library Journal* 61 (January 1936): 7–9.

This article, written shortly after the establishment of the National Archives and the construction of its building, describes the Archives' mission to provide a central depository for all inactive archival records of the federal government, and to make them available for administrative and scholarly purposes. Librarians benefit from greater accessibility to source material for reference, from publication programs, from the publication of the *Federal Register* (the official organ of administrative and executive law), and from the maintenance of comprehensive library services. The aim of the Archives' library division is to be a comprehensive source of information regarding archives at home and throughout the world, and to provide a consulting service for all problems in this field.

\ **20.** Jacobsen, Edna L. "State and Local Government Archives." *Library Trends* 5 (July 1956–April 1957): 397–401.

This is a discussion of the administrative and processing problems facing state librarians who also act as archivists. The question is how to serve both scholars and government agencies efficiently. The author takes issue with those archivists who regard library techniques as superfluous or unsuitable for archival holdings. She argues for the maintenance of both descriptive inventories and subject catalogs, to which librarians can contribute their expertise. The assumption that archives, defined as noncurrent records, are of interest only for historical research is erroneous. Archival documents frequently assume crucial importance in current administrative and legal matters. Judicious appraisal of records requires thorough knowledge of the history of all phases of state government. It also requires familiarity with records groups, the series within them, and most important, the relationship between them. The largely permissive nature of most public records laws makes close cooperation between the librarian–archivist and the state agencies essential for the effectiveness of archival programs.

21. Kahn, Herman. "Librarians and Archivists: Some Aspects of Their Partnership." *American Archivist* 7 (October 1944): 243–251.

This article deals with the problems of applying the librarian's subject approach and resulting techniques to archival material. It exposes such fallacies as confusing historical manuscripts with archives, and assuming that archival material has outlived administrative usefulness and is to be maintained for historical research only, which becomes the rationale for breaking up the organic integrity of such records in favor of a subject arrangement. Herman Kahn argues that subject arrangements must of necessity be arbitrary, since it is not possible to anticipate the use of records. Because the breakup and physical intermingling of groups of archives render them meaningless, it is best to maintain the integrity of record groups, and to provide subject approaches through various kinds of finding aids.

22. Lamb, W. Kaye. "The Modern Archivist: Formally Trained or Self-Educated?" *American Archivist* 31 (April 1968): 175–177.

Giving his reasons why library schools can make only limited contributions to archival training, the author stresses the need for both theoretical and practical courses. The theoretical portion of the professional education of the archivist should be obtained in a department of history, in collaboration with a nearby archival institution for the necessary practical training. The establishment of such educational programs must be preceded by the development of archival standards and basic principles.

23. Mearns, David C. "The Nitid Crimson." *American Archivist* 15 (April 1952): 139–145.

Calling himself a centaur-like creature, part librarian and part archivist, the author regales his audience of assembled members of the Society of American Archivists with his whimsey, wit, and erudition. In a "nitid crimson" style—a phrase derived from an eighteenth-century manuscript—he discusses archival development over two decades. After overcoming the problems of custody, arrangement, and restoration, and assembling large holdings, archivists still face problems of literary property rights in unpublished papers, and indexing. In closing, the author urges archivists not to succumb to arid professionalism, but to remain in some respects eager amateurs.

24. Morgan, Dale L. "The Archivist, the Librarian, and the Historian." *Library Journal* 93 (December 15, 1968): 4621–4623.

Generalizing from his own introduction to the archival profession as editor for the Historical Records Survey in Utah and from his experience doing research in the National Archives, the author writes of the need to publicize the archival labor of organizing primary source materials so they may be turned into written history, and of the need to give archivists an opportunity to grow professionally, to become "practicing historians" rather than mere technicians. The article criticizes those public-relations efforts which stress the housekeeping aspects of the profession by focusing on the money-conscious incentives of records management. Without downgrading the importance of economy, the author believes it is not the main value and ultimate goal of archives administration. The author goes on to stress the scholarly aspects of the profession by asking some searching questions regarding the relationship of both archives and libraries to the entire educational process.

25. Mumford, L. Quincy. "Archivists and Librarians: Time for a New Look." *American Archivist* 33 (July 1970): 269–274.

The author, former librarian of congress, acknowledges the needs of earlier American archivists to stress the distinctness of their functions and practices from those of librarians, in order to achieve a sense of professional identity, to focus public attention on the importance of preserving records, and to gain support from scholars and government for their activities. He insists, however, that the time has come to acknowledge the similarities in the two occupations, and he calls for increased cooperation. Areas of common concern are media, proliferation of records due to the evolution of electronics, concerns for physical and intellectual control over holdings, problems and potentials of automatic data processing, public relations, and professional recruitment. The author describes the work done in those areas by the Library of Congress and other large federal libraries. In public relations, in particular, he feels joint efforts could increase effectiveness tremendously. The thrust should be to gain the support of both scientists and humanists, and above all to reach young people.

26. Norton, Margaret C. "Archives and Historical Manuscripts." *Illinois Libraries* 21 (August 1939): 26–28.

Margaret Norton demonstrates that the method of collection and arrangement of archives differs from that of historical manuscripts because archives are legal documents first, and of historical value only secondarily. The archivist is a custodian of records on behalf of the people; his chief duty is to maintain the integrity of those records and to protect their value as evidence. This is the basis for the adoption of provenance as the primary principle in the organization of archival material.

27. Norton, Margaret C. "Archives and Libraries: A Comparison Drawn." *Bluebook* (Illinois: Secretary of State, 1939–1940), pp. 427–443.

The author, in her discussion of the relationships between archives and libraries, stresses the uniqueness of archives as potential legal evidence; from that uniqueness archival methodology is logically derived. Appraisal of records necessitates up-to-date knowledge of the history and functions of agencies or organizations, and of their record-keeping laws and policies. Libraries, with their different scopes and purposes, make use of different techniques, some of which, however, can be adapted to archives. The author recommends such modifications, because users are not concerned with methodology but see both libraries and archives as information sources. The article compares all aspects of archival and library activities, including the handling of government documents, which have certain archival characteristics and are consequently of concern to both institutions.

28. Rhoads, James B. "The Role of Archives in the 1970's." In *Louisiana State University Lectures in Library Science*, No. 17 (Baton Rouge: Louisiana State University, 1971), pp. 1–7.

James B. Rhoads, the Archivist of the United States, affirms the common purpose of librarians and archivists. Conceding fundamental differences in collections and methods, he states that together the two professions are engaged in preserving and rendering accessible the collective recorded knowledge of the human race. Dr. Rhoads paints a cautiously optimistic picture of archival development in general and enthusiastically outlines the programs started or projected by the National Archives in honor of the Bicentennial of the American Revolution, programs designed for a broad spectrum of users. He discusses the stepped-up activities of the six presidential libraries, administered by the National Archives and Records Service, and developments in records management and data archives.

29. Ricks, Artel. "Can a Computer Help the Archivist and Librarian?" *Records Management Journal* 9 (Summer 1971): 2–17.

This is a state-of-the-art discussion of the utilization of computers in libraries and archives. Areas susceptible to automation are administrative and clerical work, current awareness (i.e., the dissemination of information regarding new acquisitions), and information retrieval. The article describes the use of computers by the Library of Congress, the National Library of Medicine, and the National Agricultural Library, as well as the current and future automation projects of the National Archives and Records Service. It argues for selective dissemination of information, such as the service of the Legislative Reference Service of the Library of Congress, as one way to cope with the information explosion. Another is information retrieval, which makes coordinate searches possible through various types of indexing, including SPINDEX II, developed by Frank Burke of the National Archives.

30. Robison, Dan M. "Archival Services in State Libraries." *American Archivist* 22 (April 1959): 197–202.

This article weighs the arguments for and against the inclusion of archival services among the responsibilities of state libraries. Although they share an information function, the professions differ basically in the nature of the material with which they deal, and consequently in their methodology and techniques, so that traditional library training cannot adequately equip archivists for their task. Moreover, for better or worse, archivists are increasingly becoming involved in records management, a function which seems to have little to do with librarianship. Though he readily admits these disadvantages, the author uses his own institution, the Tennessee State Library and Archives, as an example for the powerful arguments in favor of joining state libraries and archives—greater convenience to the public, as well as greater flexibility in budgeting, staffing, and in the use of space and equipment. Finally he offers a practical lesson in government, where the tendency to create independent agencies to carry out specialized functions periodically invites government reorganization and consolidation. Smaller agencies are swallowed up by large departments, or they disappear altogether—their various duties dispersed among other departments.

31. Scammell, Joseph M. "Librarians and Archives." *Library Quarterly* 9 (October 1939): 432–444.

Written at a time of great change in archival method and organization, this article outlines the involvement of librarians with archives, a related field. Librarians are involved directly when they are charged with responsibility for the administration of noncurrent records essential for governmental continuity, and indirectly when increasing interest in local history creates a demand for primary source materials. Clearly defining archives, the author urges librarians and historians to take an active interest in archival methodology and functions, to counteract the widespread confusion of archives with historical manuscripts, and of the purposes of archives with those of libraries, historical societies, and museums. Archival development is described briefly, with particular emphasis on the Historical Records Survey then in progress, which, together with European activities in the field, indicates to the writer the direction of United States archives and of librarians' involvement with them.

32. Schellenberg, T. R. "Archival Training in Library Schools." *American Archivist* 31 (April 1968): 155–165.

Unlike their European counterparts, whose work involves them with the auxiliary sciences of history, American archivists need courses in historical research, archival methodology, techniques of document preservation, repair, and reproduction, as well as auxiliary courses in library science and records management. Thus archival training will always necessitate the collaboration of several departments. Since the formulation of the principles of provenance, archival institutions have stressed historical training, which gives archivists the analytical capabilities needed to learn how records came into existence; such analysis is a prerequisite to appraisal. There is danger, however, of a wrong emphasis, since the historian's objective is the interpretation of source materials, rather than the mere accumulation of information from them. Librarians teaching such courses may also project wrong emphasis because of their orientation toward the single-record item and the subject approach. They also de-emphasize the scholarly aspects of archival work, because librarians have rationalized the manipulation of their collections beyond a point desirable or even feasible for archivists. Nevertheless, Dr. Schellenberg urges that library schools undertake archival training, if only because so many librarians administer records. He also believes archivists could benefit from traditional library attitudes of public service.

33. Schellenberg, T. R. "Factors Influencing Archival Methodology." In *The Management of Archives* (New York: Columbia University Press, 1965), Chapter 2, pp. 20–31.
The main factors influencing the development of archival methodology were the types of repositories in which records accumulated, the volume of records, and their character. Colonial collections were private. Institutional preservation of such material in historical societies, archives, and libraries began only after the federal government was established. Each of these institutions contributed its own orientation toward the arrangement and description of the manuscripts and archives in its holdings. In addition the Historical Manuscript Commission and the Public Archives Commission, established by the American Historical Association in 1895 and 1899, respectively, tended to separate the manuscript curator from the archivist, with significant consequences for methodology. The volume of records, small in the first half of the nineteenth century, grew rapidly in its last decades. The geometric increase of record volume did not occur until World War I; it is a serious problem for twentieth-century archivists. The preoccupation of early American historians with political and historical matters, which determined the character of early collections, has given way to a constant broadening of historical interests and of the scope of manuscripts and records being acquired. Scholars in disciplines other than history have also become interested in primary sources, and scholarly inquiry has been extended forward in time. Today contemporary history, once controversial in its contradiction in terms, has become accepted.

34. Schellenberg, T. R. "Library Relationships, Principles and Techniques." In *Modern Archives* (Chicago: University of Chicago Press, 1956), Chapter 3, pp. 17–25.
Chapter 3 of this book deals with the relationship between the archival and library professions, arising from differences in the origins and acquisition of the materials handled by each. The consequent divergence in methodology applies to appraisal, arrangement, and description. The archivist, working with groups of records produced in connection with a governmental or organizational function, requires techniques different from those of the librarian, working with discrete items dealing with a variety of subjects. The basic differences between the two professions do not, of course, detract from their common objective of making information accessible. Each profession has much to contribute to the other, particularly in techniques of preserving audiovisual, pictorial, and cartographic material and in the matter of training.

35. Shannon, Mike. "Local Historical Records—Out of Chaos Comes Order." *RQ* 12 (Fall 1972): 44–49.

Citing New York City as an example, the author states that the neglect of local records is as widespread and as old as the records themselves. Printed local documents fare no better. Together these materials constitute an invaluable source of information, providing community profiles useful for a wide range of research topics. The problem of local historical records is treated in its totality, from the acquisition and preservation of the materials, to making them physically and intellectually accessible. Suggested solutions begin with increasing public awareness of the problem, and include the training and education of local librarians and historians, the establishment of communication among local archives, museums, and libraries, and the expansion of standard bibliographic tools to deal with local materials.

36. Sharman, R. C. "Library Control of Archives." *Australian Library Journal* 9 (July 1960): 125–128.

The author voices his objection to a statement, in a text used in archivist training, to the effect that the archival function is only one of many for a library and therefore commands only a small fraction of the library's commitment and funds, and that library administration of archives is therefore the main impediment to archival development. Acknowledging certain disadvantages of the association of archives with libraries, the article asserts that the development of archives can be successful only when sponsored by library systems. It cites as benefits the proximity of library collections, and the insistence of librarians on high educational standards for archivists. The author believes the animosity displayed by archivists to library control will evaporate with the rise of archivists within the library hierarchy, and with the recognition of the basic differences in the two professions which attract different types of persons, require different kinds of training, and result in distinctive kinds of services. (For a rebuttal see No. 5.)

37. Taylor, Hugh A. "Clio in the Raw: Archival Materials and the Teaching of History." *American Archivist* 35 (July/October 1972): 317–330.

Hugh Taylor, using English schools as an example, advocates greater use of documentary material in the teaching of history. He goes a step further and suggests that undergraduates and even high school students be given the opportunity to share in the pleasure of handling manuscripts and groups of records, a pleasure which has something to do with personal discovery. The result of such unstructured exposure may well be a genuine historical experience, one which only the archivist, working with teachers and students, can provide.

38. Trevers, Karl I. "Local Archives and the Public Library: A Proposal for Consideration by Archivists and Librarians." *Library Journal* 71 (March 1, 1946): 301–304, 306.

Public records of local communities represent gold mines of information for historical, governmental, and social science research. Between 1935 and 1942 the Historical Records Survey made a heroic effort to render local records accessible, but since the conclusion of the program some of its gains have been nullified by the disappearance of the records listed therein, under pressure of new records creation. The author suggests that public libraries are in a favorable position to alleviate some of the problems, because they represent a national network of stable local institutions with trained personnel. If archival principles are adhered to, some libraries could become repositories, while others could act as referral and consulting services for the preservation of local records.

INDEX